Adaptive Behavior

Adaptive Behavior:
Concepts and Measurements

Edited by

W. Alan Coulter
Henry W. Morrow, Ed. D.

Texas Regional Resource Center

Grune & Stratton

A Subsidiary of Harcourt Brace Jovanovich, Publishers
New York / San Francisco / London

Library of Congress Number 78-19685
International Standard Book Number 0-8089-1092-2

Printed in the United States of America

Contents

Acknowledgments   vii

Foreword   ix

Contributors   xi

I   THEORETICAL ASPECTS OF ADAPTIVE BEHAVIOR   1

  1. A Contemporary Conception of Adaptive
     Behavior within the Scope of Psychological
     Assessment   3
     W. Alan Coulter,
     Henry W. Morrow

  2. Theoretical Considerations of Adaptive Behavior   21
     Henry W. Leland

  3. Factorial Descriptions of the AAMD Adaptive
     Behavior Scale   45
     Kazuo Nihira

  4. Theoretical Constructs of Adaptive Behavior:
     Movement from a Medical to a Social–Ecological
     Perspective   59
     Jane R. Mercer

**II   POLICIES AND PRACTICES IN THE ASSESSMENT OF
ADAPTIVE BEHAVIOR**   83

  5. A Survey of State Policies Regarding Adaptive
     Behavior Measurement   85
     Henry W. Morrow,
     W. Alan Coulter

  6. One Year after Implementation: Practitioners'
     Views of Adaptive Behavior   93
     W. Alan Coulter,
     Henry W. Morrow

III   MEASURING ADAPTIVE BEHAVIOR   113

      7. A Practitioner's Approach to Selecting Adaptive
          Behavior Scales   115
          Henry W. Morrow,
          W. Alan Coulter

      8. A Collection of Adaptive Behavior Measures   141
          W. Alan Coulter,
          Henry W. Morrow

      9. The Adaptive Behavior Scale—Public School
          Version: An Overview   157
          Nadine M. Lambert

     10. The System of Multicultural Pluralistic
          Assessment: SOMPA   185
          June Lewis,
          Jane R. Mercer

IV   RESEARCH CONSIDERATIONS IN THE STUDY OF
      ADAPTIVE BEHAVIOR   213

     11. The Future of Adaptive Behavior: Issues
          Surrounding the Refinement of the Concept and
          Its Measurement   215
          W. Alan Coulter,
          Henry W. Morrow

     12. An Annotated Bibliography of Research in
          Adaptive Behavior   277
          W. Alan Coulter,
          Henry W. Morrow,
          Judi L. Coulter

      Index   253

Acknowledgments

Many persons were indispensable in producing this document. James A. Tucker, Director of the Texas Regional Resource Center, provided administrative and emotional support as well as intellectual and creative stimulus. He laughed and scowled at all the right times. He asked questions and volunteered innumerable ideas, references, and other gems.

The members of the National Association of State Consultants in School Psychology also deserve thanks for their support, encouragement, and generous advice. This group is composed of the elite among pupil appraisal practitioners and its members always ask the toughest questions. The association's hard nosed view of reality is, we hope, reflected in much of the content of this document. In a similar vein, those pupil appraisal practitioners in Texas who not only participated in our survey but often followed-up to make certain we stayed on track have our gratitude (especially Ertie Lou Rhinehart).

Judi Coulter, is a patient, persistent interviewer and fellow researcher who pursued essential interviewees across the country to insure a reasonable representation for the national survey. She carefully compiled data and later meticulously wrote many of the annotations in the bibliography section. Judy Oakland, our resident Edwin Newman and astute editor, patiently edited all the chapters and tenaciously defended the English language against our many abuses. Without her shepherd-like devotion, the diverse elements of this document would have been lost. Carolyn Hildebrandt carefully typed all manuscripts, often assisted and consoled by other members of our secretarial staff (Pat and Dianne). The staff of the Texas Regional Resource Center listened to the editors debate (argue) and deliberate (hassle) vast arrays of vital concepts (trivial minutae).

Nadine Lambert, Henry Leland, June Lewis, Jane Mercer, and Kaz Nihira are true friends. They contributed the major substance of the document and their ideas influenced our very approach. They represent a most vital resource in solving some of the complex problems currently present in special education and psychological assessment.

Foreword

It must be remembered that the object of the world of ideas as a whole is not the portrayal of reality—this would be an utterly impossible task—but rather to provide us with an instrument for finding our way about more easily in this world.

—Vaihinger, 1924, p. 15

Adaptive behavior is either the most fascinating idea or the greatest hoax ever put on diagnosticians.

Anonymous Appraisal Practitioner
in Texas

Our investigation into adaptive behavior measurement began as part of a technical assistance effort by the Texas Regional Resource Center (TRRC) for the Texas Education Agency. We were puzzled by the widespread confusion (including our own) regarding not only the measurement of adaptive behavior, but the very development of the concept itself. The TRRC received requests from pupil appraisal practitioners for assistance in locating appropriate instruments for the measurement of adaptive behavior; these practitioners also expressed concern that the existing instruments did not adequately meet all the measurement requirements surrounding the concept. Indeed, adaptive behavior measurement in public schools appeared to involve more than one intent and to be associated with several social and psychological assessment issues. To resolve our own confusion and misunderstanding and to assist in making sense of a particularly complex concept, we sought to uncover some structure or organization (or "instrument," Vaihinger, op. cit.) by which all the ideas and issues could be comprehended. Knowing that the concept of adaptive behavior was not reality in Vaihinger's sense, we nonetheless found a satisfactory conceptual base for understanding adaptive behavior in a functional definition of psychological assessment through its intent or purpose. Much of what follows is based upon that functional definition (i.e. our schema or organization).

The concept of adaptive behavior has become a composite of theoretical, political, and practical realties. Amid the concern for broader participation of the handicapped in mainstream society (Gold, 1972) and the movement toward a more pluralistic assessment of minority groups (Mercer, 1972), adaptive behavior offers some answers to questions that were previously thought unanswerable.

This book will consider the concept of adaptive behavior, its measurement within psychological assessment, and its varied implications.

References

Gold, M. W. *An adaptive behavior philosophy: Who needs it?* Unpublished manuscript, 1972. (Available from Institute for Child Behavior and Development University of Illinois, Champaign, Illinois)

Mercer, J. R. I. Q.: The lethal label. *Psychology Today*, 1972, 6 (4), 44

Vaihinger, H. *The philosophy of as if.* London, England: Routledge, Kegan and Paul, Ltd., 1924

Contributors

W. Alan Coulter
Technical Assistance Consultant
Texas Regional Resource Center
211 East 7th Street
Austin, Texas 78701

W. Alan Coulter is technical assistance consultant and an associate school psychologist with the Texas Regional Resource Center, and a National Trainer of Magic Circle, Innerchange, and Conflict Management for the Human Development Training Institute and a National Instructor for SOMPA workshops. He has served as Coordinator of Project ASSIST (a rural school psychological services delivery system) and as an associate school psychologist with the Region IX Education Service Center, Wichita Falls, Texas. He has had instructional/teaching experience for four years at the secondary level and has also served as a special education consultant, juvenile probation group worker, visiting editor of a national newsletter, and an appraisal systems consultant. Alan Coulter is certified as a psychological associate and an associate school psychologist in Texas.

Alan Coulter has presented papers at various national, regional, and state professional conventions. He has conducted workshops for general awareness and specific skill training in pupil appraisal, behavioral programming, delivery of school-based psychological services, affective education, etc. Alan Coulter's publications include co-authorship (with James A. Tucker and Henry W. Morrow) of *The Comprehensive Screening System*, articles in journals such as *The Texas Psychologist*, various workshop handbooks, teacher information handouts, and a chapter in *The School Psychologist: Dynamics within a Role*.

Judi L. Coulter
Judi L. Coulter is a pupil appraisal and educational consultant. She has worked for Region IX Education Service Center, Witchita Falls, Texas, and the Wise County Coop in Decateur, Texas. She is the coauthor of *Screening Student Talents for Assessment and Resource Services: Teacher Roles in Screening, Identifying and Serving Gifted and Talented Students*, as well as numerous teacher oriented intervention handouts. She

has presented at state and national professional meetings and her workshops for teachers receive high ratings.

Nadine M. Lambert
Professor of Education
University of California
Berkeley, California 94720

Nadine M. Lambert is Professor of Education and Director of the School Psychology Training Program, University of California, Berkeley. Currently she is the principal investigator on a major project to study factors associated with the identification and treatment of hyperactive children. She has been principal investigator on several extramurally funded projects such as Validation on a Process for In-school Screening of Children with Emotional Handicaps, Stress of School Project, Public School Standardization of the AAMD Adaptive Behavior Scale, and Manual for the Diagnosis of Educable Mentally Retarded Pupils. Contributions include articles on the concurrent and predictive validity of noncognitive attributes, manuals for the naturalistic observation and data processing of observable pupil and teacher behaviors, the dimensionality of school behavior, and measures of environment associated with school performance.

Henry Leland
Director, Adaptive Behavior Project
Nisonger Center
The Ohio State University
Columbus, Ohio 43210

Henry Leland is currently Professor of Psychology at The Ohio State University and principal investigator for the Children's Adaptive Behavior Project (BEH/HEW). He has published articles and books covering a wide range of topics within psychology, including *Mental Retardation: Current and Future Perspectives* (with D. B. Smith) and the *Adaptive Behavior Scales—1969* (Revised 1974) (with K. Nihira, F. Foster, and M. Shellhaas). Dr. Leland is currently a member of many professional organizations and serves on a number of executive honored positions, such as a member of the Executive Committee of Division 33 of the American Psychological Association (President of Division 33 in 1976) and Councilor, American Psychological Association (1977–1980). He received his doctoral degree from the Sorbonne, Paris, France, after completing a bachelor's degree at San Jose State University.

June F. Lewis
Senior Writer and Editor, PRIME
Department of Sociology
University of California, Riverside
Riverside, California 92502

Prior to her present position, June Lewis served for seven years as
Director of the Pluralistic Assessment Project and as projects director/
coordinator of PRIME (Program Research in Integrated Multiethnic Education), with Dr. Jane R. Mercer as Principal Investigator. She served her
apprenticeship as a research sociologist under Dr. Mercer on the staff of
the Community Research Project, which conducted the epidemiology of
retardation in Riverside, California from 1963–1965, and she became field
director of follow-up studies conducted in 1968. She received her master's
degree in sociology from the University of California in 1970. From
1972–1975 Lewis served as Director of the Pluralistic Assessment Project
and was intimately involved in the development of the measures of
the SOMPA (System of Multicultural Pluralistic Assessment), including the
Adaptive Behavior Inventory for Children; she was also involved in the
collection and analyses of pretest, standardization, and field test data. She
became projects director/coordinator of PRIME in 1975. In June 1977 she
assumed the position of Senior Writer and Editor on the PRIME staff. Her
publications include the SOMPA *Parent Interview Manual*, The Psychological Corporation, 1977, with Jane R. Mercer; the SOMPA *Student
Assessment Manual*, The Psychological Corporation, 1977, with Jane R.
Mercer; "Community Attitudes toward Mental Retardation: A study in
Social Ambivalence," Monograph of the AAMD #1, 1973; and "Alternative to a Density Function Definition of Overcrowding," *Land Econom-
ics*, May, 1969.

Jane R. Mercer
Professor of Sociology
University of California, Riverside
Riverside, California 92502

Jane R. Mercer was the principal investigator in the "Epidemiology of
Exceptionality in School Children," which became the empirical basis for
the System of Multicultural Pluralistic Assessment (SOMPA). Currently
she is the principal investigator for an NIMH project entitled "Student
Mental Health in Desegregated Schools"; the primary trainer and designer
of SOMPA workshops for the Institute for Pluralistic Assessment, Research, and Training (IPART); and a member of numerous task forces and
special committees. Jane has written more than 60 articles, chapters, and

research reports, including a book entitled *Labeling the Mentally Retarded* (1973). She received her Ph.D. from the University of Southern California following the receipt of a master's degree at the University of Chicago. From 1975 to 1977 Dr. Mercer was chairperson of the Sociology Department at the University of California, Riverside; she is currently on sabbatical leave in order to prepare a book on SOMPA profiles of children in the original standardization sample.

Henry W. Morrow
Program Coordinator
Texas Regional Resource Center
211 East 7th Street
Austin, Texas 78701

Prior to his present position, Henry W. Morrow served as Pupil Appraisal Consultant for Region III, Education Service Center; Lecturer at the University of Houston at Victoria; and school psychologist for the Abilene, Texas, Public Schools. Dr. Morrow received his Ed.D. degree in educational psychology from Oklahoma State University. His master's degree was in clinical psychology from North Texas State University. Dr. Morrow taught at the University of Houston, conducted and participated in numerous teacher in-service programs, and served as a consultant to special education and regular classroom teachers concerning behavior problems in the classroom. Among his presented papers are "The Rural School Psychologist: Training and Service," with P. G. Warden and R. McCarthy at the National Association of School Psychologists in Chicago, 1972; "A Reaction: The Role of Research in Classroom Instruction," as part of a panel presentation entitled "Auditory Perception: Current Research," with S. C. Larsen, P. Newcomer, D. Hammil, and H. Sanford at the International Conference of the Association for Children with Learning Disabilities, Houston, 1974. He was major investigator and co-author of two relevant studies: "Placement or Placebo: Does Additional Information Change Special Education Placement Decisions" in the *Journal of School Psychology*, 1976, *14*; and *Pupil Appraisal 1975 to 1990: A Delphi Study*, 1976, Texas Regional Resource Center Technical Report No. 2.

Kazuo Nihira
Professor of Psychiatry
University of California, Los Angeles
Los Angeles, California 90024

Kazuo Nihira is co-author of the Adaptive Behavior Scale (1974) and is a consultant to a number of projects and professional associations involving mental retardation and psychological measurement. He has published more than 60 papers, monographs, and psychological tests. Nihira received his master's and doctoral degrees from the University of Southern California in the area of psychology. His experience with adaptive behavior measurement and research is extensive and includes studies both in the United States and Japan. His most recent publication is "Development of Adaptive Behavior in the Mentally Retarded," in P. Mittler (Ed.), *Research to Practice in Mental Retardation: Proceedings of the 4th Congress of IASSMD* (Vol. 2). Baltimore, Md.: University Park Press, 1977.

Adaptive Behavior

PART I

Theoretical Aspects of Adaptive Behavior

The intellectual problem of mental retardation [and adaptive behavior] is, ultimately a problem of classification and nomenclature. The perspective from which human behavior is viewed determines its meaning. (Mercer, 1973, p. 1.)

The discussants "speak as if their differences were confined to the specific question at issue around which the present disagreement crystallized. They overlook the fact that their antagonist differs from them in his (her) whole outlook and not merely in his (her) opinion about the point under discussion" (Mannheim, 1936, p. 751).

The four chapters presented in this part draw the reader's attention to both general and specific issues concerning the theory or concept of adaptive behavior. Chapter 1 provides a brief review of the various definitions of adaptive behavior in addition to tracing the historical development of the concept, particularly over the last 15 to 20 years. A conceptual scheme of psychological assessment is offered that is especially critical to understanding the confusion surrounding adaptive behavior. The scheme is the basis for much of the analysis in later chapters. It allows the reader to understand "the whole outlook and not merely . . . opinions" (Mannheim, 1936, p. 751) of the views presented.

Leland (Chapter 2) offers an overview of the theoretical development of adaptive behavior that ultimately resulted in the most popularly used measure—the Adaptive Behavior Scale (ABS). Henry Leland is an indispensable intellect in any discussion of adaptive behavior theory. He is an active participant in its recent emergence in psychological assessment. In Chapter 2, he shares his own broad-based view of mental retardation.

1

Leland's theoretical viewpoint is buttressed by his careful recollection of the history of his work in this area.

Nihira (Chapter 3) compliments Leland's theoretical approach with a review of the factor analysis research conducted using the Adaptive Behavior Scale developed by Nihira, Leland, and others. He carefully shows where many aspects of adaptive behavior formulated theoretically be Leland can now be substantiated empirically. Nihira also reports studies conducted in Japan and elsewhere that have produced results similar to those found in the United States.

Mercer (Chapter 4) presents what she considers to be the most recent state of development of her ideas concerning adaptive behavior. A noted sociologist often associated with recent changes in views of labeling and assessment of mental retardation. Mercer gives a detailed analysis of her conception of adaptive behavior. With Lewis, she is coauthor of the System of Multicultural Pluralistic Assessment (SOMPA), of which an adaptive behavior measure is a part. She carefully extends her theory beyond the existing adaptive behavior measure that she has developed to lead the reader to the cutting edge of theoretical development.

REFERENCES

Mannheim, K. *Ideology and utopia*. London: Kegan Paul, 1936.
Mercer, J. R. *Labeling the mentally retarded: Clinical and social system perspectives on mental retardation*. Berkeley: University of California Press, 1973.

W. Alan Coulter,
Henry W. Morrow

1

A Contemporary Conception of Adaptive Behavior within the Scope of Psychological Assessment

The manner in which persons perform the tasks expected of their particular age group can be broadly conceived as their adaptive behavior. How adaptive behavior is defined and applied in psychological assessment is the subject of this chapter. It is the central contention of the authors that a parsimonious concept of adaptive behavior requires not only a knowledge of the definition(s), but also an understanding of the function of the particular assessment tool being used to evaluate a given person.

Adaptive behavior may be viewed from a number of different perspectives. Persons with varying social, professional, and political frames of reference have produced a significant impact on the direction of research, preparation of measurement instruments, and the implementation of the concept of adaptive behavior in professional practice. At least two different but related trends in present society have contributed to the current concept of adaptive behavior. First, criticism of society because it unfairly restricts or prohibits the participation of mentally handicapped citizens has served as part of the impetus to formulate and expand a technology for training adaptive behavior (President's Committee on Mental Retardation, 1975a). The theory of normalization (Nirje, 1969) asserts the desirability of providing mentally retarded citizens a pattern of life as similar as possible to the normal citizen of society. Technology for training adaptive behavior is integral to this theory because the mentally retarded citizen must acquire skills that will support a minimum level of independent functioning required for normalization to be successful (Leland, 1973).

A second social trend is reflected in current federal legislation (Public

3

Law 94–142) and strong professional support (Tucker, 1976) to establish a nonbiased assessment process to ensure equal treatment to all children within the public schools. Equal treatment means that ethnic minority children will not be disproportionately labeled as mentally handicapped and thereby unfairly stigmatized. Nonbiased assessment seeks to modify traditional assessment procedures by ensuring that professional judgments are based on data which do not discriminate against ethnic minorities. Adaptive behavior has been proposed as part of a nonbiased assessment system (office of Civil Rights, 1976) to prevent unfair labeling (see Chapter 5). Adaptive behavior in this context emphasizes the behavior of an individual outside the school environment. By evaluating out-of-school behavior there is less likelihood of unfairly labeling a minority ethnic group child where traditional school-based measures emphasize the majority culture (Mercer, 1973).

The two trends mentioned have an obvious point of overlap. The same legislation that requires nonbiased assessment also mandates the development of intervention plans to promote the optimum development of mentally handicapped students, of which adaptive behavior is an essential component. It is at this point that confusion begins to develop regarding adaptive behavior. Does adaptive behavior mean nonbiased assessment or training? The answer is not easy to obtain and understand.

Additionally, given this prominent base of attention, one would expect adaptive behavior to be a familiar and extensively discussed topic in psychological assessment. However, a search of recent texts on psychological assessment (Anastasi, 1968; Horrocks, 1964; Robb, Bernardoni, & Johnson, 1972; Sattler, 1974; Wolman, 1965) failed to unearth one mention of adaptive behavior or its measurement. In the absence of any substantial reference to adaptive behavior in the literature on psychological assessment, how is adaptive behavior to be defined for the pupil appraisal professional?

DEFINITIONS OF ADAPTIVE BEHAVIOR

A recent review of the available definitions (Coulter & Morrow, 1976) reported nine sources and at least as many definitions of adaptive behavior. From Table 1–1 it is obvious that theoreticians and professional/governmental organizations serve as the two basic and obviously related origins of adaptive behavior definitions. Professional/governmental type definitions are especially relevant to appraisal practitioners because regulatory policies governing appraisal practices utilize these definitions.

Table 1–1
Definitions of Adaptive Behavior

I. Theoreticians of Adaptive Behavior

Mercer:

The child's ability to perform the social roles appropriate for persons of his/her age and sex in a manner which meets the expectations of the social systems in which he/she participates. Thus, social role performance is viewed in relation to specific social systems and their roles. (1977.)

An individual's ability to play ever more complex social roles in a progressively widening circle of special systems (1973, p. 13).

The working definition of *abnormal* adaptive behavior, like that for intelligence, is based on a statistical model of "normal," uses three criteria levels, and varies in content with the age of the person being evaluated:

Adaptive behavior in the young child is the extent to which he has acquired the self-help and social skills upon which more complex role performance can be built.

Adaptive behavior for the older child and adult is the extent to which that person is playing a full complement of social roles appropriate to his age and is performing in those roles in a manner comparable to that of other persons of his age in society. (1973, pp. 136–37.)

Leland et al.:

For the purposes of scale development, ability to adapt to environmental demand (Heber, 1961) was seen to be represented by three behavioral formations:

1. Independent functioning, defined as the ability of the individual to successfully accomplish those tasks or activities demanded of him by the general community, both in terms of the critical survival demands for that community and in terms of the typical expectations for specific ages.

2. Personal responsibility, defined as both the willingness of the individual to accomplish those critical tasks he is able to accomplish (generally under some supervision) and his ability to assume individual responsibility for his personal behavior. This ability is reflected in decision making and choice of behaviors.

3. Social responsibility, defined as the ability of the individual to accept responsibility as a member of a community group and to carry out appropriate behaviors in terms of these group expectations. This is reflected in levels of conformity, socially positive creativity, social adjustment, and emotional maturity. It was further analyzed in terms of the acceptance of some level of civic responsibility leading to complete or partial economic independence. (Leland, Nihira, Foster, Shellhaas, & Kagin, 1968, p. 14.)

Table 1-1 (Continued)

Nihira:

The effectiveness of the individual in adapting to the natural and social demands of his environment. . . . Adaptive behavior consists of two major facets—personal independence and a culturally oriented sense of personal responsibility. (1969, p. 869).

A composite of many aspects of behavior and a function of a wide range of specific abilities and disabilities (1976, p. 215).

Balthazar:

Comprises those behaviors which occur in response to a specific program (1973, p. 5.)

Robinson and Robinson:

"Impairment in adaptive behavior" is seen as the individual's ineffectiveness in adapting to the demands of his environment and is viewed from a developmental standpoint. It may be reflected during infancy and early childhood mainly by impairment in maturation manifested by retarded development in sensory motor behavior, self-help skills, and language. During the school years, the predominant area of impairment is in learning the skills that are of special importance in the academic setting. At the adult level, impairment in adaptation is reflected primarily in social adjustment, specifically in the ability of the individual to maintain himself economically and to meet and conform to the standards of the community. (1970, pp. 615–616.)

II. Professional/Governmental Agencies

American Association of Mental Deficiency:

(former definition)

The effectiveness with which the individual copes with the natural and social demands of his environment. . . . Two major facets: (1) the degree to which the individual is able to function and maintain himself independently, and (2) the degree to which he meets, satisfactorily, the culturally imposed demands of personal and social responsibility. (As quoted in Heber, 1961, p. 61.)

(present definition)

The effectiveness or degree with which the individual meets the standards of personal independence and social responsibility expected of his age or cultural group (Grossman, 1973, p. 11).

Office of Civil Rights:

The degree with which the student is able to function and participate effectively as a responsible member of his family and community (1976, p. 2).

6

Table 1-1 (Continued)

Department of Health, Education, and Welfare:

The effectiveness or degree with which individual meets the standards of personal independence and social responsibility expected of his or her age and cultural group (1976).

Texas Education Agency:

The effectiveness or degree with which the individual meets the standards of personal independence and social responsibility expected of the age and cultural group (1976, p. 1).

President's Committee on Mental Retardation:

Simply stated, adaptive behavior refers to the way an individual performs those tasks expected of someone his (her) age in his (her) culture (1975(b), p. 6).

For each theorist different aspects of adaptive behavior are important. Mercer (1977) emphasizes the social context of adaptive behavior, while Leland (1968) emphasizes the fit of the individual to environmental demands. Nihira (1976) implies that adaptive behavior is a wide-ranging concept applicable to diagnosis of disabilities, while Balthazar (1973) restricts his definition to the effects of training programs. Robinson and Robinson (1970) combine the concept of fit to environmental demand with varying tasks during the developmental sequence.

Basic Elements of the Definitions

All definitions (except Balthazar's) have commonalities. First, all place varying degrees of emphasis upon adequate development of skills for (1) functioning independently in meeting basic physical needs (i.e., eating, personal hygiene, toileting, dressing, etc.) and as an integral member of a community (able to travel, handle money, express language, maintain a healthy living environment, etc.) and (2) maintaining responsible social relationships (able to cooperate and interact with others, initiate and persist in purposeful activities, manage and care for personal belongings, etc.). Second, definite developmental trends are implied in the definitions, but these are rarely articulated, a fact that confuses appraisal personnel when they attempt to adapt the definition to their professional judgments.

Mercer (1973) sought to clarify her definition by delineating expectancies for certain age groups:[1]

Infancy: Birth through 2 Years. Measures of adaptive behavior cannot actually evaluate role performance in children this young. However, it is possible to identify certain developmental and maturational abilities and certain embryonic social skills that must be achieved and that are the building blocks from which later social role performance is formed.

Preschool: 3 through 5 Years. Assumes more responsibility for his own cleanliness and toileting: for dressing and undressing himself; for being able to distinguish harmful and dirty objects from edible ones; for using tools such as crayons . . . scissors without harming himself and others; . . . performing simple household tasks and running errands . . . expected to be able to move about his house and neighborhood with minimal supervision. . . . This greater independence assumes that he can manage most of his social interactions with minimal adult direction, can relate events that have happened to him, and can communicate his desires to others. . . .

School: 6 through 15 Years. Must comprehend a social structure containing unfamiliar roles such as teacher, principal, secretary, custodian . . . must learn the roles and values of his peers and simultaneously meet the ever increasing demands of the teacher . . . expected to perform more complex family roles and to learn many new roles in the community . . . (e.g., customer in a store, handling his own money and making his own selections) . . . driver of wheeled vehicles, whether they be bikes, or scooters. . . .

The Adult: 16 and over. The primary new role is occupational . . . expected to play a productive occupational role and to be financially self-sufficient. . . . For adults, adaptive behavior is measured by the number of roles the adult is playing and by his level of performance in those roles. (Pp. 134–136.)

The developmental trends implied in the definitions are further supported by the majority of factor analysis studies reported to date (Lambert & Nicoll, 1976; Nihira, 1969a, 1969b, 1976). Nihira (1976), utilizing a sample of 3354 institutionalized mentally retarded children and adults for whom ABS (Adaptive Behavior Scale) scores were available, found several developmental trends. Physical development emerged as a factor only within the age groups of 4 through 7. The items that made up the

[1] Note that Mercer includes out-of-school behaviors during school ages, which is an important component of a least-biased measure for diagnosis of mental retardation.

factor were found in the personal self-sufficiency factor at later ages, reflecting the fact that the skills were developmentally prerequisite to self-sufficiency but were undifferentiated once higher order skills were acquired. Also, factors such as community self-sufficiency and personal–social responsibility did not emerge in the sample until age 10. Nihira (1976) comments on the developmental phenomenon and the problem it may present the appraisal practitioner by cautioning "one of the problems with the concept of IQ or social quotient is that they tend to be interpreted as measuring the same thing over a wide span of ages and ability range. This is fallacious" (p. 225). It is important to emphasize that adaptive behavior scales are measuring different aspects of behavior at different ages.

General Agreement on a Definition

From the preceding discussion of the available definitions, it appears that there is general agreement regarding a definition of adaptive behavior. The American Association of Mental Deficiency, the Department of Health, Education, and Welfare, and Texas Education Agency (as an example of a state department of education) all substantially agree in their definitions. Since there is given this general agreement, it should be a relatively simple task to understand the development of measures of adaptive behavior. Historically the application of the definition in the development of adaptive behavior measures for psychological assessment has resulted, however, in two distinct types of adaptive behavior measures. Prior to a discussion of the history and the two types of adaptive behavior measures, it is necessary first to define explicitly what is meant by psychological assessment and where adaptive behavior measurement belongs.

A FUNCTIONAL DEFINITION OF PSYCHOLOGICAL ASSESSMENT

For the purposes of this discussion, the term "psychological assessment" will be defined as the psychological assessment of students directed toward either or both identification/placement (e.g., educable mentally retarded, emotionally disturbed, etc.) and intervention/programming (remediate vowel confusion, build paragraph comprehension, etc.).

Because administrative data collection, federal (93-380, 94-142) and/or state funding, and allocation of available resources are usually based upon the specific labeling of children to classify and signify eligibility for further services, indentification/placement is the assessment intent most frequently pursued. The results of this focus yield information (IQ score, etc.) that enables the professional to make a discrete judgment for identification (e.g., a child is or is not mentally retarded). State and federal administrative agencies often specify detailed criteria for professionals to follow (93-380, 94-142), the end product of which is a determination of specific eligibility (e.g., a child is or is not eligible for special education services as mentally retarded, emotionally disturbed, etc.).

Psychological assessment, the intent of which is the specification of a program for intervention (i.e., intervention/programming), requires an estimate of individual abilities, fund of knowledge, recommended methods for intervention, and potentially useful materials and media. The optimum goal is an individualized intervention plan which specifies (1) objectives to be accomplished for appropriate intervention, (2) circumstances under which the objectives will be accomplished, (3) criterion level for success in measurable terms, and (4) anticipated date of completion. Particular assessment techniques may include standardized and norm-referenced tests and informal data collection, observation in situation-specific activities, and criterion-referenced tests (Drew, 1973; Mercer & Ysseldyke, 1976; Williams, 1975). This assessment process yields an increased specification of problem areas and outlines the steps and chronology of events needed to intervene and remediate.

The distinction of two intents or purposes of psychological assessment within the field of special education is arbitrary, but is nevertheless helpful. Oakland and Matuszek (1976) describe assessment as having two functions: (1) classification and (2) intervention planning and evaluation. Bernal (1976) specifies the functions of assessment as classification and educational programming, and decision making and intervention; he says testing is conducted toward these goals. However, for the purposes of this discussion, identification/placement (i.e., classification/labeling and intervention/programming (of which educational programming is one facet of a total individual program) are the central intents or purposes of assessment. Assessment provides, at various points in the educational process, the information necessary for the decision making Bernal mentions.

Considering these two distinct purposes of assessment, we can select tests, as well as procedures, that will yield the desired information. But these distinct purposes, although compatible in meeting the needs of the referral, are not necessarily accomplished by using the same tests,[2] as

[2] It should be noted that in selecting which particular tests or procedures are best for identifications/placement versus intervention/programming, the answer is usually never precise, as some tests may have relative value for both types. The efficacy of a dual function test has not been thoroughly investigated at this point. In general, though, a test which is designed for this dual purpose usually suffers in overall effectiveness. Most tests and procedures, such as a criterion-referenced test of reading abilities, are specifically designed

reported in the literature concerning nonbiased assessment models (Tucker, 1976).

Using the conceptual framework of the two purposes of assessment, we can examine a number of issues within psychological assessment more easily. For instance, criticism of testing on the basis that is unfairly labels members of minority ethnic groups can be seen as directed toward tests used in assessment for identification/placement (Bernal, 1975; Jackson, 1975). The contention that tests should furnish information relevant for practical classroom application (Faur, 1974; McKenna, 1977; Mercer & Ysseldyke, 1976; Tucker, 1976) is directed at tests used in assessment for intervention/programming. It is the basic contention of the authors that assessment of adaptive behavior (given the particular purpose, procedure, and instrumentation) can be used in either assessment for identification/placement or assessment for intervention/programming. Much of the current controversy and debate surrounding the concept and measurement of adaptive behavior (Clausen, 1972b; Leland, 1972; Mercer, 1976; Tucker, 1977) can be more easily understood and to some extent resolved by utilizing this premise. To better understand the concept of adaptive behavior within this context of psychological assessment, it is necessary to examine the history of the concept. By learning how the concept developed historically the reader will see how the current state of confusion developed.

A BRIEF HISTORICAL PERSPECTIVE OF THE CONCEPT OF ADAPTIVE BEHAVIOR

The attempt to define the relevant aspects of individuals' behaviors that enable them to function efficiently in society (the ultimate objective of adaptive behavior, Leland, 1973) has long been an objective of psychological assessment. "Itard and Haslan in 1819, Sequin in 1837, Voisin in 1843, Howe in 1858, and Goddard in 1912 spoke essentially about 'adaptive behavior,' using such terms as social competency, skills training, social norms, the power of fending for oneself in life, adaptability to environment, and efficiency of social value" (Lambert, Windmiller, Cole, & Figueroa, 1974, p. xi). Binet, originator of the concept of intelligence testing, viewed an individual as normal "if he is able to work sufficiently remunerative to supply his own personal needs, and finally if his intelligence does not unfit him for the social environment of his parents" (1909). Binet was referring to what we now define as adaptive behavior.

In 1959 the American Association on Mental Deficiency introduced

---

for the precise remediation of a problem or deficit area. Others are appropriate only for designating presence of absence of particular handicapping conditions and thus are useful for determining eligibility for placement.

the concept of adaptive behavior as a classification dimension in mental retardation (Heber, 1959). In 1961 the concept was broadened to include terms such as maturation and social adjustment. The definition of mental retardation was expanded to read: "Refers to subaverage general intellectual functioning which originates during the developmental period and is associated with *impairment in adaptive behavior*" (authors' italics) (Heber, 1961, p. 3). Most of the early major professional comments specific to the concept centered on the vagueness of the definition, the lack of empirical measurement of this hypothetical construct, and the relationship of it to the measurement of intelligence (Clausen, 1972a; Dayan & McLean, 1963; Leland, Shellhaas; Nihira, & Foster, 1967). Other peripheral comments highlighted the relationship between adaptive behavior as social adjustment versus maladaptive behavior and its need for remediation (Leland et al., 1967, Philips, 1966). Adaptive behavior, originally conceived as an adjunct to assessment of intelligence (Heber, 1961), was considered by some to be an alternative to traditional IQ testing (Clausen, 1972b; Leland, 1972; Leland et al., 1967; Philips, 1966)

Recent discussions regarding the identification of mental retardation (Clausen, 1972a, 1972b; Leland, 1972; MacMillian & Jones, 1976; Nagler, 1972; Wilson, 1972) give more contemporary significance to this long-standing history. These discussions revolved around whether to include the concept of adaptive behavior in the definition for identification of mental retardation and what proportion of the population (3 percent or 16 percent) should be labeled mentally retarded. Some would contend that the original concept of intelligence (i.e., Binet) is more closely aligned with the present concept of adaptive behavior than with the traditional concept of intelligence (Kamin, 1974; Oakland, 1976). The social and professional forces that influence the identification of the mentally retarded and the manner in which the mentally retarded are managed by government and social agencies were the initiators of the debate. The central issue in the debate to include a measure of adaptive behavior for the identification of mental retardation was that the IQ test did not furnish enough descriptive information of relevance for training mentally retarded persons for normalization. To provide additional information regarding the concept and to develop a satisfactory measure of adaptive behavior, a project was funded which subsequently clarified one purpose of adaptive behavior measurement.

THE PARSONS STATE HOSPITAL PROJECT

In 1965 Parsons State Hospital (Kansas), in cooperation with the AAMD (American Association on Mental Deficiency) began a project (MH-14901) concerning adaptive behavior that would (1) review the relevant literature, (2) develop methods and procedures for validating adaptive behavior as an *independent* dimension, (3) develop a more concise definition of the concept, (4) build a reference library, and (5) develop a measurement manual that would be useful in planning for the organization of residential centers and other services in the community (Leland, 1973). The project produced two adaptive behavior scales, Forms I and II (Nihira, Foster, Shellhaas, & Leland, 1969), which were revised and coalesced into one scale called the Adaptive Behavior Scale (ABS)—1975 Revision (Nihira, Foster, Shellhaas, & Leland, 1975). Much of the validation of the ABS and its supporting literature was conducted by the Parsons Project.

Leland, project director, characterized the majority of the research literature done by the project as "almost entirely institutional in origin" (1973, p. 92). Financial support was not available for both institutional and community data. Therefore, the former was chosen, and plans were announced to establish a community research base in the future. From the inception of the project (as documented in Leland et al., 1967), the purpose of the measurement of adaptive behavior was for the *treatment* or remediation of deficit behaviors among retardates in *institutions*. The issue of identification of mental retardation without ethnic or socioeconomic bias (as implied nonbiased assessment) was not important to the project. The project adopted the definition of adaptive behavior as noted by Heber (1959) with no substantial modifications.

Another project relevant to understanding adaptive behavior utilized a similar definition adaptive behavior but adopted a different operational procedure and, subsequently, a different purpose.

THE PACIFIC STATE HOSPITAL PROJECT

In 1954 Pacific State Hospital (California) began a study (MH-5687) of the families of the mentally retarded as part of a broader study of the importance of the community aspects of mental retardation. In the early 1960s Jane R. Mercer joined the research staff as a field director. Procedures were developed for interviewing, surveying, and sampling the general population in Riverside, California (the research site). The objective was to identify those people in the community who were mentally retarded, regardless of whether they were known as mentally retarded to social agencies (Dingman, 1973). Thus, the project's emphasis was to identify the mentally retarded in the community, whereas the Parsons State Hospital's emphasis was to program already identified mentally retarded persons.

The definition of mental retardation which the Pacific research team chose to use contained both a clinical component of intellectual subnormality and a social systems component of impaired ability to meet the demands of the social world (Mercer, 1973). "Adaptive behavior" was the term selected to describe this ability or inability to meet the demands of the social world (Mercer, 1973). Mercer noted that this definition of adaptive behavior corresponded closely with Heber's but that it incorporated the concept of social role (1973, p. 133). Because the task of the project was to find mentally retarded persons in the community, Mercer incorporated the definition of adaptive behavior as part of assessment for identification/placement. This point is critical in order to understand the present confusion concerning adaptive behavior. Although Mercer was using essentially the same definition of adaptive behavior as Leland and the Parsons Project, the function or purpose of the assessment was quite different.

Results of the study showed that public schools labeled more people than any other agency. Black and Mexican-American children were "overlabeled" as mentally retarded by public schools, while Anglo children were "underlabeled" as mentally retarded. Additionally, children from lower socioeconomic backgrounds were overlabeled, while children from higher socioeconomic backgrounds were underlabled. These results documented the need to develop a multicultural, pluralistic method of assessment for schools that would evaluate children as multidimensional persons within particular sociocultural settings rather than maintain a bias toward the majority culture (Mercer, 1975).

A new project to extend the work begun at Pacific State was funded in 1969 and housed at the University of California–Riverside (UCR) under the direction of Mercer to develop the System of Multicultural Pluralistic Assessment (SOMPA). One scale within this system of assessment was a measure of adaptive behavior. The purpose in developing the Adaptive Behavior Inventory for Children (ABIC) was to provide an instrument that would identify those children who were retarded in their ability to meet the demands of various social roles (e.g., assessment for identification/placement). A corresponding identification of mental subnormality (measured intelligence below two standard deviations) with a significantly low score on adaptive behavior would identify a mentally retarded child. For Mercer the central issue regarding adaptive behavior measurement was its inclusion as part of a system for least-biased assessment for identification purposes rather than for intervention/programming. The content of the ABIC was designed primarily to measure out-of-school role behaviors. This emphasis reflects Mercer's particular purpose of adaptive behavior measurement and her concern for least-biased assessment.

ADAPTIVE BEHAVIOR AND THE
NONBIASED ASSESSMENT CONTROVERSY

As mentioned earlier, adaptive behavior was included in a controversy regarding the appropriateness of the IQ test and its use in making a differential placement in public school programs (i.e., special education versus regular education). Related to the controversy were the results of Mercer's preliminary study, which found overlabeling of minority group children by traditional assessment practices (Mercer, 1972, 1973).

The controversy took on crisis dimensions in California when in 1971 the California State Education Code was modified to include a measure of adaptive behavior in the evaluation of students for placement as educable mentally retarded (Lambert, Windmiller, Cole, & Figueron, 1975). The measure of adaptive behavior was added as a function of administrative policy in an attempt to make the identification of mental retardation less biased by ethnic differences. An implementation problem was created because no specific measure or accepted nonbiased assessment procedures were available in public schools to carry out the policy. A manual was developed, through support of the California State Department of Education, for pupil appraisal personnel (chiefly school psychologists) to expand the scope of the psychological assessment process (Lambert, Wilcox, & Gleason, 1974). Lambert et al. (1975) stated that the adaptive behavior scale most capable of satisfying the state education code mandate was the AAMD's ABS. The only modifications necessary to insure its applicability for pupil appraisal personnel were the preparation of public school norms and the deletion of some items of the scale (Lambert et al., 1975, p. 3). Using this premise, the ABS—Public School Version (ABS—PS) was developed for use by school psychologists in California (Lambert, Windmiller, et al., 1974). The ABS—PS authors agree with the basic contention that the scale was based on remediation rather than classification and/or labeling (p. xi), but they contend that their deletion of certain items and their standardization assist in determining whether a child's score is more or less comparable to known groups within the public schools (p. 10). Some debate is now emerging among appraisal practitioners regarding the applicability of the ABS, a programming instrument, as a test for identification/placement (Fitzpatrick & Rogers, 1977; also Chapter 6 of this volume) to satisfy a similar legislative mandate in Texas. Since the test's authors stated certain disclaimers and cautions regarding use of the ABS—PS, the debate surrounding it seems unwarranted. The greatest strength of the ABS (Nihira et al., 1975) is that it is a frequently used measurement in programming and remediation for the mentally retarded (see Chapter 6).

The larger controversy of ethnic bias in intelligence testing has not

diminished. Recent court action (*Larry P.* v. *Riles*) and related professional debate (Lambert, Meyers, & Opton, 1977) have further intensified
the dilemma of providing special services to meet educational needs
versus the need to identify and classify children for administrative purposes. The concept and measurement of adaptive behavior is integral to a
resolution of the controversy, but it is not the only component. The
pressure of court action, state and federal legislation, and professional
examination of current testing practices (Oakland & Laosa, 1976) shows
no sign of quick resolution.

TWO APPROACHES TO ADAPTIVE BEHAVIOR
MEASUREMENT

This chronology of the two projects, seminal to the contemporary
concept of adaptive behavior, indicates two distinct differences in purpose. The Parsons State Project, in an effort to assist the mentally retarded in reentry as viable, independently functioning members of the
community, began its study in the institution with the institutionally
placed mentally retarded. Leland (Leland et al., 1967) outlined the project's objective in these words: "The need for the assessment of adaptive
behavior originated in an attempt to obtain more useful information for
the *treatment and training of the mentally retarded*" (authors' italics) (p.
366). In other words, the purpose of the assessment was intervention/
programming. The Pacific State Project (which became the University of
California-Riverside Project) sought to identify the mentally retarded in
the community. Mercer (1973) stipulates the specific use of their adaptive
behavior scale as "important in evaluating persons from ethnic minorities
and lower socioeconomic statuses—persons from backgrounds that do
not conform to the model pattern for the community" (p. 191). In other
words, the emphasis here is identification. The different social settings
(institution versus community) profoundly affected the articulation of
each project's operational definition of adaptive behavior, the development of the measurement instrumentation, and eventually the purpose of
each adaptive behavior measure (ABS and ABIC) within the field of
psychological assessment.

In summary, although the general concept of adaptive behavior is not
new, the integration of a systematic measure of adaptive behavior as a
component of psychological assessment is a more recent development.
The 1959 inclusion of adaptive behavior as part of its classification system
of mental retardation gave the American Association on Mental Deficiency the distinction of reviving adaptive behavior as a relevant concept
(Heber, 1959). More recently, the use of adaptive behavior in least-biased

assessment procedures (Mercer, 1973; Tucker, 1976) has been advocated. These two related but distinct origins (Parsons State and Pacific State/ UCR) and their subsequent development have had a profound effect upon varying policies and methodology of implementation regarding the concept of adaptive behavior. Not only are these two events of historical importance, but they are integral to explanation of the use of adaptive behavior in current practices in psychological assessment. The resulting confusion from at least two different intents or purposes of adaptive behavior (Leland et al., 1967; Mercer, 1977) within the broad scope of psychological assessment may have confused appraisal practitioners in their selection and implementation of a measure of adaptive behavior.

REFERENCES

Anastasi, A. *Psychological testing* (3rd ed.). London: Macmillan, 1968.
Balthazar, E. E. *Balthazar Scales of Adaptive Behavior: II. Scales of Social Adaptation*. Palo Alto, Ca.: Consulting Psychologists Press, 1973.
Bernal, E. A response to educational uses of tests with disadvantaged subjects. *American Psychologist*, 1975, *30*, 93–95.
Bernal, E. Perspectives in nondiscriminatory assessment. In T. Oakland (Ed.), *With bias toward none: Non-biased assessment of minority group children*. Lexington, Ky.: Coordinating Office for Regional Resource Centers, 1976.
Binet, A. *Les idees modernes sur les enfants*. Paris: Flammarion, 1909.
Clausen, J. Quo vadis, AAMD? *Journal of Special Education*, 1972, *6*, 51–70. (a)
Clausen, J. The continuing problem of defining mental deficiency. *Journal of Special Education*, 1972, *6*, 97–106. (b)
Coulter, W. A., & Morrow, H. W. *A collection of definitions of adaptive behavior*. Austin: Texas Regional Resource Center, 1976.
Dayan, M., & McClean, J. Gardner behavior chart as a measure of adaptive behavior of the mentally retarded. *American Journal of Mental Deficiency*, 1963, *67*, 887–892.
Dingman, H. F. Foreword. In J. R. Mercer, *Labeling the mentally retarded*. Berkeley: University of California Press, 1973.
Drew, C. J. Criterion-referenced and norm-referenced assessment of minority group children. *Journal of School Psychology*, 1973, *11*, 323–329.
Faur, P. *Train, don't test*. Champaign, Il.: Children's Research Center, 1974.
Fitzpatrick, A., & Rogers, D. *A critique of the AAMD Adaptive Behavior Scale, Public School Version*. Unpublished manuscript, 1977. (Available from the Northside Independent School District, Pupil Appraisal Center, 1827 Westridge, San Antonio, Texas 78227.)
Grossman, H. J. (Ed.). *Manual on terminology and classification in mental retardation* (Special Publication No. 2). Washington, D. C.: American Association on Mental Deficiency, 1973.
Heber, R. A. A manual on terminology and classification in mental retardation. *American Journal of Mental Deficiency* (Monograph Supplement), 1959, *64*.

18   Coulter and Morrow

Heber, R. A. A manual on terminology and classification in mental retardation. *American Journal of Mental Deficiency* (Monograph Supplement), 1961, *66*.

Horrocks, J. E. Assessment of behavior: *The methodology and content of psychological measurement.* Columbus, Ohio: Merrill, 1964.

Jackson, G. Another psychological view from the Association of Black Psychologists. *American Psychologist,* 1975, *30*, 88–93.

Kamin, L. J. *The science and politics of IQ.* New York: Wiley, 1974.

Lambert, N. M., Meyers, C. E., & Opton, E. From California: Two views. *APA Monitor,* 1977, *8*(4), 4–5.

Lambert, N. M., & Nicoll, R. C. Dimensions of adaptive behavior of retarded and nonretarded public school children. *American Journal of Mental Deficiency,* 1976, *81*, 135–146.

Lambert, N. M., Wilcox, M. R., & Gleason, W. P. *The educationally retarded child: Comprehensive assessment and planning for slow learners and the educationally mentally retarded.* New York: Grune & Stratton, 1974.

Lambert N. M., Windmiller, M., Cole, L., & Figueroa, R. *AAMD Adaptive Behavior Scale: Public school version* (1974 Rev.). Washington, D. C.: American Association on Mental Deficiency, 1975.

Lambert, N. M., Windmiller, M., Cole, L., & Figueroa, R. Standardization of a public school version of the AAMD Adaptive Behavior Scale. *Mental Retardation,* 1975, *13*(2), 3–7.

Leland, H. Introduction and theoretical considerations. In E. Kagin (Ed.), *Conference on measurement of adaptive behavior: III.* Parsons, Ks.: Parsons State Hospital and Training Center, 1968.

Leland, H. Mental retardation and adaptive behavior. *Journal of Special Education,* 1972, *6*, 71–80.

Leland, H. Adaptive behavior and mentally retarded behavior. In C. E. Meyers, R. K. Eyman, & G. Tarjan (Eds.), *Sociobehavioral studies in mental retardation: Papers in honor of Harvey F. Dingman,* Washington, D. C.: American Association on Mental Deficiency, 1973.

Leland, H., Nihira, K., Foster, R., Shellhaas, M., & Kagin, E. *Conference on measurement of adaptive behavior: III.* Parsons, Ks.: Parsons State Hospital and Training Center, 1968.

Leland, M., Shellhaas, M., Nihira, K., & Foster, R. Adaptive behavior: A new dimension in the classification of the mentally retarded. *Mental Retardation Abstracts,* 1967, *4*, 359–387.

MacMillian, D. L., & Jones, R. L. Lions in search of more Christians. *Journal of Special Education,* 1976, *6*, 81–90.

McKenna, B. What's wrong with standardized testing. *Today's Education,* 1977, March–April, 35–38.

Mercer, J. R. IQ: The lethal label. *Psychology Today,* 1972, *6*(4), 44.

Mercer, J. R. *Labeling the mentally retarded: Clinical and social system perspectives on mental retardation.* Berkeley: University of California Press, 1973.

Mercer, J. R. Sociocultural factors in educational labeling. In M. J. Begab & S. A. Richardson (Eds.), *The mentally retarded and society: A social science perspective.* Baltimore: University Park Press, 1975.

Mercer, J. R. Personal communication, November 10, 1976.

Mercer, J. R. Personal communication, April 28, 1977.
Mercer, J. R., & Ysseldyke, J. Designing diagnostic-intervention programs. In T. Oakland (Ed.), *With bias toward none: Non-biased assessment of minority group children*. Lexington, Ky.: Coordinating Office for Regional Resource Centers, 1976.
Nagler, B. A change in terms or in concepts? A small forward or a giant step backward? *Journal of Special Education*, 1972, *6*, 61–64.
Nihira, K. Factorial dimensions of adaptive behavior in adult retardates. *American Journal of Mental Deficiency*, 1969, *73*, 868–878. (a)
Nihira, K. Factorial dimensions of adaptive behavior in mentally retarded children and adolescents. *American Journal of Mental Deficiency*, 1969, *74*, 130–141. (b)
Nihira, K. Dimensions of adaptive behavior in institutionalized mentally retarded children and adults: Developmental perspective. *American Journal of Mental Deficiency*, 1976. *81*, 215–226.
Nihira, K., Foster, R., Shellhaas, M., & Leland H., *AAMD Adaptive Behavior Scale*. Washington, D. C.: American Association on Mental Deficiency, 1969.
Nihira, K., Foster, R., Shellhaas, M., & Leland, H. *American Association on Mental Deficiency Adaptive Behavior Scale, 1975 revision*. Washington, D.C.: American Association on Mental Deficiency, 1975.
Nirje, B. The normalization principle and its human management implications. In R. Kugel & W. Wolfensberger (Eds.), *Changing patterns in residential services for the mentally retarded*. Washington, D. C.: President's Committee on Mental Retardation, 1969, 179–195.
Oakland, T. (Ed.) *With bias toward none: Non-biased assessment of minority-group children*. Lexington, Ky.: Coordinating Office for Regional Resource Centers, 1976.
Oakland, T., & Laosa, L. M. Professional, legislative, and judicial influences on psychoeducational assessment practices in schools. In T. Oakland (Ed.), *With bias toward none: Non-biased assessment of minority group children*. Lexington, Ky.: Coordinating Office for Regional Resource Centers, 1976.
Oakland, T., & Matuszek, P. Using tests in nondiscriminatory assessment. In T. Oakland (Ed.), *With bias toward none: Non-biased assessment of minority group children*. Lexington, Ky.: Coordinating Office for Regional Resource Centers, 1976.
Office of Civil Rights. Memorandum from OCR to state and local edcation agencies on elimination of discrimination in the assignment of children to special education classes for the mentally retarded. In T. Oakland (Ed.), *With bias toward none: Non-biased assessment of minority group children*. Lexington, Ky.: Coordinating Office for Regional Resource centers, 1976.
Philips, I. *Prevention and treatment of mental retardation*. New York: Basic Books, 1966.
President's Committee on Mental Retardation. *Mental retardation: Century of decision*. Washington, D. C.: Superintendent of Documents, 1975. (a)
President's Committee on Mental Retardation. *Mental retardation: The known and the unknown*. Washington, D. C.: Superintendent of Documents, 1975. (b)

Public Law 94–142. Washington, D. C.: Ammendments, 1974.

Robb, G. P., Bernardoni, L. C., & Johnson, R. W. *Assessment of individual mental ability.* Scranton, Pa.: Intext Educational Publishers, 1972.

Robinson, H. B., & Robinson, N. M. Mental retardation. In P. H. Mussen (Ed.), *Carmichael's manual of child psychology* (3rd ed.), Vol. II. New York: Wiley, 1970.

Sattler, J. *Assessment of children's intelligence* (Rev. ed.). Philadelphia.: Saunders, 1974.

Texas Education Agency. *Proposed revision 3572.5a administrative procedure.* Austin: Author, Special Education Division, 1976.

Tucker, J. A. Operationalizing the diagnostic intervention process. In T. Oakland (Ed.), With bias toward none: Non-biased assessment of minority group children. Lexington, Ky.: Coordinating Office for Regional Resource Centers, 1976.

Tucker, J. A. Personal communication, January 16, 1977.

Williams, R. L. The bitch-100: A culture-specific test. *Journal of Afro-American Issues,* 1975, *3,* 103–116.

Wilson, J. B. Is the term "adaptive behavior" educationally relevant? *Journal of Special Education,* 1972, *6,* 93–95.

Wolman, B. B. (Ed.) *Handbook of clinical psychology.* New York: McGraw-Hill, 1965.

Henry W. Leland

2
Theoretical Considerations of Adaptive Behavior

Looking at the manner in which individuals cope with their environment is not a new idea, but it is still very difficult. The various factors that go into coping behaviors often are not known, nor is it known how to relate them to observable behaviors which are not easily amenable to measurement. It is simple to set up very specific behavioral dimensions such as toileting, feeding, dressing, etc., except that there are other equally specific behavioral dimensions which come under a broad heading of "what the individual is doing instead," and although these are also observable, it is difficult to systematize them into a rating scale. Thus, if one asks, "Does a child feed him/herself with a spoon?" the answer may be no, but this may be only half the answer. At the same time the child may be throwing the food, smearing it, putting his/her face in it, or squeezing it through a fist. There are a variety of things which may be going in "instead,"all of which represent observable discrete behaviors that demonstrate how this particular individual is attempting to cope with the fact that there is food in front of him/her. In many respects the "instead" behaviors are, in terms of program planning, more important than the "expected" behaviors. One of the reasons that adaptive behavior measurement is basically different from IQ measurement is that it is not tied to standardized or expected behaviors, but, rather, it is a combination of anticipated behaviors and idiosyncratic behaviors. The real measurement of the individual's adaptive behavior comes from this combination.

Here we find a theoretical relationship to Piaget's (1952) discussion of adaptation, where he refers to the balance between accommodation (which in this instance can be taken in terms of standardized or expected behaviors) and assimilation (which in this instance can be taken to be representative of the idiosyncratic responses), and in that sense this very fine balance is the area where measurement is being attempted by the adaptive behavior scales.

Further, the level of the individual's adaptive behavior is of more than just academic interest. It is information that people in the helping professions, administrators, legislators, and individuals in the service delivery system need in order to establish some sort of habilitative classification system. Since the individual's IQ cannot be considered an appropriate way to diagnose or classify a person because of the aspects of IQ measurement which, in the long run, emerge as destructive to the handicapped person, it has been decided by the American Association on Mental Deficiency (Grossman, 1973), as well as by the legislatures of various states, that some concordance between measured intelligence and deficit in adaptive behavior be required before labels or designations of mental retardation should be applied. This means that adaptive behavior measurement must take into consideration the "bookkeeeping" aspects of the classification problem. It is not sufficient merely to measure the basic functional independence or cognitive progress or social and personal motivation of the person, nor is it sufficient to outline levels of social maladaptation (Leland, Shoaee, & Vayda, 1975). While all of these areas are very closely related to the development of an appropriate individual habilitation plan, they do not give generalized kinds of information which will permit legislators, other governmental bodies, school systems, etc., to plan for the number of individuals who are going to require a specialized kind of help.

BASIC FACTORS FOR AN ADAPTIVE BEHAVIOR SCALE

From the frame of reference just noted an appropriate measurement must take four things into consideration: (1) the factors being measured, (2) the special requirements of the population being measured, (3) the personal and social consequences of such measurement, and (4) the community needs for the results of the measurement. Any scale which fails to touch all four of these bases fails in its underlying and basic purpose and may in the long run become more destructive to the individual than helpful.

It is important to consider the individual's right to privacy, the individual's right to personal space, the individual's right not to be unnecessarily intruded upon, and the individual's right not to have his personal ecology unnecessarily disturbed. An ethical dictum for measurement should exist whereby information that is not needed or usable should not be acquired. Therefore, it is necessary to conceptualize a measurement scale which asks only those questions which are specifically relative to individuals' abilities to cope with the demands of their personal environments, i.e., those behaviors which are considered by that environment to be necessary for survival. Within the framework of the social responsibility of the test makers, all such items should also have some practical relationship to the daily living needs of the client and should have some opportunity for being modified if the "instead" behaviors predominate over the required behaviors.

With these considerations in mind, an effort was made by the American Association on Mental Deficiency's Adaptive Behavior Project to develop an adaptive behavior scale which dealt with discrete observable behaviors in areas that were generally considered socially necessary within the framework of a typical living environment. Those behaviors which would differentiate between clients were also taken into consideration, giving some potential for leveling; a concerted effort was made to insure all items were essentially reversible.

INDEPENDENT FUNCTIONING

In order to accomplish this measurement needed that items be reversible, items were grouped into basic domains and subdomains. The first was Independent Functioning. This domain grouped those items which are considered necessary for the individual to function in almost any environment. It also included a number of items which may be considered only "desirable," e.g., table manners. We further recognized that, while the standard culture has many subcultural variations within it, items such as toileting, feeding oneself, carrying out certain kinds of required activities in relationship to the rest of society, etc., seemed to run through most areas of the American culture. The variations occur through specific refinements of these behaviors and, more importantly, through the level of social tolerance around certain aspects of them. Thus, most of our cultural areas consider it necessary that the individual be clothed to some loosely defined extent. There are, however, many regional, cultural, social, and national differences as to what would necessarily be called "appropriate" clothing; even those differences are modified by geographical considerations, such as the difference between downtown and on the beach. Thus, being able to function with clothing is a necessary adaptive behavior. The quantity of clothing, the percentage of the body to be covered, and the nature and composition of this clothing comes under a broader heading of "desirable," and this varies greatly from place to place.

The broad domain of Independent Functioning takes both of these elements into consideration, with major emphasis given to those demands which are "necessary," but with continued consideration given to those demands which are considered "desirable." As an aside, it is our experience with problems relating to institutionalization, special class placement, and other program considerations which involve labeling and separation of exceptional or handicapped persons from other portions of society, that it is often the inability to stay within the tolerance level of the "desirable" behaviors that brings about requests for separation. At that point, there also needs to be a consciousness of which aspect of the individual's community is to be given priority, e.g., the child's behavior and clothing habits may be much different at home than they would be in school.

Independent functioning, however, is not just the completion of self-help skills. Various other mediating elements have been included in Part I of the scales. These include domains such as Physical Development, which identifies the tie-in between the presence or absence of a physically handicapping problem and the inability to perform certain of the expected skills. There is a relationship between cognitive learning and adaptation. The three domains of Economic Activity, Language Development, and Number and Time Concepts give some indication of how these elements interact with the broader aspects of independent functioning (Page, 1970). Further, as we move from childhood into adolescence and adulthood, various aspects of the question which have been generally defined under the domain and subdomains of Independent Functioning become modified in terms of the "chores" and other daily living activities required for the maintenance of a social unit. Thus, the domain of Domestic Activity becomes an additional reflection of the ability to perform at a functionally independent level in the contest of the living environment, and these activities become one basis for judging the development of an adult level of adaptation.

Social and personal motivation play an important role in the maintenance of functional independence. This is another maturation area which helps separate the mere learning of self-help skills from the utilization of skills and ability as part of a daily living pattern at a level of personal responsibility. There is an underlying ethic that all mentally retarded persons should have the "same basic rights as other citizens of the same country of the same age" (Declaration of General and Special Rights . . ., 1969). This statement has become the basic "normalization" statement in relationship to development of the rights of the retarded. It is obviously one thing to have rights, however, and something else to be able to exercise them. The adaptive behavior scales do not become representative of the ethical issue, but in terms of the responsibility of the helping professions to make it possible for the mentally retarded and developmentally delayed persons to exercise their rights, the work on personal responsibility as represented through personal and social motivation becomes an essential part of program planning. This measurement is reflected in the domains of Vocational Activity, Self-Direction, Responsibility, and Socialization (Leland, Shoaee, & Vayda, 1975).

Part II of the scales was established to determine what role various maladaptive behaviors played in the disruption of independent functioning, personal responsibility, and social responsibility. Individuals may have a high or low level of skills, they may respond well or poorly to training, and they may represent good or imperfect levels of growth and development, but all of these estimations have to be further mediated against the existence or absence of evidence of emotional disturbance, antisocial behaviors, antiself behaviors, and other similar functions which interfere regularly with both the learning process and all efforts through either training or treatment to bring about change. As in other aspects of adaptive behavior measurement, however, these behaviors are also reversible, and their identification permits the establishment of appropriate programs of intervention.

RELATIONSHIPS BETWEEN INTELLIGENCE AND ADAPTIVE BEHAVIOR

In the latter regard there is a very obvious relationship between adaptive functioning and intelligence. Without doubt individuals with higher levels of intelligence learn to perform skills sooner, are able to assume greater personal responsibility, and have a high capacity for social adjustment. There are mentally retarded and developmentally disabled persons in our environment, however, who do not have high levels of intelligence, nor do they necessarily have a potential for high levels of intelligence. They do, though, have a very good potential for high and effective levels of adaptive behavior, so one must understand both what the relationship between intelligence and adaptive behavior would seem to be and also what the differences are.

There is or should be an area of overlap with the relationship of adaptive behavior to measured intelligence. The immediate observation in a residential setting is that the elements being observed under the heading of adaptive behavior are in most instances similar to elements being observed under the heading of measured intelligence. This observation, however, should not be generalized, for as the classification of the mentally retarded moves out of the institution into the general community, other elements appear. Thus, if only the institutionalized retarded individuals (in the residential institutions in the United States) are considered, there would be a very close correlation between the estimated level of adaptive behavior and the measured level of intelligence as based on current psychometrics. Part of this is due to the shaping or molding effect of the institution, part to the selection factors in the community in terms of who becomes institutionalized, and part to imperfection in psychometric measurements. There is an indication that the IQ level and the adaptive behavior level would be very similar for a great number of institutionalized persons. This does not rule out adaptive behavior as a separate dimension for institutional classification because we are classifying for more than "bookkeeping" reasons; we need to learn specific behavioral responses to specific types of stimuli and to learn, even among those individuals remaining in institutions, which of the "necessary" social-community demanded behaviors are being met. Thus, the measurement does not appear primarily for the purpose of labeling or for the continuation of warehousing procedures but, rather, to help set up individual habilitation plans. In that regard the information derived from adaptive behavior measurement or from any criterion-based measurement is much more appropriate to the development of plans for the individual than are mere scores derived from irrelevant behaviors based on some previous rate of learning, as is the case in most IQ measurement.

While there is overlap between measured intelligence and adaptive behavior within institutional settings, at least 50 percent of the patients' measured intelligence and adaptive behavior are different. This represents a major consideration in terms of program planning and community transition. Even in the institutional setting where the concept would be most challenged, adaptive behavior emerges as a separate dimension.

As we move into the community, a new phenomenon appears. The mentally retarded still resemble their counterparts in institutions in measured intelligence but, because they have not been institutionalized, they present a different distribution of adaptive behaviors, and the correlations which appear in institutional figures tend to disappear in favor of a large group of individuals who are still mentally retarded in terms of their IQ scores (i.e., they present significant subaverage levels of general intellectual functioning) but who, nonetheless, often present adaptive behavior levels very similar to those found in the normal population. Thus, the correlation between measured intelligence and adaptive behavior is an attributed of the residential setting, and as more and more community information is available, the broad picture verifies the original notion that adaptive behavior as defined is a separate dimension.

RELATIONSHIP BETWEEN ADAPTIVE BEHAVIOR AND DEVELOPMENT

In regard to the relationship of adaptive behavior to development, an entirely different approach is required. It is probably true that most ideas which are historically related to the measurement of adaptive behavior are based primarily on notions of skills; thus, when Heber (1961) suggested that "at the preschool level" the Vineland Social Maturity Scale was "fairly adequate as a measure of adaptive behavior" and suggested further that it may be "supplemented by specific selected items from the Gesell Development Schedules or the Cattel Infant Intelligence Scale or the Kuhlmann Tests of Mental Development" (p. 63), he was saying that these scales, which are essentially measurements of child development skills, are representative of what is attempted to be measured by adaptive behavior measurement today. The essential question, however, is, Do the measurements of child development currently available answer the needs of the measurement of adaptive behavior as it is currently defined? The answer is a qualified no. Many aspects of the scales listed measure the behaviors classified under the heading of adaptive behavior. They measure them very well and represent an extremely important milestone in the total development of the concept. If one considers, however, that adaptive behavior applies to all mentally retarded individuals regardless of age, schedules based on child development notions very quickly expire when looking at behaviors which are derived primarily from those learned in the developmental period and then translated into what is now chronologically a later period. This area is not measured by the currently available instruments.

Thus, adaptive behavior does correspond in many instances to levels of measured intelligence, but this is primarily true of institutionalized retarded persons. It becomes increasingly less true as more and more community-based individuals are observed. Further, neither the IQ nor the etiology of the retardation are specifically pertinent to the planning of individual habilitation programs or to the diagnosis of individuals when these diagnoses are made with an eye on the reversal or modification of their behaviors. Those aspects of behavior which are based on development are very closely related to adaptive behavior, but this is not a sufficient answer to the total problem of measurement in adaptive behavior because a great number of behaviors which we wish to measure are derived from the relationship of individuals to the demands of their environments after the completion of the developmental period. Further, one major criterion of adaptive behavior is the kinds of behaviors the individual performs, not whether the individual is able to achieve certain preconceived functional levels. The determination of these behaviors becomes one of the major aspects in knowing the kind of adaptive skill and coping strategies the individual has acquired. It is impossible to determine these from any standardized form of psychometric measurement.

Therefore, when the dimension of adaptive behavior is described as referring to the effectiveness with which individuals cope with the natural and social demands of their environments, it indicates a different aspect of intellectual growth. For this reason a number of clinical dimensions have been postulated in the concept of intelligence, and adaptive behavior needs to be considered as one of those separate clinical dimensions, different, on one hand, from the measurement of the previous rate of learning and different, also, from measurements of cognition or sensory-motor development or social awareness. Obviously each contains elements of the other and one would anticipate and hope for a great deal of overlap, for without such overlap it is impossible for the individual to function as any sort of integrated whole (Leland & Smith, 1974).

COPING

When one speaks of coping, the notion is essentially one of movement—what individuals do or do not do at any given moment and how appropriate the behavior is to the immediate or long-range needs of the situation. Thus, this is not a static measurement, nor is it an achievement measurement. It presumes and individuals' adaptive behavior will change; and assuming that they were able, either through their own devices or through treatment or training procedures, to learn from previous experiences, they will change in a positive direction. An area where an individual has failed to cope in one instance might become an area of highly successful coping the next time because of learning experience. Thus, adaptive behavior is the reversible aspect of mental retardation, and it reflects primarily those behaviors which are most likely to be modified through appropriate treatment or training methods.

Coping refers to the manner in which an individual responds to the environment and to the interactive behaviors which are produced by this response. In a biological sense the more successful the coping, the greater the expectancy for life; unsuccessful coping would yield more immediate death. In the realm of adaptation these coping procedures may not always be life-and-death matters, but they still are related to the kinds of behaviors required for the individual to survive psychologically in any given situation. There are instances where behavior would be acceptable, and there are instances where the same behavior (such as undressing) would not be acceptable.

Effective coping would imply that the individual was able to read successfully the available environmental cues present in the situation and respond appropriately. Failure to read these cues appropriately often results in public disapproval. A more appropriate reading of these cues leads to more successful psychological survival. Thus, when the author refers to the effectiveness with which individuals cope, he is speaking essentially of the manner in which individuals are able to respond properly to behavior-producing cues in their environment and to the effectiveness with which they are able to adapt their behavior to the situation for the purpose of social-psychological survival. The alternative to this survival has traditionally been institutionalization or some other form of removal from the community (Shellhaas & Nihira, 1969). When one considers the relationship between adaptive behavior and long-range planning for the retarded, it is immediately evident that the individual who does not cope effectively is inevitably the one who becomes the prime candidate for removal.

One also needs to look at the natural and social needs of the environment in terms of effective coping. An individual may have learned or may have been trained to cope effectively under certain circumstances, but because of the rigidity of behavior or other factors, that persons may not be able to apply this learning to new circumstances. Persons brought up in small towns without stoplights, for example, may have learned effectively to cross the street by watching for cars. If brought to a large city where their street-crossing behavior is controlled by stoplights, however, they may follow the behavior learned in their rural environments, and because they ignored the light, they would be guilty of an infraction and would thus be said to be coping unsuccessfully with the needs of their new environment. Part of the question of effective coping is very closely tied to the flexibility of individuals, i.e., their ability to modify their behavior in terms of changing environmental needs.

The natural and social demands of the environment concern the social and cultural elements which normally evolve from any grouping of individuals. These groupings impose various types of demands. It is apparent that the demands for survival in a large city are different from the demands for survival in a small town. The demands for survival between different national cultures creates another type of coping. The demands for the survival of young persons in terms of expectations of their environments are different from the demands for adults in exactly the same environment. These survival behaviors evolve around the critical demands of that environment, which involves some highly subjective questions. Even the critical demands of one child's family may be entirely different from the demands of another, and it is not unusual for a child who comes from a family or poor educational background, for example, to demonstrate a somewhat different mode of survival than a similar child who has come from a family with a higher educational background. Thus, the needs of the environment must also be considered as shifting and variable and as representing elements that are constantly modifying themselves from within.

ADAPTATION AND CONFORMITY

The approach that we have just considered to the problem of coping as it relates to the demands of the environment raises the issue of the relationship between adaptation, on the one hand, and the notion of conformity, on the other. Originally, Heber included conformity as one of the aspects of adaptation, saying "on subjective clinical evaluation of the degree to which the person's behaviors *conform* to the standards and norms of the individual's chronological age group" (author's italics) (Heber, 1961, p. 65). When one speaks of adaptation and coping, conformity is not really the issue. The individual is expected to conform to a large variety of different standards—one in the home, one in the school, one in the neighborhood. This is not an unusual situation for the normal or nonhandicapped person, but again, recognizing the difficulty that the handicapped individual has in coping with cues in the environment, this expectation of easy movement between different demand areas is obviously inappropriate when dealing with handicapped persons. If we say that they must conform with each demand area, we are eliminating the elements of judgment and the utilization of personal responsibility and often create a new kind of undesirable visibility. Actually, it is this concept of "visibility versus invisibility" (Leland, 1964) which becomes the major question in adaptive behavior rather than the concept of conformity as such. For example, if an individual is on a street with a gang stealing hubcaps, he/she would be demonstrating a high degree of conformity if he/she went along with them and stole hubcaps. If the individual recognized that stealing hubcaps was not appropriate behavior, however, and learned to be invisible in that group, he/she would be at a much more successful level of adaptation and, in terms of the ability to cope with the police, at a much higher level of survival.

The problem is that retarded individuals have difficulty in being acceptably creative. Often retarded persons' creativity merely makes them visible without improving their acceptability. The answer lies in finding a level of creativity which is consistent with the retarded individual's ability to perform and in finding some way of reinforcing and accepting that behavior even though it does not necessarily conform completely to the behavior or the norm for his/her chronological age group. The ability of mentally retarded individuals to survive in their communities is usually centered around how visible they are in that community. The highly visible retarded individual is labeled; as various failure experiences accumulate, the community becomes more and more aware of the label, and eventually the individual is removed. Conversely, invisible retarded persons are able to meet, to some degree of community tolerance, the expected demands of that community. They are not being labeled in terms of their retardation. The community is not aware of their presence, and they are able to remain and be absorbed by the community, often performing a useful function in relationship to this absorption. Thus, the question of creativity versus conformity is highly related to this invisibility– visibility continuum. Since invisibility also demands some creativity, retarded individuals must learn when not to conform. For example, conformity to the schoolroom would be carrying out the daily assignments. Retarded individuals cannot always do this. If they could, they would not be considered mentally retarded; so they are going to be visible. The question is how visible. If they are attempting to cope with the procedures of the rest of the classroom, if they have developed a process of cooperation, if they can interact with other children at an acceptable level, and if they do not constantly annoy the teacher, they will be given a much better chance of survival in the school situation than if their inability to do the lessons also results in antisocial outbreaks and other types of maladaptive behavior. This invisibility is dependent upon creativeness in the areas of social interaction as substitutes for their inability to conform in the academic processes where, if the demand were merely conformity, they would begin with a failure experience which had no possibility of redemption.

If these questions are related to social-cultural aspects of the environment in which individuals find themselves, the primary question is how individuals behave in relationship to critical demands of the environment, and if individuals cannot respond to them, what they do instead.

AGE-RELATED BEHAVIORS AND THE MEASUREMENT OF ADAPTIVE BEHAVIOR

It is from the questions just considered that the functional areas were divided into personal independence, personal responsibility, and social responsibility. (Note that after the scales were developed and the material was subjected to factor analysis, the factors of personal independence and social maladaptation emerged, as well as another factor of personal maladaptation [Nihira, 1969a, 1969b]. These are not the same elements necessarily as the three philosophical areas just cited.) In looking at these functional areas, there is one additional concern: the question of age-related behaviors. This approach to the measurement of adaptive behavior permits us to utilize most of the interactive and interlocking elements which go into the coping behavior of individuals, taking into consideration what individuals are able to do, what they are motivated to do, what is expected of them at their ages, and what society expects in general of all of its members under a variety of circumstances. These are based on measures of competency, but in terms of adaptive behavior measurement, social priorities must be dealt with over and above the mere question of achievement. Thus, in one setting it may be extremely important for individuals to feed themselves properly using all utensils, while in another it is only necessary that persons be able to feed themselves regardless of how. It is difficult to give an accurate catalog of "necessary" behaviors, but they range around the broad subdomains of eating, toileting, dressing, mobility, communication, and similar types of activities. As we said, it is often behaviors deemed "desirable" whose failure produces social annoyance. Society is often prepared to adapt to an individual who lacks certain "necessary" abilities, but it has a very low tolerance for individuals who lack abilities which a specific social unit or subcultural group considers high priority even though it may not be that universally necessary. Thus, adaptive behavior measurement in this area is a combined relationship between the ability to do what is expected and the ability to fit within the priority system of the social unit making the judgment.

Achievement measurement counts the number of successes in a particular succession in a particular topic area or group of topic areas. It is based on a normative assumption that this learning occurs in a specific succession. It is the practical experience of anyone working with handicapped individuals that they have specific proficiencies and specific abilities which may typically be based on order of difficulty, in terms of ease in completing the task. This order of difficulty may not always be consistent with growth and development norms, so that profile of their proficiencies is often different from a predicted profile in a normal achievement pattern. This is particularly true if the handicapped person has an orthopedic or sensory deficiency.

Thus, one cannot say that an individual should be doing something because other persons the same age are doing it; nor can one say specifically that tasks should be ordered in a certain succession because that is the way they occur with the usual person. One rather has to look at the situation in terms of what the specific individual is doing in terms of his/her own proficiencies and what particular succession this particular person followed in reaching that level. This latter element is not cumulative, and it cannot be based on adding a line of proficiencies in that specific area. Rather, the highest level of competency or proficiency that the individual can achieve must be determined, and one must then assume that all previous behaviors are irrelevant and not part of the consideration of the person's current functioning level of adaptive behavior. Thus, specific criteria based on both levels of difficulty and, when they are consistent, levels of growth and development must be determined. The major question is whether the individual being measured meets those criteria, and if he/she does not, the extent to which it is possible to determine what he/she is doing instead. The result is an ordered set of criterion-referenced items which may be similar to or may differ greatly from the same order of items based on a norm reference.

RELIABILITY AND VALIDITY MEASUREMENTS FOR AN ADAPTIVE BEHAVIOR SCALE

The establishment of items and utilization of priority criteria (which in themselves subsume a large number of unmeasured activities) raises important questions concerning the establishment of reliability and validity measurements appropriate for this type of scale (Leland, 1972). The need for a different concept of reliability based on criterion-referenced measures exists, and this reliability must put greater emphasis on inter-rater responses at the level of two persons observing the same behavior in a third person and greater emphasis on construct and face validity. The comparison point in each instance is the observed behavior of the individual as it occurs in a field situation under usual circumstances in what is, for this specific individual, a standard environment. The standard environment is the one in which it is most important for the individual to function, e.g., home, neighborhood, school.

In addition, this question of the age-related demands becomes one of the major elements in identifying the difference between adaptive measurement and IQ measurement, on the one hand, and adaptive measurement and achievement measurement, on the other. Humans are, roughly speaking a "standard model," e.g., two arms , legs, eyes, etc., and these parts function in approximately the same manner, develop at the same rate; it is from this fact that the concept of "normal growth and development" was derived. The approximate similarities of humans differ drastically from individual to individual. When speaking of a "normal" person, one is referring either to the individual's place on a curve or to someone who falls within a wide range of social tolerance for specific differences. Persons who fall outside that range of social tolerance are considered handicapped if society judges the difference to be negative or, idiosyncratically, superior if society judges the difference to be positive, e.g., scientists, musicians, philosophers.

A CONCEPTION OF COMPETENT BEHAVIOR

In the development of the adaptive behavior scales the project was dealing only with the handicapped population. Therefore, the differences were on the level that society typically considers negative. When using a norm-referenced approach to examine age-related expectations, one is comparing the handicapped population with the nonhandicapped population, and the growth and development patterns are based on the pattern of body parts and functions which go with the "standard model." Individuals who either lack some of those parts or who have them and are unable to use them in the usual manner cannot be expected to develop in the same pattern. Therefore, any estimations of behavior based on typical age norms will only reveal that the individual in question does not behave according to "typical age norms." If psychologists ask how individuals are behaving or what they are doing instead (and these are the major adaptive behavior questions when one attempts to measure the manner in which the individual copes), the knowledge that they are not behaving in accordance with typical age norms or expectations is of no value. It is not important to know what individuals would have done had they been normal but, rather, what individuals are doing at the time of evaluation, so that, given their current patterns of behavior, the next learning step can be identified.

Some type of highly individualized competency is necessary, based precisely on the individual's current level of functioning, the steps that lead to that line of behavior, and the next expected behavior. Also, by examining negative behaviors one can determine additional alternative routes and options in an attempt to help the individual toward the next level of behavior, rather than merely judging whether the person is competent.

This element relates to the concept of invisibility versus visibility, and the word "competent" can be used synonomously with "invisible" in the sense that the only "competency" behaviors which really preoccupy society are those which create negative visibility. This is a concept of competency which is different from the relationship to a school system or a sheltered workshop or other agency-type activity which requires a different set of demands that is also related to adaptive behavior. This is why functional independence, personal responsibility, and social adaptation are considered entities, each requiring its own kind of competency.

We shall consider these separately. The first group of behaviors represents those which come under the heading of the functional areas. These are observable behaviors of the individual as they are met either in a testing situation or in a free field of activity. The first category, which includes independent functioning, is essentially a measure of whether individuals are able to do the things expected of them. Unless the observer has actually seen them performed or knows absolutely because of other information that they can be performed, it cannot be assumed that the individual is able to do them. It is not relevant that the person has done them in the past. This approach differs from many other adaptive behavior scales (e.g., Vineland Scale of Social Maturity) which assume the ability to perform. The difference is based on the fact that this is not an achievement test nor a measure of growth and development. If because of interfering elements from other aspects of personality development, individuals are no longer able to cope with specific critical community demands at the time they are being examined and, therefore, they do not perform certain behaviors, it becomes the major information. Individuals are not penalized by being marked down (because the score is not the basis for decisions), but they are being given the best possible opportunity to be seen in the total context of the current relationship with the environment, thus permitting the best plan for modification of the behavior to emerge. This approach obviously broadens the scope of adaptive behavior measurement into vast areas of developmental and functional disability, which would include residents of mental hospitals and psychiatric institutions as well as other persons involved in treatment through mental health facilities. The measurement of adaptive behavior in the area of independent functioning can become a major adjunct to the classification of mental illness as well as to the classification of mental retardation and developmental disability.

This is particularly true in the relationship between the first functional area (independent functioning) and the second functional area (personal responsibility). After individuals have learned to carry out a large group of behaviors, if they are able to assume personal responsibility, they will be able to do these activities on their own with only a minimum of supervision, e.g., communicate, carry message, practice personal hygiene, etc. The key to this area is essentially how much responsibility individuals will assume for their own behavior in terms of general day-to-day activities. A subquestion might be, Is the individual a responsible individual in relationship to the rest of his/her environment? This is related to areas such as interpersonal relationships, cultural conformity, and responsiveness in terms of the ability to delay gratification.

The area of personal responsibility is tied to the psychological construct of motivation: what individuals can do as opposed to what they will do. This is an exceedingly important aspect which establishes one of the differences with measured intelligence because the question of motivation is not usually reflected in psychometric measurement. In order to judge fully an adaptive behavior, however, this question must be raised and, to the extent possible, measured. (In this regard, social and personal motivation are measured by domains 7, 8, 9, and 10 of Part I [Leland, Shoaee, & Vayda, 1975].)

The third functional area (social responsibility) involves the ability of the individual to carry out behaviors because they are supposed to be done without constant reminder or constant threat of immediate reprisal. Social responsibility is not performed without fear of punishment; rather, the punishment is not immediately available as a motive for carrying out the behavior. The situation is one both of delay and reward and delay and punishment. Social responsibility can be subdivided into three fairly clear-cut categories: (1) social adjustment, which includes most of the factors relating to antisocial behavior, (2) intrapunitive behaviors, and (3) a combination of intra- and extrapunitive behaviors.

Under social adjustment, behaviors are primarily extrapunitive in nature, aimed at and against society, its customs, and its mores. Impairment in social adjustment is represented by the presence of delinquent behaviors or total social withdrawal. The difference between this aspect of the question and personal responsibility rests not so much on the success of interpersonal relationships but on the willingness of the individual to maintain socially acceptable relationships because society expects it and not because they are specifically personally gratifying. This again addresses the question of conformity, and appropriate social adjustment from an adaptive behavior frame of reference would be represented partly by the ability of the individual to make appropriate social decisions over and above the ability to maintain adequate interpersonal relationships.

Another question which relates to positive aspects of social adjustment is civic responsibility, which involves questions of family management, marriage, children, etc. This one area where *social* visibility is a major source of the difficulty. The individual may be able to get along well on a personal basis, but having to take responsibility for others becomes a problem. Another aspect of civic responsibility is the ability of the individual to live in a community in keeping with the mores and standards of the community. The retarded individual, because of the visibility problem, has to be expected to maintain these norms as closely as possible.

Economic responsibility centers around the ability to find and keep a job or some other socially acceptable means of obtaining economic independence within the community. This involves many of the rehabilitation goals and training areas of most agencies, and one of the major functions of measurement in this area relates to the judgment of potential job success, eligibility for halfway-house residential training, and sheltered-workshop placement. This area also involves planning in the sense of budgeting, paying bills, not overusing credit, etc. Finally, economic responsibility ties onto the problems of both social interaction and civic responsibility in terms of maintaining family units at some level of stability.

These areas are not measured by the adaptive behavior scale because the scale tries to look at ongoing currently occurring behaviors; but, without seeming to set up any kinds of predictions, there is still an unwritten assumption that an individual who is coping successfully with the natural and social demands of the environment in the current situation can be considered a relatively good risk for the appropriate kinds of training, leading to experiences which meet the demands of civic and economic responsibility. From this frame of reference adaptive behavior represents not only the reversible aspects of mental retardation, but success represents the road map to an acceptable level of social independence and appropriate social living.

These considerations, tied into elements of age-related behaviors and critical social demands, become the warp and woof of adaptive behavior measurement. If it can be understood that these kinds of individualized behaviors reflect a growth and development pattern regardless of the fact that this pattern may be completely out of line with growth and development expectations for certain age groups, it can be seen that the adaptive behavior approach can be a very systematic way of ordering programs for change. Thus, if growth and development are to be seen in terms of orderly steps of progression, when one is working with the mentally retarded, developmentally disabled, or severely emotionally disturbed, one must recognize that the nature of the handicapped may vary the order of difficulty of these behaviors, but (in broad general terms, over time) the patterns of development should occur, taking into account the specific nature of the handicap.

There is still a role for age-related expectations. That is, there is a need to know when not to expect certain behaviors (in terms of the fact that the general population does not act in certain ways until a certain age has been reached) and to know when the absence of certain behaviors makes the individual appear to be significantly subaverage in the broad areas of adaptation and learning. Many developmentally disabled adults, however, have not achieved certain levels of behavior typical of young, normal children. These adults cannot be said to be performing as though they were young children because they have alongside of their handicaps and difficulties another group of alternative behaviors which are often quite consistent with their body size and physical age, even though the behaviors themselves may be socially undesirable and unwanted.

If the current level of functioning can be determined, our knowledge of growth and development makes it possible to see if the antecedent behavior was consistent with the current behavior. This makes it further possible to ascertain what the next behavior to be trained should be. In this way adaptive behavior measurements lead directly to individual habilitation planning.

The second category of social responsibility consists of intrapunitive behaviors. These are negative behaviors which are aimed at the self rather than at society: frightening, obnoxious behaviors; disgusting, annoying behaviors; self-abusive behaviors; hyperactive behaviors, etc. These all make the individual extremely visible within the social context; this visibility is due to the peculiarity of the observed behavior rather than to the danger that it may pose to other persons. Any person performing such behaviors consistently or frequently becomes a source of concern to all persons who have to observe them. Some of these behaviors may be associated with other aspects of difficulty or disability, e.g., certain individuals with orthopedic handicaps or sensory handicaps may perform a number of stereotyped or intrapunitive behaviors as part of their response to their handicap. These cannot automatically be presumed to represent severe mental retardation or other automatic categories; regardless of their source, the presence of such behaviors inevitably makes the individual exceptionally visible, and society typically intrudes.

The third category of social responsibility consists of behaviors which have both intra- and extrapunitive implications but are essentially centered around the way individuals respond when they fail to cope to social stimulus. That is, these become the "instead" behaviors related to Part II of the scale. This third group of behaviors does not make the individual continually visible, but if they are carried out with any frequency, they produce a level of visibility which makes it very difficult for society to cope with that individal. This is a reversal in the basic definition and this third group of behaviors makes it difficult for society to demonstrate appropriate adaptive behavior. These are behaviors which, while not in themselves demonstrative of social or personal danger, nonetheless, are sufficiently immature and maladaptive that they make it almost impossible for individuals to gain acceptance if they continue to perform in this way.

The measurement of these areas must, of necessity, be stated in a negative manner; so one is measuring social maladaptation rather than social adjustment. The absence of maladaptive forms is taken as presumptive evidence of the existence of social adjustment, but social adjustment itself cannot be measured because one cannot readily ask if individuals perform a vast number of adjusted behaviors. All that can readily be asked is what persons do to increase visibility and cause others to label them "obnoxious." When these items were being searched, various agencies in the community and institutions were requested to report those behaviors which, if their clients did not stop performing them, would not enable the clients to remain in their current program. From this it was possible to derive a group of negative behaviors which a large number of professionals reported as making it impossible for them to work with certain individuals. It was these behaviors, grouped into Part II of the adaptive behavior scales, that became the measure of social maladaptation. Obviously, the frequency at which these behaviors were performed became a major aspect of judging the criticalness of these behaviors. Also, it was recognized that the behavior itself, taken as a discrete entity, was not in every instance maladaptive. The negative aspects of the behavior are based on how inappropriately it is performed and in what context. In looking at this in terms of adaptive behavior, it is necessary that when Part II of the scale is used, the behaviors reported are seen in this critical context.

Some behaviors (e.g., rape, arson, murder) are always evil, and these have a special context, not only because they are obviously not measured in terms of their frequency, but also because they establish an identification for the individual which has many social implications. Thus, a person who commits arson once is still a major source of concern many years later. In the adaptive behavior context the consideration of such behaviors has to be given special planning and analysis in programming for the individual. Thus, the Part II behaviors reflect things far beyond the basic aspects of social adjustment and are not just the opposite side of the social adjustment coin.

DEFINING ADAPTIVE BEHAVIOR FOR SCALES OF MEASUREMENT

Early in the project it was found that all of these areas (both Part I and Part II) lacked appropriate operational definitions. Consequently, part of the effort has been the development of more specific parameters. Here we have had to move slowly because there is a two-way interaction required between the establishment of a definition from a theoretical frame of reference and the development of a working definition based on the collection of data. The working definitions derived from our theoretical considerations, however, included the initial reference that adaptive behavior refers primarily to the manner in which the individual copes and that, therefore, "an impairment in adaptive behavior" would imply unsuccessful of incomplete coping. This concept of coping is represented by three major facets:

1. *Independent functioning:* The ability of the individuals to accomplish successfully those tasks or activities demanded of them by the general community both in terms of the critical survival demands for that community and in terms of typical expectations for specific ages, recognizing that these typical expectations are themselves divided into "necessary" and "desirable" types of behavior.

2. *Personal responsibility:* The willingness of individuals to accomplish those critical tasks they are able to accomplish (generally under some supervision) and their ability to assume individual responsibility for their personal behavior. This ability is reflected in decision making and choice of behaviors.

3. *Social responsibility:* The ability of the individual to accept responsibility as a member of a community and to carry out appropriate behaviors in terms of group expectations. Social responsibility is reflected in levels of conformity, socially positive creativity, social adjustment, and emotional maturity. It can be analyzed further in terms of the acceptance of some level of civic responsibility leading to complete or partial economic independence. (Leland, 1973).

The concept of adaptive behavior must be considered in two realms. The first involves the relationship between adaptation and learning, which is essentially a research realm. An adaptive approach to specific problems such as education, training, or treatment will require a modification in some of the basic approaches traditionally used. More specifically, this dimension is not only valuable in the measurement and classification of the mentally retarded, but it also opens a broad new area of understanding in work with all individuals functioning at an "impaired" level.

The second realm, the question of measurement, involves both the utilization of an adaptive behavior scale in terms of the manner in which the material is presented and the treatment and training programs which may evolve from the information derived from the scale. This involves the problem of establishing diagnostic profiles and weighing the information with the underlying recognition that certain aspects of the data are more meaningful in some situations than they are in others. Thus, a professor without arms can still have an extremely high level of social and personal responsibility even though his independent functioning is impaired. Conversely, another adult who is unable to function without her arms may have to be institutionalized. One essential measurement clue leading to a classification profile is centered around whether the observing public thinks the individual is able to complete the function successfully rather than whether he/she is actually able to do it. The essential difference between an adaptive behavior scale and an achievement test resides in this aspect. An achievement test reflects the actual ability of the subject. An adaptive behavior scale in addition reflects the observer's opinion of that behavior. This is a valid approach to the subject since the eventual disposition of the individual in the long run is dependent on that observer's opinion.

Beyond this it is still necessary to report to central data-collecting agencies and to classify individuals for the purpose of placing them in living units, treatment programs, and training areas; it is even necessary to decide whether they should be institutionalized or should remain in their community. As research develops around the theoretical realm of adaptation and learning, it will be possible to group individuals in terms of adaptive skills. All this leads to the necessity of maintaining a "level system" for description and classification of the retarded as a "shorthand or bookkeeping" basis for grouping individuals into program areas. Such a classification system, however, should be derived in terms of (1) the existing behavioral history of the individual, including information from currently available tests, (2) the observable present level of functioning as noted in ongoing daily field situations, (3) the level of functioning as defined by the adaptive behavior scales, and (4) a comparison with behavior generally expected of individuals of similar age, social origin, geographical position, etc.

Experience indicates that it is most valuable to consider levels of functioning in terms of their relationship to independence starting with "no evidence of impairment" through a level of almost total dependence. This concept of independence versus dependence needs to be based on community expectations rather than institutional expectations and can, in a sense, become the main basis for deinstitutionalization (Bennett, 1976).

Further, these levels reflect long-range general program objectives around which individual programs can evolve. It is thoroughly understood, however, that adaptive behavior represents the reversible dimension within the behavioral aspects of mental retardation and developmental disability. It is also expected that an individual once classified within a certain level would be put into an appropriate training or treatment program to deal with the priority behaviors being considered. Let us assume that this program was properly conceived; then the individual should be able to move from one level to a higher one. It may also be assumed that if retarded individuals are left to their own devices, they may sink to a lower level.

CONCLUSION

This chapter is a brief overview of the early theoretical considerations. Some of these will certainly change as improved data becomes available, but the overall objective remains one of achieving a generalized view of society's observations of the manner in which an individual copes. Any one of the scale's subdomains can and should be sharpened for use in specific programs, and the author expects that a number of highly specialized scales will evolve for use in individual settings. The author hopes that the more general scale will be able to serve the classification purposes for which it was designed.

REFERENCES

Bennett, F. A. *Levels of community residential living and its relationship to adaptive behavior among trainable mentally retarded adults.* Unpublished doctoral dissertation, The Ohio State University, 1975.
Declaration of general and special rights of the mentally retarded. *Mental Retardation,* 1969, *7*(4), 2.
Grossman, H. J. (Ed.). *Manual on terminology and classification in mental retardation* (Special Publication No. 2). Washington, D. C.: American Association on Mental Deficiency, 1973.
Heber, R. A. (Ed.). A manual on terminology and classification in mental retardation. *American Journal of Mental Deficiency* (Monograph Supplement), 1959, *64;* (Rev. *1961, 66*).
Leland, H. What is a mentally retarded child? *Journal of Psychiatric Nursing,* 1964, *2,* 21–37.
Leland, H. Mental retardation and adaptive behavior. *Journal of Special Education,* 1972, *6,* 71–80.
Leland, H. Adaptive behavior and mentally retarded behavior. In C. E. Meyers, R. K. Eyman, & G. Tarjan (Eds.), *Sociobehavioral studies in mental retardation: Papers in honor of Harvey F. Dingman.* Washington, D. C.: American Association on Mental Deficiency, 1973.
Leland, H., Shellhaas, M., Nihira, K., & Foster, R. Adaptive behavior: A new dimension in the classification of the mentally retarded. *Mental Retardation Abstracts,* 1967, *4,* 359–387.
Leland, H., Shoaee, M., & Vayda, S. *Guidelines for the clinical use of the AAMD Adaptive Behavior Scales.* Columbus: Nisonger Center, Ohio State University, 1975.
Leland, H., & Smith, D. E. *Mental retardation: Present and future perspectives.* Belmont, Ca.: Jones, 1974.
Nihira, K. Factorial dimensions of adaptive behavior in adult retardates. *American Journal of Mental Deficiency,* 1969, *73,* 868–878. (a)

Nihira, K. Factorial dimensions of adaptive behavior in mentally retarded children and adolescents. *American Journal of Mental Deficiency,* 1969, *74,* 130–141. (b)

Page, E. R. *Comparisons of the Illinois Test of Psycholinguistic Abilities and the Adaptive Behavior Checklist with institutionalized mentally retarded children.* Unpublished doctoral dissertation, The Ohio State University, 1970.

Piaget, J. *The origins of intelligence in children.* New York: International Universities Press, 1952.

Shellhaas, M., & Nihira, K. Factor analysis of reasons retardates are referred to an institution. *American Journal of Mental Deficiency,* 1969, *74,* 171–179.

Kazuo Nihira

3
Factorial Descriptions of the AAMD Adaptive Behavior Scale

Adaptive behavior is a composite of many aspects of behavior and a function of a wide range of specific abilities and disabilities. The manual for terminology and classification by the American Association on Mental Deficiency (AAMD) defines adaptive behavior as "the effectiveness or degree with which the individual meets the standards of personal independence and social responsibility expected of his age and cultural group" (Grossman, 1973). Interest in this concept has stemmed from the general recognition that the IQ score, in and of itself, is inadequate, and, indeed, potentially misleading when used as the sole basis for an individual's evaluation.

The AAMD Adaptive Behavior Scale was developed in late 1960s in order to provide operational specifications for measuring and describing the adaptive behavior of mentally retarded individuals (Nihira, Foster, Shellhaas, & Leland, 1969). The scale consists of two parts. Part I (see Table 3–1) is the product of a comprehensive review of the existing behavior rating scales designed to assess the traditional notions of social competency or personal and social adjustment. This part of the scale is organized along developmental lines and is designed to evaluate an individual's skills and habits in ten behavior domains, i.e., coherent groups of related activities. These behavior domains cover most of the behaviors recognized by the existing rating scales as important indicators of the degree of personal independence of mentally retarded individuals.

Part of this chapter was presented at the annual meeting of the American Association on Mental Deficiency, New Orleans, June 1977.

Table 3–1
AAMD Adaptive Behavior Scale—Part I

Domain	I.	*Independent Functioning*

(Subdomains)

    A. Eating
    B. Toilet Use
    C. Cleanliness
    D. Appearance
    E. Care of Clothing
    F. Dressing and Undressing
    G. Travel
    H. General Independent Functioning

Domain II. *Physical Development*
(Subdomains)

    A. Sensory Development
    B. Motor Development

Domain III. *Economic Activity*
(Subdomains)

    A. Money Handling and Budgeting
    B. Shopping Skills

Domain IV. *Language Development*
(Subdomains)

    A. Expression
    B. Comprehension
    C. Social Language Development

Domain V. *Numbers and Time*

Domain VI. *Domestic Activity*
(Subdomains)

    A. Cleaning
    B. Kitchen Duties
    C. Other Domestic Activities

Domain VII. *Vocational Activity*

Domain VIII. *Self-direction*
(Subdomains)

    A. Initiative
    B. Perseverance
    C. Leisure Time

Domain IX. *Responsibility*

Domain X. *Socialization*

Table 3–2
AAMD Adaptive Behavior Scale—Part II

Domain	I.	*Violent and Destructive Behavior*
Domain	II.	*Antisocial Behavior*
Domain	III.	*Rebellious Behavior*
Domain	IV.	*Untrustworthy Behavior*
Domain	V.	*Withdrawal*
Domain	VI.	*Stereotyped Behavior and Odd Mannerisms*
Domain	VII.	*Inappropriate Interpersonal Manners*
Domain	VIII.	*Unacceptable Vocal Habits*
Domain	IX.	*Unacceptable or Eccentric Habits*
Domain	X.	*Self-abusive Behavior*
Domain	XI.	*Hyperactive Tendencies*
Domain	XII.	*Sexually Aberrant Behavior*
Domain	XIII.	*Psychological Disturbances*
Domain	XIV.	*Use of Medications*

Part II of the scale consists of 14 domains of maladaptive behavior related to personality and behavior disorders (see Table 3–2). Specific items in these domains were derived from an extensive survey of the social expectations placed upon retarded persons, both in residential institutions and in the community. The description of these social expectations was obtained empirically fron an analysis of a large number of "critical incident" reports provided by ward personnel in residential institutions, by day-care instructors, and by special education teachers in public school systems.

Part II is designed to provide measures of maladaptive behavior related to personality and behavior disorders. Domain XIV, Use of Medications, of course, is not a behavior domain, but it does provide information about a person's adaptation to the world.

PREVIOUS FACTOR ANALYTIC STUDIES

Since the publication of the Adaptive Behavior Scale (ABS) several factor analytic studies were done by different investigators that used different subject populations in order to provide empirical definitions of the components of adaptive behavior (Guarnaccia, 1976; Lambert & Nicoll, 1976; Nihira, 1969a, 1969b, 1976; Thomas, 1974; Tomiyasu, 1974,

1976). These studies uncovered several important characteristics concerning the factorial structure of the ABS.

1. In earlier studies with institutionalized children and adults factor analyses of domain scores in both Part I and Part II have yielded three orthogonal dimensions labeled Personal Independence, Social Maladaptation, and Personal Maladaptation (Nihira, 1969a, 1969b). Personal Independence was defined by (1) seven behavior domains in Part I which represented the individual's skills and abilities required to maintain independence in daily living, e.g., Independent Functioning, Physical Development, Language Development, Vocational Activity, etc.; and (2) three behavior domains in Part I which indicated that presence of autonomy or motivation to manage personal and interpersonal affairs, e.g., Self-direction, Responsibility, and Socialization. This dimension was recognized to have some resemblance to the traditional notion of social competency as measured by the Vineland Social Maturity Scale. Social Maladaptation was defined by behavior domains in Part II that represent extrapunitive, antisocial behavior disorders, e.g., Violent and Destructive Behavior, Rebellious Behavior, Untrustworthy Behavior, Psychological Disturbances, etc. Personal Maladaptation was defined by several behavior domains in Part II that represent intropunitive autistic behavior syndrome, e.g., Stereotyped Behavior, Self-abusive Behavior, Unacceptable or Eccentric Habits, etc. Thus, Part II of the scale can be described in terms of two orthogonal dimensions: aggressive or conduct-deviant behavior and withdrawn or personality-deviant behaviors. These factors have been identified repeatedly in institutionalized populations of mentally retarded individuals, i.e., children and adults, and both in the United States and in England (Thomas, 1974). These earlier studies indicated the need for inclusion of maladaptive dimensions for a broader conceptualization of adaptive behavior.

2. More recent studies examined the factorial structure of the adaptive behavior of mentally retarded populations in the community rather than of those in residential institutions. Lambert and Nicoll (1976) applied the Public School Version of the AAMD Adaptive Behavior Scale (Lambert, Windmiller, Cole, and Figueroa, 1975) to samples of school children in TMR, EMR, and regular classes. The study delineated two orthogonal clusters of domains in Part I of the scale. The first cluster, labeled Functional Autonomy, represented qualities of adaptive behavior characterized by independent functioning supported by cognitive and physical development. The second cluster, labeled Social Responsibility, consisted of behavior domains that reflected autonomy or motivation to manage personal and interpersonal affairs. The study delineated the motivational components called Social Responsibility from the aspect of cog-

nitive and physical development within the traditional concept of social competency. The study also confirmed the two dimensions of maladaptive behavior, social and personal, previously discovered in Part II of the scale.

3. Guarnaccia (1976) analyzed the ten Part I domain scores and a measure of productivity (the average weekly earning) of mentally retarded adults working at a vocational training center in the community. The study reported the existence of four factors labeled Personal Independence, Personal Responsibility, Productivity, and Social Responsibility.

There is a good deal of resemblance between the Personal Independence factor and the factor of Functional Autonomy described by Lambert and Nicoll (1976) in their study of public school children. The separation of Personal Responsibility and Social Responsibility is a unique finding of this study. Perhaps the use of a relatively homogeneous population of well-adjusted adults in the mild and moderate range of retardation may have contributed to the separation of these specific factors. The emergence of productivity as an independent factor seems to make sense in terms of the sample studied. For retarded adults employed in a work-shop setting, productivity may be considered a prime indication of maturity and adaptability.

Since the productivity measured by the individual's weekly earnings is not a part of the AAMD Adaptive Behavior Scale, this factor may not be replicated in other studies. Nevertheless, this study confirmed the existence of at least two broad dimensions—personal independence skills as well as responsibility in personal and interpersonal affairs—in Part I of the Adaptive Behavior Scale or in the traditional notion of social competency.

4. In search for more basic factors of adaptive behavior which permit generalization across various populations, Nihira (1976) turned to the identification of oblique factors using the 25 subdomain scores instead of the 10 domain scores as in the previous studies. A series of factor analytic studies of a large sample of institutionalized mentally retarded populations has demonstrated three oblique dimensions in Part I of the scale which emerged across a wide span of age ranges from childhood through senility. These factors have been labeled Personal Self-sufficiency, Community Self-sufficiency, and Personal-Social Responsibility.

Personal Self-sufficiency was defined by subdomains labeled Eating, Toilet Training, Grooming, Dressing and Undressing, and Motor Development. These subdomains represent an individual's basic skills that contribute to the manner in which the person attends to immediate personal needs. Community Self-sufficiency was defined by subdomains representing various skills expected of an individual to be self-sufficient in community living, e.g., communication skills, number and time concepts, economic activity, domestic skills, etc. These two factors seem to represent the degree of independence and self-sufficiency accompanied by cognitive and physical development. The former is an expression of self-sustaining adequacies in the personal sphere, while the latter emphasizes self-sufficiency as reflected in relationship with other members of a social environment. Together, they represent a more general dimension of adaptive bahavior variously labeled in previous studies as Functional Autonomy (Lambert & Nicoll, 1976) and Personal Independence (Guarnaccia, 1976).

Personal-Social Responsibility represented a broad spectrum of motivational attributes that included the initiative to engage in purposeful activities, autonomy in conducting one's own affairs, responsibility for self and for others, and interest in group activities. The factor is almost identical to Social Responsibility found in school children (Lambert & Nicoll, 1976) and appears to be the combination of the two factors—Personal Responsibility and Social Responsibility—reported in a study of mentally retarded adults in a vocational training center. Similar factors have also been reported in studies which used different behavior rating scales: Social Participation (Halverson & Waldrop, 1976) and Prosocial Behavior (Ross, Lacey, & Parton, 1965).

Results of the subdomain analysis indicated the need for reexamination of the present classification of certain subdomains in Part I of the scale. For example, Travel and Other Independent Functioning subsumed currently under the domain of Independent Functioning have shown consistently significant factor loadings on Community Self-sufficiency, while the rest of the subdomains under Independent Functioning have all been loaded on the Personal Self-sufficiency factor. A close inspection of specific items in these subdomains suggests that items such as "sense of direction" and "use of public transportation" would be classified more appropriately under Community Self-sufficiency rather than Personal Self-sufficiency.

FACTOR ANALYSIS OF THE ABS ITEMS

The accumulated knowledge about the factorial structure of the scale provided a new frame of reference for analysis of the functional relationship between the domains and the subdomain scores. There may be another meaningful way to classify the items in Part I of the scale. The present study attempts to explore a new system for classification of Part I items.

Method

Factor analyses of the 66 item scores in Part I have been performed separately on 750 children between 4 and 9 years of age, 947 adolescents between 10 and 18 years of age, and 734 adults between 19 and 67 years of age. The subjects were sampled from 68 state institutions for mentally retarded individuals representing 39 states across the country. The subjects represent a wide range of mental retardation from the Measured Intelligence (MI) levels I through IV. The individuals at the MI level V were not included in the samples because a previous study indicated that they were distinctly different in their adaptive behavior from those at higher MI levels and that some items were inappropriate for identifying salient dimensions of individual difference among these individuals. The subjects were rated by their ward personnel, using Part I of the AAMD Adaptive Behavior Scale. The correlation matrices were submitted to the principal component extraction program with multiple R^2 for estimate of communalities. The principal axes were then rotated obliquely toward the direct oblimin criterion (Dixon, 1973). Because most aptitude traits are known to be moderately correlated with each other, e.g., moderate correlations among the WISC subscales, it seems reasonable to assume some degree of correlation among the factors of adaptive behavior. Therefore, a rotation to an oblique criterion may yield a meaningful pattern of correlated factors.

The number of significant factors was estimated to be approximately ten, based upon a statistical criterion suggested by Kaiser (1970). Therefore, four separate rotations using different numbers of factors, i.e., the first 8, 9, 10, and 11 principal axes factors, were performed. The same procedure was applied to each of the three age groups, i.e., children (4 to 9 years), adolescents (10 to 18 years), and adults (19 to 69 years). The ten-factor rotation for the children and the nine-factor rotations for the adolescents and adults yielded most meaningful factors.

Description of Obtained Factors

Factors that emerged at different age groups were matched on the basis of the similarity of item cluster which defined each factor. Factors are grouped in Table 3–3 under each of the three general dimensions established by the previous factor analytic investigation of domains and subdomain scores.

Neuromotor Development, Self-help Skills, and Sensory Development have been identified as specific factors which constitute the dimension of Personal Self-sufficiency. Neuromotor Development and Sensory

Table 3–3
Personal Self-sufficiency

Factor I.	*Neuromotor Development*	
	(all three age groups)	

Item No.
1	Use of Table Utensils
3	Drinking
24	Body Balance
25	Walking and Running
26	Control of Hands
27	Limb Function

Factor II.   *Self-Help Skills*
(all three age groups)

Item No.
5	Toilet Training
6	Self-care at Toilet
7	Washing Hands and Face
8	Bathing
10	Tooth Brushing
11	Menstruation
15	Dressing
16	Undressing
17	Shoes

Factor III.   *Sensory Development*
(children and adolescents)

Item No.
22	Vision
23	Hearing

Development may be considered as two basic prerequisites for the development of Personal Self-sufficiency. However, the appearance of these three factors in this study imply that the maturation in neuromotor and/or sensory development does not automatically guarantee the acquisition of self-help skills. It should be noted that Use of Table Utensils and Drinking, which have been subsumed under the domain of Independent Functioning, seem to be more closely related to the Neuromotor Development factor. In the children's group Toilet Training is also loaded on Neuromotor Development rather than on Self-help Skills, as in the adolescent and adult groups.

Some items currently subsumed under Independent Functioning, e.g., Eating in Public, Care of Clothing, Use of Public Transportation, etc., did not appear on any of these three factors. Instead, these items have been classified under the Community Living Skills to be described later.

Four factors have been delineated in the area of Community Self-sufficiency (Table 3–4). These factors are Community Living Skills–I, Community Living Skills–II, Cognitive Development, and Language Development. Factor VIII, Speech Development, has been found in the adult group only and is a part of the Language Development factor.

Table 3–4
Community Self-sufficiency

Factor	IV.	*Community Living Skills–I*
		(all three age groups)

Item No.

2	Eating in Public
18	Sense of Direction
21	Misc. Independent Functioning
30	Errands
31	Purchasing
46	Table Setting
47	Food Preparation
48	Table Clearing
49	General Domestic Activity
50	Job Complexity

Factor	V.	*Community Living Skills–II*
		(children and adolescents)

Item No.

9	Personal Hygiene
13	Clothing
14	Care of Clothing
19	Public Transportation
20	Telephone
45	Laundry

Factor	VI.	*Cognitive Development*
		(children and adults)

Item No.

28	Money Handling
29	Budgeting
32	Writing
37	Reading
41	Numbers
42	Time
43	Time Concept

Table 3-4 (Continued)

Factor VII.   *Communication Skills*
              (children and adolescents)

       Item No.
       33   Preverbal expression
       34   Articulation
       35   Sentences
       36   Word Usage
       38   Complex Instructions
       39   Conversation
       40   Mis. Language Development
       41   Numbers

Factor VIII. *Speech Development*
              (adult group only)

       Item No.
       23   Hearing
       33   Preverbal Expression
       34   Articulation
       35   Sentences
       36   Word Usage

Community Living Skills–I and II have both been defined by clusters of items reflecting a variety of functional skills expected of an individual to maintain self-sufficiency in home and community environments. The Community Living Skills–I seems to represent essential skills for community living, while the Community Living Skills–II is concerned with relatively complex skills for personal grooming and indicates the geographical horizons of a person's widening activities and locomotion.

The Cognitive Development factor consists of academic skills, e.g., Reading, Writing, Numbers, and Time, and the ability to handle money and budget. It is not apparent why the Cognitive Development factor failed to appear from the adolescent group.

Factor VII, Communication Skills, emerged from the children and adolescent groups but not in the adult group. Instead, the analysis yielded the factor of Speech Development in the adult population. It should be noted that this factor is a component of the Communication Skills, which emphasize the development of expressive oral communication.

Factors IV through VIII are listed together in Table 3-4 because most of the items in these factors have been included in the subdomains which defined the Community Self-sufficiency factor in previous factor analytic studies. The general dimensions of Community Self-sufficiency have been described as (1) self-sufficiency beyond immediate personal needs as in factors I through III, and (2) self-sufficiency as reflected in relationships with other community members.

Table 3-5 lists three specific factors in the general dimension of Personal-Social Responsibility. The Self-direction and Socialization factors have been delineated in the adult group only. The former indicates

Table 3-5
Personal-Social Responsibility

Factor IX.	*Self-direction* (adult group only)	
	Item No.	
	51	Job Performance
	52	Work Habits
	53	Initiative
	54	Passivity
	55	Attention
	56	Persistence
	57	Leisure Time Activity
	58	Personal Belongings
	59	General Responsibility
Factor X.	*Socialization* (adult group only)	
	Item No.	
	60	Cooperation
	61	Consideration for Others
	62	Awareness of others
	63	Interaction with Others
	64	Participation in Group Activities
Factor XI.	*Personal-Social Responsibility* (children and adolescents)	
	Item No.	
	53	Initiative
	54	Passivity
	55	Attention
	57	Leisure Time Activity
	58	Personal Belongings
	59	General Responsibility
	60	Cooperation
	61	Consideration for Others
	62	Awareness of Others
	63	Interaction with Others
	64	Participation in Group Activities

the individual's motivation and dependability in managing personal affairs, including occupational activities, while the latter expresses motivation and effectiveness in interpersonal affairs.

These two factors did not appear as separate dimensions in the children and adolescent groups. Instead, the factor analysis yielded a combined factor labeled Personal-Social Responsibility. This seems to indicate that the personal and social responsibilities have not yet been separated between the children and adolescent groups, at least in the mentally retarded population. The lack of development and/or social expectations in the work and occupational activities for these age groups may have been the reason for emergence of the combined factor.

The items loaded on each of the three factors have jointly defined a more general dimension labeled Personal-Social Responsibility in a previous factor analytic study of subdomain scores. For this reason the three specific factors are listed under Personal-Social Responsibility in Table 3–5.

Implications

It has been known that the traditional notion of social competency reflected in Part I of the AAMD Adaptive Behavior Scale is not an unidimensional phenomenon. Previous factor analytic studies repeatedly indicated that there are at least two or possibly three general dimensions in Part I of the scale. The present study further delineated specific components within each of these general dimensions, providing more precise descriptions of the components of the Adaptive Behavior Scale. The effort also contributes to the evolution of a standard taxonomy of the basic attributes of adaptive behavior.

A factorial description of a measurement tool such as the AAMD Adaptive Behavior Scale specifies the nature of its component parts and provides conceptual explanations concerning the functional relationship among them. Thus, the profile of an individual or a group on the basis of domains or factor scores can be interpreted in more meaningful ways and can provide a potential source of testable hypotheses for formulation of strategies for training and program development. It is hoped that the present paper will provide some theoretical and empirical basis for the development of hypotheses as well as contribute to the understanding of the nature of Part I of the AAMD Adaptive Behavior Scale.

REFERENCES

Dixon, W. (Ed.). *BMD biomedical computer programs*. Berkeley: University of California Press, 1973.
Grossman, H. J. (Ed.). *Manual on terminology and classification in mental*

retardation (Special Publication No. 2). Washington, D. C.: American Association on Mental Deficiency, 1973.

Guarnaccia, V. Factor structure and correlates of adaptive behavior in noninstitutionalized retarded adults. *American Journal of Mental Deficiency*, 1976, *80*, 543–547.

Halverson, C., & Waldrop, M. Relations between preschool activity and aspect of intellectual and social behavior at age 7½. *Developmental Psychology*, 1976, *12*, 107–112.

Kaiser, H. A. A second generation little jiffy. *Psychometrika*, 1970, *35*, 401–415.

Lambert, N. M., & Nicoll, R. C. Dimensions of adaptive behavior of retarded and nonretarded public school children. *American Journal of Mental Deficiency*, 1976, *81*, 135–146.

Nihira, K. Factorial dimensions of adaptive behavior in adult retardates. *American Journal of Mental Deficiency*, 1969, *73*, 868–878. (a)

Nihira, K. Factorial dimensions of adaptive behavior in mentally retarded children and adolescents. *American Journal of Mental Deficiency*, 1969, *74*, 130–141. (b)

Nihira, K. Dimensions of adaptive behavior in institutionalized mentally retarded children and adults: Developmental perspective. *American Journal of Mental Deficiency*, 1976, *81*, 215 226.

Nihira, K., Foster, R., Shellhaas, M., & Leland, H. *AAMD Adaptive Behavior Scale, 1974 Revision*. Washington, D. C.: American Association on Mental Deficiency, 1975.

Nihira, K., Foster, R., Shellhaas, M., & Leland, H. *AAMD Adaptive Behavior Scale*. Washington, D. C.: American Association on Mental Deficiency, 1969.

Ross, A., Lacey, H., & Parton, D. The development of a behavior checklist for boys. *Child Development*, 1965, *36*, 1013–1027.

Thomas, D. *The use of the ABS in an assessment survey in England.* Paper presented at the preconvention workshop of the American Association on Mental Deficiency, Toronto, Canada, June 1974.

Tomiyasu, Y., & Matsuda, K. *Assessment methods of adaptive behavior.* Tokyo; Nihon Bunka Kagakusha, 1974.

Tomiyasu, Y. *Measurement of adaptive behavior Japan: A factor analytic study.* Paper presented at the Fourth Congress of the International Association for the Scientific Study of Mental Deficiency, Washington, D.C. , August 1976.

Jane R. Mercer

4

Theoretical Constructs of Adaptive Behavior: Movement from a Medical to a Social-Ecological Perspective

The most enduring basis for assessing human competence has been the evaluation of an individual's ability to adapt to the physical and social environment. Long before intelligence tests or social maturity measures were invented, persons in all human societies observed the role performance of others and made judgments about their fitness to assume various social responsibilities. Based on these observations, they identified the wise man and the fool, the clever and the bumbling, the competent and the incompetent.

Legal definitions of competence still reflect such evaluations of social-role performance. Relatively few legal codes have incorporated psychological tests into their definitions of competence and incompetence. For example, the California code defines mentally deficient persons as those who are "incapable of managing themselves and their affairs independently, with ordinary prudence, of being taught to do so, and who require supervision, control, and care for their own welfare or for the welfare of others, or for the welfare of the community" (California Code Ann., 5250, 1952). In South Dakota the mentally deficient are those persons who "are incapable of making the proper adjustments of life for one of their chronological age" (South Dakota Code 30.0402, 1939). The state of Washington code describes the mentally deficient as individuals who are "mentally incapable of assuming those responsibilities expected of the socially adequate person such as self-direction, self-support, and social participation" (Washington Rev. Code 72.33.020, 1958). Judgments about the quality of an individual's performance in relation to these criteria are left to the courts and the due process of law.

Psychological definitions of abnormality have diverged dramatically from legal definitions. With the introduction of standardized tests which purported to measure "intelligence," psychological definitions of subnormality and of incompetence narrowed sharply to the evaluation of behavior in a testing situation. Binet (Binet & Simon, 1905), who invented the concepts "mental age" and "intelligence" tests, was concerned with identifying those children who would not benefit from the regular school program and should be placed in special programs for the mentally deficient. Hence, his perspective was that of a pathological or deficit model. "Intelligent" behavior came to be equated with the ability to succeed in an academic program. The criterion of social competence, in the broader sense of social-role performance, was replaced by a criterion that centered almost exclusively on the individual's adaptivity to a single social role, the academic role in the public school.

The narrowing of the clinical definition of mental retardation to focus primarily on the academic types of performance sampled in intelligence tests occurred soon after Binet's tests were modified for use in the United States. Henry Goddard, Research Director of of the Vineland Training School in New Jersey, discovered Binet's test while traveling in Europe and brought out an American standardization of that scale in 1910. A new classification of feeblemindedness was formulated by Goddard and was adopted by the American Association on Mental Deficiency in 1910. "The older terms, idiot and imbecile, were retained—differentiated now at the upper limit of mental age 2 by a variety of performances rather than by the earlier single criterion of speech. For the highest grade of social inadequacy—reaching MA 8 to MA 12—Goddard coined a new word, moron, from the Greek, meaning "deficient in judgement, sense, or intelligence" (Doll, 1962). Thus, a new category of social deviant, the moron, was created and immediately legitimated by the major national association of professionals in the field of mental deficiency.

The use of intelligence tests to identify morons was quickly accepted as a legitimate procedure. For example, in 1915 the California Political Code was amended to require appointment of a "competent, clinical psychologist" to the staff of the home for the mentally deficient who, among other duties, "shall conduct a mental and psychological examination of each patient and . . . shall classify and group the said inmates according to their mental capacity. . ." (California Political Code, Title V, Section 2153b, 1915). In 1947, when the first state law was passed making "special training classes for mentally retarded minors" mandatory, placement procedures were specified in terms of test performance. "Before any child is placed in a school or class for mentally retarded children, he shall be given a careful individual examination by a competent psychologist holding a credential" (California Education Code, Chapter 11, 9805, 1948). By 1964, when we of The Riverside Project first studied procedures by which children were labeled mentally retarded in a typical California community, we found that the schools placed almost total reliance on intelligence test scores in making placement decisions. Other community agencies also relied primarily on intelligence tests in labeling the mentally retarded (Mercer, 1973). Clinicians assumed that intelligence tests were tapping some general ability which encompassed the individual's overall competence in a variety of situations and roles. Although the American Association on Mental Deficiency advocated that both intellectual functioning *and* adaptive behavior be evaluated in identifying the mentally retarded (Heber, 1961), little systematic attention was actually given to assessing nonacademic skills in the process of diagnosing mental retardation until after 1970.

The AAMD monograph supplement (Heber, 1961) and others have used the term adaptive behavior (Gesell & Amatruda 1941; Grossman, 1973; Lambert, 1975; Leland, Nihira, Foster, & Shellhaas, 1967; Leland, Nihira, Foster, Shellhaas, & Kagin, 1966; Leland, Shellhaas, Nihira, & Foster, 1969; Mercer, 1965, 1970, 1973; Nihira & Shellhaas, 1970; Robbins, Mercer, & Meyers, 1967). Others have used the terms social maturity (Doll, 1953), adaptive capacity (Fullan & Loubser, 1972), and social competence (Cain, Levine, & Elzey, 1963; Doll, 1953). In this chapter the terms will be treated as essentially synonymous.

In spite of the fact that the designation adaptive behavior has been utilized for more than a quarter century, relatively little theoretical work has been done on the construct of adaptive behavior, although various attempts have been made to measure behaviors related to the term (Cain, Levine, & Elzey, 1963; Doll, 1953; Gesell & Amatruda, 1941; Lambert et al., 1975; Mercer, 1965; Nihira et al., 1969). This lack of theoretical interest is in marked contrast to the effort that has been spent in developing alternative constructs of intelligence. Such constructs range from Spearmen's early concept of a "*g*," or general intellectual factor (Spearman, 1927), to Guilford's concept of a structure of intellect (1956) based on a factor analytic model.

The purpose here is to review some of the writings of those who have developed scales to measure adaptive behavior or related concepts and to abstract from their work their implicit assumptions and the conceptual models from which they were operating. These models will then be contrasted with a social-ecological perspective which is emerging as an alternative model for conceptualizing human adaptivity (Carlson, 1976).

THE MEDICAL MODEL

Doll (1953) and Gesell and Amatruda (1941) were among the first to attempt to measure behaviors relating to social competence. They leaned heavily upon the conceptual tools developed to deal with intelligence tests. They operated essentially from a medical model in conceptualizing the phenomenon which they were attempting to assess.

The medical model has also been called the pathological model, the disease model, and the deficit model. It was developed in medicine to conceptualize biological malfunctioning and disease processes. (A more complete discussion of the medical model appears in Chapter 10.) In a medical model abnormal is defined as the presence of organic pathology indicated by biological symptoms. Normal remains a residual, undefined category consisting of those individuals who do not manifest biological symptoms.

The medical model assumes that pathological symptoms are caused by some biological condition in the organism. Because the biological organism of the human species is similar for its members, sociocultural factors are not relevant to diagnosis when using a medical model. Tuberculosis can be diagnosed without knowing what language patients speak or the nature of their cultural heritage. In addition, pathology is viewed as a characteristic of the organism of persons being diagnosed, a trait they carry with them into all social situations. When one uses a medical model, the verb "to be" is appropriate, e.g., a person "is" tubercular or "has" the measles.

Cause-and-effect reasoning is appropriate in this model because it hypothesizes a biological cause for observed symptoms and seeks for biological explanations. Finally, within a medical model a pathology can exist unrecognized and undiagnosed. For example, a person could have tuberculosis and not be aware of the pathology. Thus, within a medical model it makes sense to speak of "hidden" illnesses and to undertake epidemiologic studies in which the investigator seeks out undiagnosed illnesses by screening a sample population for high blood pressure, cancer, or other biological conditions.

The medical model has been one of the most powerful conceptual tools developed for dealing with organic anomalies. However, when it is used to conceptualize social behaviors, it tends to influence the perceptions of the observer in predictable ways. There is a tendency to interpret behaviors which deviate negatively from the investigator's expectations as symptoms of some underlying biological condition. There is a tendency to favor biological explanations for behavioral phenomena in conducting research and in making clinical interpretations. A corollary to such biological hypotheses is the tendency to regard sociocultural factors as irrelevant or of minor importance in explaining behavior and to minimize the impact of learning on behavior. Sociocultural factors are considered important only when it can be demonstrated that they are implicated in producing organic damage which, in turn, produces the negatively evaluated behavior. For example, if it can be demonstrated, as in the case of pellagra, that the dietary habits of a particular group are producing organic damage which, in turn, is precipitating the unacceptable behavior, then sociocultural factors are relevant to diagnosis and treatment of the behavior. If no link between sociocultural factors and organic damage can be established, then the factors are regarded as irrelevant to diagnosis and treatment.

Furthermore, when a medical model is used to conceptualize social behaviors, the "condition" believed to be associated with those behaviors is viewed as a characteristic of the person, a trait that is carried by the person into many different social situations. Intervention focuses on changing the individual. Since a condition may or may not be manifested in behavior in all social situations, it is conceivable that an undiagnosed condition may exist awaiting recognition and diagnosis by a properly trained professional. Research focuses on identifying the biological cause of the change-worthy behavior and treating that condition.

Gesell and Amatruda were both medical doctors concerned with clinical methods and pediatric problems. They called their procedures "developmental diagnosis" because they conceptualized development as an orderly maturational process unfolding in a similar fashion in all human infants. They described "normal child development" in order to identify "abnormal child development." They viewed the development of behavior, defined as "all reactions whether reflex, voluntary, spontaneous, or learned" as "the result of growth which produces progressive changes in structure and correlated changes in function" (Gesell & Amatruda, 1941, p. 37). They identified four fields of behavior: motor behavior, adaptive behavior, language behavior, and personal-social behavior. The latter "comprises the child's personal reactions to the social culture in which he lives. These reactions are so multitudinous, so variegated and contingent upon environment that they would seem to be beyond the reach of developmental diagnosis. But here, as elsewhere, we find that the patterning of behavior is fundamentally determined by intrinsic growth factors" (pp. 5–6).

It is important to note that these authors were focusing almost exclusively on infants and preschool children. They accepted the following organic assumption:

Development yields to diagnosis because the construction of the action-system of infant and child is determined by lawful growth forces. Behavior patterns are not whimsical or accidental by-products. They are authentic end-products of a total developmental process which works with orderly sequence. They take shape in the same manner that the underlying structures take shape. They begin to assume characteristic forms even in the fetal period for the same reasons that the bodily organs themselves assume characteristic forms. . . . All behavior patterns both in prenatal and postnatal life take shape in a comparable manner . . . . Throughout all infancy this same morphogenesis is at work, creating new forms of behavior, new and more advanced patterns. These patterns are symptoms. They are indicators of the maturity of the nervous system. (Gesell & Amatruda, 1941, p. 4)

Doll (1953) places more emphasis on possible sociocultural variation, but he still operates implicitly from a medical perspective. He sees his measure of social competence as "a standardized method for the quantitative estimation of personal social maturation which presents a unique device for the overall evaluation of human behavior. Social competence is a universal human attribute" (p. 1). He sees social competence as a "functional composite of human traits" which "entails both phylogenetic and ontogenetic evolution and it varies with physical and cultural conditions according to time, place, and circumstance. Social competence may therefore be expressed in terms of age, status, opportunity, talent, health, degree of freedom, and so on" (p. 2). Doll postulated a "developmental central factor (corresponding to their judgment or Spearman's "g") operating in combination with various specific or group factors. This central factor we loosely conceive as progressive, self-direction culminating in the direction and protection of others." Assuming that a general factor of social competence exists, he followed "the principle of sampling representative performances from which general performance might be inferred" (p. 6). He formulated a systematic performance schedule arranged as a progress chart.

Doll's major premises clearly reflect the biological assumptions underlying his view of social competence. He sees it as "the functional ability of the human organism for exercising personal independence and social responsibility" which may be "measured progressively in terms of maturation by sampling its genetic stages by means of representative performance at successive life ages . . . . He sees "such maturation . . . as a practicable measure of the changing organism as a whole" (p.10). Social maturation parallels biological maturation. Doll, however, carefully points out that "the formulation of this scale is related to the central North American [United States] environment" and "it would obviously be absurd to endeavor to apply the standard items of this scale, designed for the typical cultural environment of our day and country, without appropriate modification for other environments or times" (p. 20).

Reflected in the writings of both Gesell and Amatruda and Doll is the implicit perspective of the medical model. Marked deviation from the developmental schedule established on "normal" children is interpreted as a pathological sign relating to some biological condition in the child.

Gesell and Amatruda minimize the impact of sociocultural factors, and Doll sees environmental factors as important primarily in determining the types of items that are appropriate. The underlying assumption of a general adaptivity dimension which depends primarily on maturational processes is evident in their discussion. Developmental normality and social competence are viewed as characteristics of the individual organism which can be rated using a relatively universal standard.

It is important to recognize that these researchers focused on the study of infants and young children and were interested in those behaviors which are less influenced by environmental factors, such as holding up the head, sitting alone, crawling, grasping, and vocalizing.

MIXED MEDICAL AND SOCIAL-SYSTEM DEFINITIONS

More recent discussions of the concept of adaptive behavior have reflected a mixture of medical and social-system perspectives. This mixture appears both at the conceptual and the operational levels.

In 1961 the American Association on Mental Deficiency adopted a two-dimensional definition of mental retardation which specified for the first time that a person should be subaverage in general intellectual functioning *and* should evidence impairment in adaptive behavior before being diagnosed as mentally retarded (Heber, 1961). The definition of adaptive behavior proposed at that time was a mixture of medical and sociological concepts.

The sociological, or social-system, model is essentially a social-deviance perspective. Derived from sociology rather than medicine, it defines abnormality as behavior which violates social-system norms. Since each role in each social system is governed by its own set of expectations, there are multiple definitions of normal. For example, the behavior expected of a child who is playing first base on the softball team differs from that expected of the same child when playing the role of drummer in the band or when playing the role of student in the fifth-grade arithmetic class. To judge whether a particular set of behaviors is normal or abnormal requires four kinds of information. One must know the system in which the child is functioning, know the role the child is playing in the system at the time the judgment is being made about his or her behavior, know the expectations which others in the system have for behavior of persons playing that role, and have information on the actual behavior of the child.

Unlike the medical model, the norms for social systems are not biologically determined. They are hammered out in a political process by which the dominant group in the system establishes the rules that govern behavior in various social roles. The social-system model has seven characteristics. It is multidimensional, i.e., there are norms for each role in each social system. It is evaluative—the values of the most powerful groups are enforced. Definitions of normality are both role-bound and system-bound. The model is both a deficit and an asset model because both the poor performers and the outstanding performers in various social roles can be identified. Consequently, test scores within a social-deviance model form a normal distribution and have high ceilings, unlike distributions of scores within a pathological model, which tend to have low ceilings and truncated distributions. Since social deviance is a judgment about an observed behavior, it is not logical to speak of "hidden" deviance or to conceptualize deviance as a "trait" of the individual. It is an evaluation of behavior. Similarly, seeking biological explanations for all behavior is inappropriate because the political process defines what types of behavior will be treated as deviant. Changes in the power relations within the social system may change the definition of "normal."

It now becomes clear that some concepts of adaptive behavior are hybrids drawing from two different perceptual frameworks. Heber (1961) writes that "adaptive behavior refers primarily to the effectiveness of the individual in adapting to the natural and social demands of his environment. Impaired adaptive behavior may be reflected in (1) maturation, (2) learning, and/or (3) social adjustment. These three aspects are of different importance as qualifying conditions of mental retardation for different age groups." By maturation, Heber is referring to sequential development in sitting, crawling, standing, walking, and talking during infancy and early childhood, essentially the same developmental sequence covered in the Gesell and Amatruda procedures and Doll scales for younger children. Learning ability refers to facility in acquiring the types of academic knowledge "most manifest in the academic situation" (Heber, 1961, pp. 3–4). "Social adjustment . . . is assessed in terms of the degree to which the individual is able to maintain himself independently in the community and in gainful employment . . ." In preschool years and school years social adjustment "is reflected in large measure in the level and manner in which the child relates to parents, other adults, and age peers" (p. 4).

Heber's concept of maturation implies a medical model, since behaviors are assumed to be primarily determined by the organic, maturational state of the organism. Learning and social adjustment are clearly linked to performance in particular social roles and imply a social-system definition of normal and a social-deviance model for analysis and measurement. Although Heber notes that adaptive behavior is related to the "culturally and socially imposed standards of acceptable behavior," he does not explore the implications of such a position, i.e., the question of differing norms for differing roles, the question of the source of the norms and the basis of their enforcement, the issue of multiple standards in a pluralistic society, and so forth. Rather, he continues to conceptualize adaptive behavior as an individual characteristic that can be carried into many situations and evaluated as a relatively unitary, general trait of the person.

The 1973 revision of the AAMD definition (Grossman, 1973) alters the language but retains the mixed definition. During infancy and early childhood the behaviors evaluated are sensory-motor skills, communication, self-help, and socialization skills which "develop in a sequential pattern reflective of the maturation process." For older children and adults adaptive behavior is defined in terms of social-role performance. The definition recognizes that expectations will vary at different ages, but it does not address the issue of expectations which vary by social role and social system in a pluralistic society nor the issue of who determines what types of behaviors are "normal." The implicit assumption is that a single set of standards exists by which the person's "ability to meet and conform to standards set by the community" may be judged. Adaptive behavior is viewed as a characteristic of the person. Interventions are viewed as programs focused on specific "deficiencies in adaptive behavior" (Grossman, 1973).

The definition of adaptive behavior used in the Riverside Project epidemiology closely paralleled the AAMD definition (Mercer, 1973). The 28 age-graded scales which were developed to measure adaptive behavior in that study focused on developmental and maturational sequences for infants and young children and shifted to an evaluation of social-role performance for older children, adolescents, and adults. The scales were designed with low ceilings for purposes of screening for deficits in adaptive behavior, evidence of an implicit pathological model. Individuals were assigned a global adaptive behavior score based on their performance relative to others of the same age. This procedure implies the concept that adaptive behavior is an individual characteristic and that age is the only crucial dimension for developing pluralistic norms.

Leland (Leland et al., 1966, 1967, 1969) has moved furthest from the medical model in conceptualizing adaptive behavior. He and his colleagues have seen adaptive behavior as related to environmental demands, treating social expectations as the independent variable and the adaptive behavior of the individual as the dependent variable. They point out that different environments have different expectations for performance and that modifying the environment may make the child more adaptive. Their Adaptive Behavior Scales (Nihira, Foster, Shellhaas, & Leland, 1969) report performance in a variety of behavioral domains rather than a global, overall score.

SOCIAL-SYSTEM MODEL OF ADAPTIVE BEHAVIOR

The System of Multicultural Pluralistic Assessment (SOMPA) conceptualizes adaptive behavior from a social-system model. It defines adaptive as the child's social-role performance in a variety of social systems in which the child is participating: the family, the peer group, the map a child's adaptive topography at one point in time in the major social systems in whcih the child is participating: the family, the peer group, the community, nonacademic school roles, earner/consumer roles, self-maintenance roles, and academic school roles. The Adaptive Behavior Inventory for Children (ABIC) is based on a particular set of concepts and premises concerning the nature of human adaptation.

The Nature of the Social Environment

The child must learn to cope with the physical and natural environment in order to survive. The uniquely human mechanism for coping with problems of survival in the physical and natural environment has been to develop intricate social organizations with a highly differentiated division of labor. Through social cooperation individual members of the species, who alone are weak, slow, and vulnerable, have been able to cope with the problems posed by the physical and natural environment and to become dominant on earth. It is through building and maintaining human social structures that the human infant and the species are able to survive. It is through adaptation to these social structures that the infant develops humanity. For this reason our concept of adaptive behavior focuses primarily on the child's adaptation to the social systems in which he or she is participating. It is the *social* environments which are centered to our concept of adaptive behavior.[1]

The Social System

The social environment is composed of a highly complex set of interlocking social systems that form the social structure into which the newborn is thrust. A social system may be a dyad, such as that formed by the mother and infant, or it may be highly elaborated. Regardless of its

[1] The author is deeply indebted to Nancy Carlson of Michigan State University and to Tom Cassel of Wayne State University for their invitation to participate in a two-day conference on the concept of adaptive behavior. This conference was based on a series of working papers developed by them and their staff. Many of the ideas expressed in this chapter were concepts introduced and/or developed during that two-day period, concepts which are more fully elaborated in the final report for the project. Persons interested in adaptive behavior should read their splendid discussion (Carlson, 1976).

size, each social system consists of certain basic elements: statuses, roles, and social norms.

SOCIAL STATUSES

The positions in a system constitute social statuses. In a formal institutionalized system statuses have names, such as teacher, principal, or custodian. In informal systems, such as friendship groups or neighborhood play groups, the statuses may not have specific names, but the individual's location vis-à-vis other members of the system can still be identified.

SOCIAL ROLES

The behaviors of individuals who occupy various statuses are their social roles. Obviously, behaviors differ according to the role that the individual is playing. A teacher behaves differently from a student or a custodian when playing the role of teacher. Although dramaturgical language is used in describing role behavior, this language does not imply that there is anything artificial in occupying particular statuses and playing the roles associated with those statuses. Indeed, negotiating entry to a status, establishing the interpersonal ties necessary to maintain one's position, and acquiring the technical skills needed to fulfill role expectations are pivotal aspects of adaptation that differentiate the human species from animals with less developed social organizations.

SOCIAL NORMS

Persons participating in any social system share some common expectations concerning how occupants of various statuses in the system ought to play their roles. These role expectations for each status involve some definition of the types of interpersonal ties it is appropriate for a person in that status to develop with persons holding other statuses in the system and the kinds of obligations and privileges system members have toward each other. The social norms also specify the contribution to the achievement of group goals that is expected of persons holding various statuses. Thus, the norms specify the types of technical skills that are expected of those playing various roles.

NORMAL BEHAVIOR

Role performance that conforms to the expectations of others in the system is considered "normal" behavior. "Deviant" behavior is behavior that varies sufficiently from the expectations of the group to trigger group strategies aimed at coping with the deviance. Both positive and negative sanctions are used to enforce the norms. The positive sanctions may be tangible rewards, such as prizes or money, or they may be symbolic, such as receiving praise from other system members or being assigned to a higher, more esteemed status in the group. Negative sanctions may take the form of physical punishment, such as spanking, imprisonment, or restriction of activity. They, too, may be primarily symbolic, such as ridicule, deprivation of privilege, or demotion to a lower, less esteemed status in the group. The most drastic negative sanction available is to strip a member of status in the group and make that individual an outsider.

SITUATED FUNCTIONING

Social systems differ greatly in the types of statuses and roles which make up each system. This is referred to as situated functioning. Social systems also differ in the content, focus, and level of their norms; the extent to which the norms have been formalized and codified; and the rigor with which the norms are enforced. For example, in the study of labeling the mentally retarded, the norms of the schools were embodied almost exclusively in the IQ test, while other agencies, such as Vocational Rehabilitation and the Department of Mental Hygiene, emphasized medical norms. While schools focused almost exclusively on learning problems, law enforcement agencies focused on acting out behavior problems, and medical agencies focused heavily on health problems. The public schools required a much higher performance on IQ tests than that demanded by other agencies, such as the Department of Mental Hygiene. The public school norms were highly formalized and codified and were rigorously enforced by teachers and school psychometrists, compared with parochial school norms, which were informal, less codified, and not systematically enforced by a corps of specialized labelers. Because of these differences in the normative structures of social systems, a child could be "situationally retarded." The same child might play the role of retardate at school but be regarded as normal by peers, family, and neighbors outside of school (Mercer, 1973, Chaps. 4–6). In a most fundamental sense, all adaptive functioning is situated functioning, and behavior can be evaluated only within the normative structure of the system in which the child is operating.

The Process of Adaptive Fitting

Adaptive fitting is a term used by Cassel (1976) to describe the process by which the individual and the social system negotiate an adaptation. The present participle form is used to convey the sense that adaptation is a dynamic, continuous process by which the individual modifies his or her behavior to fit the demands of the social system *and* the other participants in the social system modify their behavior and expectations when confronted with the unique characteristics of each individual.

Because the process of achieving an adaptive fit between the child and a particular social system is negotiated between the child and other participants in the system, the fit may be achieved by the child changing his or her behavior to meet the expectations of the system, by the system changing its expectations to accept the child's performance, or, more usually, through some mutual adaptation of child to system and system to child. It is since children are born into a world of preexisting, relatively stable social structures, a child is more likely to be socialized to meet the expectations of the system than vice versa. However, the child is not passive during this process, but negotiates entry to each system by developing the necessary socioemotional ties to other persons in the system and by learning the necessary technical skills. The bidirectional nature of the child–other interaction needs to be emphasized because the child not only adapts to the preexisting social systems, but also influences the nature of those systems by his or her responses (Bell, 1968; Sander, 1962). Thus, the child's role-specific adaptive behavior is the child's ability to negotiate entry to a specific social system, to occupy a status in that social system, and to play the role associated with that status in a manner which is acceptable to other persons in that system. It is the child's situated functioning.

For two or more persons to establish and maintain a social system, it is necessary that (1) they develop some type of continuing mutuality in the form of socioemotional ties and (2) they develop some mechanism for achieving the instrumental or task requirements of the system. To achieve an adaptive fit within a particular social system, children must acquire two types of role competencies. First, they must develop skill in creating and maintaining interpersonal ties with other members of the system. Such ties require children to generate affective attachments through negotiating patterns of mutual assistance and reciprocity that will support their continued participation in the system. Second, children must learn the instrumental skills expected of persons of their status so that they can participate at a level considered appropriate for their age and sex in the achievement of group tasks and goals. For example, children who wish to participate in the social system of a baseball team must not only develop skill in catching, hitting, and throwing baseballs (skills needed to participate in achieving group goals), but they must also develop interpersonal ties with other players on the team.

Adaptive fitting characterizes the interaction of even very young children. A series of papers by Sander (1962, 1970) report a longitudinal analysis of 22 mother–infant pairs over 18 months. Sander discovered a cyclic pattern in the sequencing of the adaptations of mother–infant pairs as each advancing level of maturity in the child demanded new adjustments in the relationship. Sander saw the process of mutual modification as a matter of interactive negotiation.

Negotiating Entry to a Social System

The newborn enters a world of pre-existing social structures and must gradually negotiate entry to the original mother–infant dyad and subsequently to each of the social systems in which the infant will participate. Negotiating successful entry to any social system is facilitated by at least three elements: the presence of a "secure base," the presence of a transition agent and/or zone, and anticipatory socialization.

THE SECURE BASE

It has been noted among birds as well as mammals (King, 1966) that the presence of the mother reduces fear of novel stimuli and encourages exploratory behavior. Harlow (1961) reports that isolated surrogate-reared rhesus monkeys explore strange settings using the surrogate as the locus around which exploration takes place. Short-term separation of the rhesus infant and its mother tends to eliminate exploratory behavior and to depress its appearance for considerable periods thereafter (Hinde, 1969; Hinde & Spencer-Booth, 1967). Cassel (1976) uses the term "secure base" to describe a situation in which the child has developed an attachment relationship in an ongoing system, usually the family. Such a relationship, especially between mother and child, provides the locus of support for the child to explore novel social situations. Carlson (1976) notes that the fear of novel situations is reduced by the presence of the mother or other attachment figures because it assures the child that the new environment is both physically and psychologically safe. Having a secure base supports the child's navigation into new social systems and the acquiring of new social statuses and roles. The absence of a secure base removes the support for exploring new environments and is likely to inhibit the child from negotiating entry to new social systems.

TRANSITION AGENT

Entry to a new social system is also facilitated by the presence of a transition agent, a person who can mediate the critical transition into the new social system. To be effective, the transition agent must be an individual with whom the child has established an attachment relationship so that the agent can function to provide a secure base for the child's exploratory behavior. Preferably, the agent should be a person who already has an established status in the new social system so that the agent can operate to introduce the child to other participants in the system, legitimate the child's presence in the system, and support the child's initial efforts to function in the system. For example, the mother may function as transition agent for the preschool child entering a day-care center. Her presence during the first few sessions provides a secure base from which the child can move out to explore the new environment, and her participation lends support to the child's initial efforts to make an adaptive fit with the other children and teachers at the center. Children from the neighborhood play group may serve as transition agents when the child first enters the neighborhood elementary school, and so forth.

A child who does not have a transition agent will have greater difficulty negotiating entry to a new social system. For example, the child of a Spanish-speaking mother who cannot serve as transition agent when the child enters public school may have more difficulty negotiating entry to the school than a child with an English-speaking mother who is familiar with bureaucratic structures. The child from a rural home who has no playmates to serve as transition agents and the child who has no older siblings can be expected to have more difficulty with transitions to new peer groups and to the public school.

ANTICIPATORY SOCIALIZATION

Anticipatory socialization occurs when a child has the opportunity to acquire some of the skills needed to perform the social roles in a particular system before attempting to negotiate entry to the system. If the child has had an opportunity to practice the new role in other settings, has already acquired some of the technical skills needed to perform the role success-fully, or already has had experience in developing interpersonal ties with persons similar to those who will participate in the new group, this child will have fewer problems making an adaptive fit. For example, the child who has learned how to develop and to maintain interpersonal ties with neighborhood children will be better able to establish ties with children at school. The child socialized by a mother who uses a teaching style similar to that used by public school teachers will have fewer difficulties coping with the teaching style of the public school teacher than a child who has been socialized to a different learning-teaching style. Ramirez and Cas-taneda (1974) conclude that children reared in non-Anglicized Mexican-American homes learn to relate to adults in a field-dependent manner and develop a field-dependent cognitive style. Their anticipatory socialization makes it difficult for them to relate to a public school teacher who uses a field-independent teaching style and expects children to respond in a field-independent manner. Adaptive fitting is also facilitated when the child has experience in a transitional system (Cassel, 1976) and has an opportunity to practice some of the new role behaviors. Preschools, Head Start programs, summer orientation sessions prior to school opening, and kindergarten, serve as transitional environments to the academic program of first grade.

Ideally, a child should be assisted through major transitions by transi-tion agents who can provide a secure emotional base for the new experi-ence as well as provide anticipatory socialization. Whenever possible, transition zones should provide gradual movement into the new status and role. Analysis of critical transitions in the child's life will provide valuable information in understanding the child's current functioning as well as useful avenues for intervention when the child is experiencing difficulties in negotiating an adaptive fit in a particular social system.

Adaptive Trajectories

A child's adaptive behavior can be conceptualized as an adaptive trajectory, a longitudinal pathway which the child traces through varying social systems in the course of development. The nature of the adaptive trajectory developed by a child is dependent not only on the characteristics of the child, i.e., the child's presenting state (Cassel, 1976), but it is also dependent on the characteristics of the social systems with which the child must deal: the nature of the statuses and roles available in each system; the nature of the role expectations; the content, focus, and level of normative expectations; and the types of sanctions typically used by each system. When there is a fit between the child's presenting state and the demands of the system, adaptation is facilitated. Where there is a mismatch, either the child, the system, or both child and system will have to be modified if an adaptive fit is to be negotiated.

The optimal way to measure adaptive behavior is to develop a careful longitudinal chart of the child's movement through the social space which comprises his or her life space. The trajectory would trace the various paths which the child has taken from birth onward through the social systems which make up his or her domain of functioning. It would start with the initial mother–child dyad, move into the family, kinship group, neighborhood, peer group, day-care center, church school, kindergarten, and so forth. The dimensions of analysis would be those discussed earlier in this chapter: the nature of the statuses, roles, and normative structures of each social system; problems encountered in negotiating entry to each system and maintaining an adaptive fit; and the presence or absence of a secure base, a transition agent, and anticipatory socialization.

ENABLING AND DISABLING TRAJECTORIES

An enabling trajectory is a trajectory that facilitates the individual's movement into ever broadening circles of social systems.

A disabling trajectory is a trajectory that takes the child into social systems which are dead ends. It prevents or impedes movement into broader social space. A disabling trajectory contains cul de sacs that consist of systems that do not provide a secure base, transition agents, and anticipatory socialization to enable the person to negotiate entry into other systems. For example, children whose adaptive trajectories have led them through accelerated educational programs and college preparatory courses are enabled by that pathway to gain entry to college programs and curricula which in turn will open doors to a wide variety of occupational roles and social systems. On the other hand, children whose adaptive trajectories have led through encapsulated educational programs or institutional settings find themselves on pathways that constrict the opportunity to enter and to participate in multiple social systems. Similarly, children who negotiate entry into a delinquent group may foreclose the possibility of gaining access to many of the social systems and resources of the larger society because the delinquent gang tends to be a cul de sac.

In the assessment of adaptive behavior it is the nature of the overall trajectory which is being assessed and the extent to which it either broadens the child's life space and enriches the child's human experience or shunts the child into peripheral social systems that matters. The thoughtful reader can readily see the utility of examining the adaptive trajectory of the individual child in planning interventions which will not place the child in a series of blind alleys, such as self-contained programs or special institutions, which limit entry to social systems that could enlarge the child's life space.

The concept of a disabling trajectory is related to the notions of primary and secondary deviance (Lemert, 1967). Primary deviance is the process by which an individual's behavior is defined as deviant by others in the social setting because it violates the norms of the system. Secondary deviance arises when the person whose behavior has been defined as deviant is forced into deviant social roles as a result of these definitions. The process of secondary deviance is complete when the individual has accepted the deviant label and the roles based on that label as an appropriate definition of the self. Such an acceptance results in a psychic restructuring of the individual, a "symbolic reorganization at the level of self-regarding attitudes and social roles" (Lemert, 1967, p. 17). At this juncture the disabling process is complete. A disabling trajectory gradually changes the individual so that he or she becomes less able to make adaptive fits in new social systems.

Adaptive Topography

Tracing a child's adaptive trajectory is a complex longitudinal process which can be done only by an extensive case study. The Adaptive Behavior Inventory for Children (ABIC) is not designed for such an in-depth analysis but focuses, instead, on securing a cross-sectional view of the child's adaptive behavior in a variety of social systems at a single point in time. Because a child's situated functioning may differ from system to system, it is useful to think of the child's current functioning as a topographical map. The topography may show a series of peaks and valleys, a broad plateau of high functioning in all systems, a flat plain of poor functioning in most systems, or any combination of these. Thus, a child's adaptive topography may be likened to a map of the child's situated functioning in a variety of social systems. A cross-sectional view provides relatively little information on the trajectory that produced the current topography, but it does make it possible to assess the child's current functioning and to work backward to try to establish the nature of the trajectory behind the present profile.

To develop a topographical view of a child's adaptive fitting, it is necessary to establish a baseline for purposes of measuring individual variation. In geographic mapping sea level is the "norm" for measuring peaks and valleys. The ABIC uses the statistical average of the responses given by the parents of the 2,100 children in our sample as the norm for measuring the peaks and valleys of adpative fitting.

Developmental Sequencing of
Adaptive Behavior

As a child matures, expectations for role performance become more demanding and the number and complexity of social roles increases. In a relatively undifferentiated society, children may progress from childhood roles to adult roles with few discontinuities. Adults may be able to master the full complement of roles available in the society to one of their age, sex, and social position. Having once achieved adult status and having mastered the appropriate roles, adults may seldom be required to develop interpersonal ties in additional social systems or to master the skills required for acceptable performance in a new role. Such is not the case in a pluralistic, urban society characterized by geographic and social mobility. Adults frequently find themselves negotiating entry to new social systems, learning new social roles, and internalizing new social norms. In American society socialization to unfamiliar social roles is a lifelong process of adaptive fitting.

The ABIC is concerned with the adaptive behaviors of children 5 through 11 years of age. We visualize five major social systems in which most children participate during this period of life: the family, the peer group, the community, the school, and the economy. Each of these larger structures has subsystems within it.

THE FAMILY

Cassel (1976) and Carlson (1976) view the attachment relationship in the family, especially between the mother and child, as serving four functions for the developing child. First, it provides the secure base for the exploration of novel socioecological settings, the pivot around which exploration takes place. The second function of the family is supporting "navigation" into new social systems. Members of the family can serve as transition agents or mediators who assist the child in making critical transitions between social systems. For example, older siblings may facilitate the child's entry into the neighborhood peer group through serving as advocate, teacher, and role model. Such mediators are important in helping the child acquire the skills needed to make successful transitions and to achieve an adaptive fit in new social settings. The third function of family attachment relationships is to provide a "privileged setting for combinatorial play," a setting in which the child can freely experiment with new combinations of tools and materials. Fourth, it provides a privileged setting in which the young child can master complex skills.

Negotiating and renegotiating an adaptive fit within the family is a dynamic, ongoing process in the child's adaptive behavior because maturational changes in the child and developmental changes in other family members continually modify the nature of the child's relationship with other family members. The changing circumstances and contingencies of the family situation also require constant modification of the family social structure. In addition, the child is continually developing new instrumental skills which contribute to performing family tasks relating to food acquisition and preparation, utilization and maintenance of family equipment and possessions, selection and maintenance of clothing for family members, and so forth. Thus, even as the child moves into nonfamily social systems, he or she is simultaneously engaged in the continuing process of constructing and elaborating social relationships in the family which serve as the foundation for transitions to new systems and the development of more complex role performances within the family. In a sense, the developing child is like a juggler who must keep the original ball in motion even while adding objects to his juggling performance.

THE PEER GROUP

Entry into a peer group is one of the first transitions most children make to nonfamily social systems, whether the peer group consists of neighborhood children, nursery school peers, or members of other community peer groups. Again, the process can be viewed as having two major dimensions. The child negotiates entry into the group by establishing relationships with the other children so that they accept rather than reject, tease, or ridicule him or her. Additionally, the child acquires the role skills valued by the peer group, whether they be throwing balls, climbing jungle gyms, or playing various childhood games so that he or she can participate acceptably in group activities and tasks. As in the family, the nature of the relationships with peers changes as the child matures. The level of skill expected in performing group tasks increases. There is greater independence from adult supervision in managing social interactions with other children. There are greater expectations that the child will cooperate with peers in playing more complicated games according to rules.

Achieving a successful adaptive fit with the neighborhood and community peer group provides a secure base for entry into the peer group at school because the child will have learned many of the role skills valued by peers and will have developed techniques for establishing relationships with peers.

THE COMMUNITY

As children gain entry to various peer groups, they are also beginning to participate in social systems within the community which involve nonfamily adults: neighbors, members of community organizations, authority figures such as the police, members of religious groups, and so forth. Again, the child negotiates adaptive fits in community social systems through developing interpersonal relationships with community persons, relationships that differ in nature from those with adults in the family or with peers. Adaptive behavior in the community also requires developing a variety of role skills, such as being able to cross streets, locate places in the community, ride wheeled vehicles, attend and participate in community events, and use public transportation. Participating in community social systems teaches the child skills needed in establishing and maintaining relationships with nonfamily adults, which may be useful in establishing relationships with teachers, custodians, secretaries, and other adults in the school system.

THE SCHOOL

School adds a new, complex social system to the life space of children. They must now comprehend a social structure containing unfamiliar adult roles, such as teacher, principal, secretary, and custodian, and must develop interpersonal ties with those adults. The child learns to play a new and demanding role—that of pupil. The child must learn to meet the behavioral expectations of the peer group and those "big" pupils who have special prerogatives and responsibilities, while simultaneously meeting the ever increasing demands of the teacher for skill in reading, writing, calculating, listening, and other academic proficiencies.

The child's performance in the role of student in the classroom has been the primary focus for traditional assessment. Undoubtedly, mastery of the role of scholar is important to a child's future because success increases a child's social options and the likelihood that a child will ultimately have an opportunity to move into a wide variety of social systems in American society. The school has a variety of subsystems, however, which tend to be overlooked in the assessment process. Nonacademic roles in the peer group during recess, on athletic teams, in the band, in the chorus, in student government, and so forth are also important aspects of achieving in adaptive fit in the social system of the school. To the child, achieving success in nonacademic roles may be of more immediate concern and have higher priority than academic achievement.

THE ECONOMY: EARNER/CONSUMER ROLES

In contemporary society achieving an adaptive fit in the economic system and its many subsystems is critical in the adaptive behavior of the individual. Although economic roles are more salient for adults than for children, such roles are emergent during childhood and become increasingly important as the child grows older. Earning money, managing money, borrowing money, lending money, spending money are all activities that take place in various subsystems of the economy. Even the elementary school child learns to establish appropriate relationships with clerks in stores, cashiers, waitresses, and other persons involved in economic transactions and learns the value of different coins and bills. The child acquires skills needed to earn money by playing the role of employee: running errands, cutting the grass, or doing chores. He or she learns entrepreneurial skills earning money by collecting bottles, running a lemonade stand, or selling scrap metal. The child learns the skills needed in the role of customer, such as making selections, counting change, or ordering food in a restaurant or hot-dog stand. Such experiences provide the foundation for the development of the more complex economic roles which the individual is expected to play during adolescence and in adult years.

SELF-MAINTENANCE ROLES

Adaptive fitting in various social systems requires a set of general interpersonal and survival skills that enhance the probability of successful negotiation in any human social system. These self-maintenance skills are not social-system specific but tend to be useful in most social settings: for example, impulse control, attending behavior, perseverance, confidence in self, recognizing dangerous situations, caring for one's personal hygiene and health, self-help skills in feeding and dressing, communicating one's needs to others. In the ABIC these more general social skills have been organized into a separate scale because they are relevant to functioning in most systems.

CONCLUSION

Although the ABIC provides a device for mapping a child's adaptive topography at one point in time, it is essential that the child's current profile be viewed as the end product of an adaptive trajectory extending backward to the moment of birth. Although the clinician or educational diagnostician can do little about those past decisions and events which placed a child on a disabling trajectory, identifying the sources of the disabling process can be useful in planning future interventions. Following are some of the questions which can be explored within the concept of adaptive behavior presented in this chapter.

1. In which specific system(s) is the child having adaptive problems?
2. What has been the source of the poor adaptive fit? The child's presenting state? The nature of the system's normative structure? A mismatch between child and system?
3. To what extent does the disabling process stem from difficulty in establishing and maintaining interpersonal ties with other system members?
4. To what extent does the maladaptive fit result from lack of the technical skills needed to fulfill role expectations?
5. To what extent does the disabling process reflect difficulties in the transition process and in negotiating initial entry to the system, i.e., lack of a secure base, lack of a transition agent, or lack of anticipatory socialization?
6. To what extent is the disabling trajectory the result of institutional decisions which have moved the child into adaptive blind alleys or encapsulated systems which constrict rather than expand the child's opportunity to participate in an ever-widening range of social systems as he or she matures?
7. Having identified the sources of the disabling process, the next step, of course, is to determine how best to intervene to place the child on an enabling rather than a disabling trajectory. How can the child be assisted in negotiating entry to additional social systems? How can a secure base and/or a transition agent or zone be provided to assist with anticipatory socialization and with the initial entry process? How can the social system be modified to support the child's entry? Are changes in the normative structure needed? The physical environment? The additudinal and interpersonal environment?

The challenge for the future in the measurement of adaptive behavior will be to develop the technology necessary to assess the behavior of the child, to assess the expectations of the social system for the child's performance, and to evaluate the adaptive fit between the two. The focus will be on the *interface* between the behavior of the child and the demands of the system rather than exclusively on the behavior of the child. Primary concern will center on the nature of the child's adaptive trajectory and on those interventions that will enhance the child's opportunity to carve a broad and varied pathway through social space.

REFERENCES

Bell, R. Q. A reinterpretation of the direction of effects in studies of socialization. *Psychological Review*, 1968, *75*, 81–95.

Binet, A., & Simon, T. Sur la necessite d'éstablir un diagnostic scientifique de états inferieurs de l'intelligence. *Année Psychologique*, 1905, *11*, 1–28.

Cain, L. F., Levine, S., Elzey, F. F. *Manual for the Cain-Levine Social Competency Scale*. Palo Alto, Ca.: Consulting Psychologists Press, 1963.

Carlson, N. A. (Ed.). *Final report: The contexts of life: A socioecological model of adaptive behavior and functioning*. East Lansing: Institute for Family and Child Study, Michigan State University, 1976. (Submitted to U.S. Department of Health, Education, and Welfare, Bureau of Education for the Handicapped, September 30, 1976. Project No. 443MH50013, contract No. 300-75-0255.)

Cassel, T. Z. A social-ecological model of adaptive functioning: A contextual developmental perspective. In N. A. Carlson (Ed.), *Final report: The contexts of life: A socio-ecological model of adaptive behavior and functioning*. East Lansing: Institute for Family and Child Study, Michigan State University, 1976.

Doll, E. A. *Measurement of social competence: A manual for the Vineland Social Maturity Scale*. Circle Pines, Mn.: American Guidance Service, 1953.

Doll, E. E. Historical survey of research and management of mental retardation in the United States. In E. P. Trapp (Ed.), *Readings on the exceptional child*. New York: Appleton-Century-Crofts, 1962.

Fullan, M., & Loubser, J. J. Education and adaptive capacity. *Sociology of Education*, 1972, *45*, 271–287.

Gesell, A., & Amatruda, C. S. *Developmental diagnosis: Normal and abnormal child development*. New York: Hoeber, 1941.

Grossman, H. J. (Ed.). *Manual on terminology and classification in mental retardation* (Special Publication No. 2). Washington, D. C.: American Association on Mental Deficiency, 1973.

Guilford, J. P. The structure of intellect. *Psychological Bulletin*, 1956, *53*, 267–293.

Harlow, H. F. The development of affectional patterns in infant monkeys. In B. M. Foss (Ed.), *Determinants of infant behavior I*. New York: Wiley, 1961.

Heber, R. A. A manual on terminology and classification in mental retardation (Rev.). *American Journal of Mental Deficiency* (Monograph Supplement), 1961, *66*.

Hinde, R. A. Analyzing the roles of partners in a behavioral interaction: Mother–

infant relations in rhesus macaques. *Annals of the New York Academy of Science,* 1969, *159,* 651–667.

Hinde, R. A., & Spencer-Booth, Y. Social influences on the mother–infant relations in rhesus monkeys. In D. Morris (Ed.), *Primate ethnology.* Chicago: Aldine, 1967.

King, D. L. A review and interpretation of some aspects of the infant–mother relationship in mammals and birds. *Psychological Bulletin,* 1965, *65,* 143–155.

Lambert, N., M., Windmiller, M., Cole, L., & Figueroa, R. *Manual: AAMD Adaptive Behavior Scale, Public School Version* (1974 Rev.). Washington, D. C.: American Association on Mental Deficiency, 1975.

Leland, H., Nihira, K., Foster, R., & Shellhaas, M. *The demonstration and measurement of adaptive behavior* (Adaptive behavior project). Parsons, Ks.: Parsons State Hospital and Training Center, 1967.

Leland, H., Nihira, K., Foster, R., Shellhaas, M., & Kagin, E. *Conferance on measurement of adaptive behavior II.* Parsons, Ks.: Parsons State Hospital and Training Center, 1966.

Leland, H., Shellhaas, M., Nihira, K., & Foster, R. *Adaptive behavior: A new dimension in the classification of the mentally retarded.* Parsons, Ks.: Parsons State Hospital and Training Center, 1969.

Lemert, E. M. *Human deviance, social problems, and social control.* Englewood Cliffs, N.J.: Prentice-Hall, 1967.

Mercer, J. R. Social system perspective and clinical perspective: Frames of reference for understanding career patterns of persons labeled as mentally retarded. *Social Problems,* 1965, *13*(1).

Mercer, J. R. Sociological perspectives on mild mental retardation. In H. C. Haywood (Ed.), *Social/cultural aspects of mental retardation: Proceedings of the Peabody NIMH conference.* New York: Appleton-Century-Crofts, 1970.

Mercer, J. R. *Labeling the mentally retarded: Clinical and social system perspectives on mental retardation.* Berkeley: University of California Press, 1973.

Nihira, K., & Shellhaas, M. Study of adaptive behavior: Its rationale, method, and implication in rehabilitation programs. *Mental Retardation,* 1970, *8,* 11–15.

Nihira, K., Foster, R., Shellhaas, M., & Leland, H. *AAMD Adaptive Behavior Scale.* Washington, D. C.: American Association on Mental Deficiency, 1969.

Ramirez, M., II, & Castaneda, A. *Cultural democracy, bicognitive development, and education.* New York: Academic Press, 1974.

Robbins, R. C., Mercer, J. R., & Meyers, C. E. The school as a selecting-labeling system. *Journal of School Psychology,* 1967, *5,* 270–279.

Sander, L. W. Issues in early mother–child interaction. *Journal of the American Academy of Child Psychiatry,* 1962, *9,* 103–123.

Sander, L. W. Early mother–infant interaction and 24-hour patterns of activity and sleep. *American Academy of Child Psychiatry Journal,* 1970, *9,* 103–123.

Spearman, C. *The abilities of man.* New York: Macmillan, 1927.

PART II

Policies and Practices in the Assessment of Adaptive Behavior

The present decade seems to be characterized more by a heighted responsiveness to political, legal, and ethical implications that derive from our conceptions of deviancy. (Baumeister & Muma, 1975, p. 294.)

Much of the recent impetus to the discussion and analysis of the concept and measurement of adaptive behavior stems from federal and state legislation and regulations which affect the practice of psychological assessment. Chapter 5 presents a compilation of state policies regarding adaptive behavior. The authors point out that although measurement of adaptive behavior is required by recent federal legislation, only half the states have policies supporting the regulation. Chapter 6 analyzes the response of a large number of pupil appraisal practitioners to a comprehensive survey regarding adaptive behavior. The results show widespread support for the concept of adaptive behavior but general dissatisfaction with available measures. These two chapters summarize the current status of governmental/administrative requirements regarding adaptive behavior.

REFERENCE

Baumeister, A. & Muma, J. On defining mental retardation. *Journal of Special Education*, **9**, 293–306, 1975.

Henry W. Morrow,
W. Alan Coulter

5

A Survey of State Policies Regarding Adaptive Behavior Measurements

The Education of the Handicapped Act, Part B, as amended by Public Law 93-380, requires each state to establish procedures concerning nondiscriminatory testing and evaluation of its public school students and to submit a plan to the federal government to show how it will comply with the law. Passage of this law created a national need to locate test instruments or testing procedures which assure nondiscriminatory testing.

In 1976 the Coordinating Office of Regional Resource Centers (COORC) sponsored a national planning conference (COORC, 1976) on the topic of nondiscriminatory assessment of handicapped children. One possible answer to nondiscriminatory assessment mentioned at this conference was the measurement of adaptive behavior. Mercer's (1973) explanation of the six-hour retardate, a student who functions in school as if retarded but who functions normally in the home environment, was the foundation for the movement to measure the student's behavior outside the school environment, that is, the student's adaptive behavior. For public school educators, specific interest in the concept of adaptive behavior was generated when Mercer (1977a, 1977b) developed the System of Multicultural Pluralistic Assessment (SOMPA), of which the Adaptive Behavior Inventory for Children (ABIC) is part (Mercer & Lewis, 1977). The SOMPA system offered a potential testing procedure that might be considered nonbiased. Furthermore, the ABIC was a specific adaptive test to be used with the system.

Continued national interest in adaptive behavior measurement was evidenced at the December 1976 Annual Meeting of the National Association of State Consultants in School Psychology (NASCSP), where a

specific request was made for a workshop on this topic. The Texas
Regional Resource Center provided a one-day workshop (see Chapter 7)
that involved, among several things, the compilation of a survey of state
policies regarding adaptive behavior measurement from the participants,
who represented 11 states. One goal of the survey was to identify
similarities and differences in definitions of adaptive behavior used at the
state level because selection of specific adaptive behavior test instruments
depends upon that definition. This goal was pursued because the term
adaptive behavior may have two distinct meanings, meanings that are
derived from a state's definition and from the intent or reason for wanting
to measure adaptive behavior. Furthermore, some states may inadver-
tently adopt or recommend adaptive behavior tests that conflict with their
definition and intent for requiring such a measure.

The first distinct meaning or intent is derived from a need to develop
nonbiased assessment procedures, and the measurement of adaptive behavior is viewed as a possible vehicle to meet this need. Currently the
only measurement device with this intent is the Adaptive Behavior Inventory for Children (Mercer & Lewis, 1977). The second meaning or intent
was developed by mental retardation professionals, who have used the
term adaptive behavior since 1961 when Heber published "A Manual on
Terminology and Classification in Mental Retardation." (Heber, 1961).
This intent was to measure behavioral skills needed by the institutionalized retarded who are to be integrated into a community outside
the institution. In other words, this measure was used to gather information for educational programming or instruction. Efforts to define the
concept and measure it in institutions were undertaken by Leland, Shellhaas, Nihira, & Foster (1967); these efforts resulted in the AAMD Adaptive Behavior Scale (Nihira, Foster, Shellhaas, & Leland, 1975), which
was extended for use in the public schools by Lambert, Windmiller, Cole,
and Figueroa (1974). Thus, diagnostic personnel in public schools who are
seeking adaptive behavior tests in order to provide a nonbiased assessment may be confused because many currently available adaptive behavior tests are designed to provide instructional programming information regarding mentally retarded students. Because the majority of available tests are for instructional programming, confusion about the concept
and measurement of adaptive behavior should not exist for diagnostic
personnel in institutions.

In order to collect information about state policies which define and
measure adaptive behavior, a brief survey was constructed and given to
participants of the one-day Texas workshop. The survey questions, administration procedures, results, and follow-up survey to include states
not represented at this workshop will be described in the following sections.

SURVEY FORMAT AND PROCEDURE

The survey was given and returned during the workshop. The participants were school psychology consultants to state education departments who would have a major role in writing policies on adaptive behavior measurement which would directly influence test selection by practitioners.

The survey contained three questions. The first question—did the consultant's state have any regulations or written policies requiring the measurement of adaptive behavior as part of the determination of any handicapping condition—was written in a yes-no format. Consultants who answered yes were asked to specify the handicapping conditions (e.g., educably mentally retarded, emotionally disturbed). If their state had no existing policy regarding adaptive behavior measurement, they were asked whether plans were currently underway to enact such a policy. The second question asked the consultants to list specific adaptive behavior instruments of which they were aware that were not necessarily used in their states. The third question asked the consultants to write their definition of adaptive behavior.

State consultants who did not attend the workshop were telephoned by the authors to elicit answers to the three survey questions. Because less than 50 percent of the states have school psychology representatives, state directors of special education were contacted and given the survey or were asked to identify a staff member who had major responsibility in the area of pupil appraisal. A total of 49 states were surveyed regarding state policies on adaptive behavior measurement. One state was contacted several times but did not respond to the survey.

RESULTS

QUESTION 1:

Does your state require an adaptive behavior measure for any of the handicapping conditions?

Of those states responding yes to the first question (Table 5–1), 80

Table 5–1
Answers to Question 1

	Frequency	Percent
Yes	25	51
No	24	49

percent require adaptive behavior measurements for the handicapping condition of mental retardation. Several other states simultaneously require such a measure for the handicapping condition of emotionally disturbed. Of those states responding yes, 28 percent include a measure of adaptive behavior in their general policy guidelines for all handicapping conditions. Only two states indicated that an adaptive behavior measure is required when students are referred for a special education assessment: (1) if the student is culturally different and/or disadvantaged and (2) if the student is bilingual.

Of those states responding no, only 25 percent have current plans to require a measure of adaptive behavior for part or all of their handicapping conditions.

QUESTION 2:

List specific measures of adaptive behavior of which you are aware.

The most frequently mentioned adaptive behavior measure was the Public School Version of the AAMD Adaptive Behavior Scale. No specific measure of adaptive behavior was noted by 30 percent of the states. Other specific measures of adaptive behavior cited by the survey participants were Behavioral Characteristics Progression Chart (Santa Cruz Co., 1974), Callier-Azusa Scale (Stillman, 1975), Camelot Behavioral Checklist (Foster, 1974), and the Denver Developmental Scale (Frankenberg & Dobbs, 1968).

Table 5–2
Answers to Question 2

Measure	Frequency of Mention
AAMD Adaptive Behavior Scale—Public School Version (Lambert, Windmiller, Cole, & Figueroa, 1974)	24
Vineland Social Maturity Scale (Doll, 1965)	15
AAMD Adaptive Behavior Scale (Nihira, Foster, Shellhaas, & Leland, 1975)	8
System of Multicultural Pluralistic Assessment—SOMPA (Mercer & Lewis, 1977)	6
Cain-Levine Social Competency Scale (Cain, Levine, & Elzey, 1963)	6
Can cite no specific instrument	15

QUESTION 3:

Does your state have an adopted definition of adaptive behavior?
Of the 25 states requiring an adaptive behavior measure, 35 percent
($N = 17$) have a state adopted definition of adaptive behavior; 14 percent
($N = 7$) or those states requiring this measure have no formal definition
but have provided for adaptive behavior in assessment/eligibility criteria
for individual comprehensive assessment; 2 percent ($N = 1$) of those
requiring this measure have no formal definition but are planning to
develop or adopt one.

Table 5–3
Answers to Question 3

	Frequency	Percent
Yes	17	35
No	32	65

Table 5–4
Frequency of States Requiring Adaptive Behavior Measurement
while Providing an Adaptive Behavior Definition

State Policies	State-adopted Definition		No Definition, Adaptive Behavior Measurement Included in General Poll		No Definition, But Planning One		No Definition, Not Planning One	
	F	%	F	%	F	%	F	%
Now Require Adaptive Behavior Measurement ($N = 25$)	17	35	7	14	1	2	2	
Planning to Require Adaptive Behavior Measurement ($N = 6$)					6	12		
Planning No Adaptive Behavior Measurement ($N = 18$)							18	37

Of the 24 states currently not requiring an adaptive behavior measure as indicated in question 1, 12 percent ($N = 6$) are planning to require this measure and are planning to adopt a formal definition of adaptive behavior. The remaining 37 percent ($N = 18$) of the states not requiring an adaptive behavior measure have no current plans to develop a state adopted definition nor to require this measure for any of the handicapping conditions. The results of questions 1 and 3 are combined in Table 5-4.

Since the term adaptive behavior may have two distinct meanings dependent upon a state's definition and intent or reason for wanting to measure adaptive behavior, a frequency count was made on general types of behaviors described in the adaptive behavior definition of those states ($N = 17$) having one.

The two distinct meanings of adaptive behavior were represented in disproportionate numbers. Seventeen percent ($N = 3$) had definitions emphasizing social role performance (Mercer's adaptive behavior definition); the remaining definitions emphasized behaviors of personal independence and social responsibility (the AAMD adaptive behavior definition) in a global environment, including behaviors inside and outside the school environment.

DISCUSSION AND CONCLUSION

Results of Question 1 reinforce the perception that adaptive behavior measurement has reached national prominence and that there is a current critical need for clarification regarding definition that will ultimately result in a demand for definitive measurement instruments. Confusion about the concept of adaptive behavior is apparent (nonbiased assessment versus instructional planning) because 28 percent of the states that require adaptive behavior measurement require such measurement for all handicapping conditions. Two distinct meanings of adaptive behavior are identifiable in the United States. The first involves the identification of those skills needed by retarded students to be successfully integrated into a community outside an institution (Leland, Shellhaas, Nihiria, & Foster, 1967). Instruments were developed to provide information for educational programming, thus facilitating community integration. The second meaning involves the use of adaptive behavior measurement as part of a nondiscriminatory or nonbiased assessment of minority group students who are being considered for special education programs. Note that the emphasis is on all of special education or its programs and not on one or two handicapping conditions. The majority of states which require a measure of adaptive behavior do so for only one or two handicapping conditions (the AAMD concept) but have considered including this measure as part of a nonbiased assessment process (Mercer's concept). Only two states have specifically related the required adaptive behavior measurement to nonbiased assessment of minority group students. These two adaptive behavior measures can be aligned with the two functions of assessment: assessment for educational placement (Mercer's concept) and assessment for educational programming (AAMD concept) (see Chapter 1).

This survey revealed that 50 percent of the states require a measure of adaptive behavior. Practitioners in states requiring a measure of adaptive behavior should be aware of the following information if the requirement's intent is to develop a nonbiased assessment process. The majority of instruments currently available which contend that they measure adaptive behavior have been developed for educational programming (AAMD concept) and not for educational placement. The measures of adaptive behavior most frequently mentioned by representatives of state departments were the AAMD Adaptive Behavior Scale—Public School Version, the Vineland Social Maturity Scale, and the AAMD Adaptive Behavior Scale (developed for educational programming use with institutional mentally retarded). The only widely known adaptive behavior measure designed to assist in making educational placement decisions when considering a minority group student's test results is Mercer's SOMPA, specifically the Adaptive Behavior Inventory for Children (ABIC).

If state departments intend to require a measure of adaptive behavior, the way they define adaptive behavior becomes critical in at least two respects. First, their definition will guide the practitioner in the selection of a test instrument. Those states that do not provide a definition must provide technical assistance to practitioners who encounter difficulties in instrument selection because they are unaware of the criteria for making decisions for placement or programming once the results are gathered. Second, their definition will clarify the *intent* of requiring an adaptive behavior measurement. Is the intent to establish a nonbiased assessment process for minority group students being considered for special education programs (assessment for placement) or to establish information that will assist classroom instructors to prepare students for integration into the community (assessment for educational programming)? Only 17 percent of those states that have adopted an adaptive behavior definition had a definition emphasizing social-role performance (Mercer's definition). Should the authors assume that the remaining states are strictly interested in adaptive behavior measurement as it relates to educational programming for one or two handicapping conditions?

In conclusion, a major problem is apparent. States are requiring that adaptive behavior be measured but have not fully investigated the two major adaptive behavior meanings currently in existence. Furthermore, the intent of such a requirement, whether for nonbiased assessment or for educational programming, might be unclear since the term adaptive behavior has two meanings.

REFERENCES

Cain, L., Levine, S., Elzey, F. *Cain-Levine Social Competency Scale.* Palo Alto, Ca.: Consulting Psychologists Press, 1963.
Coordinating Office for Regional Resource Centers. *With bias toward none: Proceedings for a conference on nonbiased assessment of minority group children.* Lexington: University of Kentucky, 1976.
Doll, E. A. *Vineland Social Maturity Scale.* Circles Pines, Mn.: American Guidance Service, 1965.
Foster, R. *Camelot Behavioral Checklist.* Bellevue, Wa.: Edmark Associates, 1974.
Frankenburg, W., & Dobbs, J. *Denver Developmental Screening Test,* Denver, Co.: Ladoca Project and Publishing, 1968.
Heber, R. P., A manual on terminology and classification in mental retardation (Rev.) *American Journal of Deficiency* (Monograph Supplement) 1961, 66.
Lambert, N. M., Windmiller, M., Cole, L., & Figueora, R. *AAMD Adaptive Behavior Scale, Public School Version (1974).* Washington, D. C.: American Association on Mental Deficiency, 1975.
Leland, H., Shellhaas, M., Nihira, K., & Foster, R. Adaptive behavior: A new dimension in the classification of the mentally retarded. *Mental Retardation Abstracts,* 1967, *4,* 359–387.
Mercer, J. *Labeling the mentally retarded: Clinical and social system perspectives on mental retardation.* Berkeley: University of California Press, 1973.
Mercer, J. *System of Multicultural Pluralistic Assessment: Technical Manual.* New York: The Psychological Corporation, 1977. (a)
Mercer, J., & Lewis, J. *System of Multicultural Pluralistic Assessment: Parent Interview manual.* New York: The Psychological Corporation, 1977. (b)
Nihira, K., Foster, R., Shellhaas, M., & Leland, H. *AAMD Adaptive Behavior Scale.* Washington, D. C.: American Association on Mental Deficiency, 1969.
Nihira, K., Foster, R., Shellhaas, M., & Leland, H. *American Association on Mental Deficiency Adaptive Behavior Scale, 1975 revision.* Washington, D. C.: American Association on Mental Deficiency, 1975.
Santa Cruz Co. *Behavior Characteristics Progression.* Palo Alto, Ca.: Vort Corporation, 1974.
Stillman, R. *Callier-Azusa Scale.* Dallas: University of Texas, Callier Center for Communication Disorders, 1975.

W. Alan Coulter,
Henry W. Morrow

6

One Year after Implementation: Practitioners' Views of Adaptive Behavior

At the 1976 Atlanta Conference—With Bias Toward None—sponsored by the Coordinating Office for Regional Resource Centers, papers were presented by Mercer and Ysseldyke (1976), Tucker (1976) and Loasa (1976) that set forth the need for a measurement of adaptive behavior in a system of nonbiased assessment. During this conference specific plans were developed for dissemination of information on nonbiased assessment in four workshops throughout Texas. The general purpose of the Texas workshops was to enable participants to make appropriate special education placement decisions regarding minority group students (Nesbit, 1976). Included in the agenda of each workshop was a session discussing a planned change in state-level pupil appraisal policies which featured the addition of adaptive behavior measurement.

In the summer of 1976 the Texas State Board of Education approved a revision of policy that included the use of a measure of adaptive behavior as part of the data required to substantiate a diagnosis of mental retardation (Texas Education Agency, 1976). This policy specified that beginning with the school year 1976–1977 all assessments of students referred for special education who were being considered for placement as mentally retarded would have to include a measure of adaptive behavior. Also, any assessment of students currently placed as mentally retarded and referred for periodic comprehensive reevaluation would include a measure of adaptive behavior (Tucker, 1977). In addition to the policy change, two scales for measuring adaptive behavior, the AAMD's Adaptive Behavior Scale—Public School Version and the Adaptive Behavior Inventory for Children (Mercer & Lewis, 1977), were added to the state-approved list of tests used in the assessment of mental retardation. The Adaptive Behavior Inventory for Children (ABIC) was not available for use by practitioners when the policy was implemented. An interim alternative used by practitioners because of the lack of approved adaptive behavior measures was to write for state approval on any other measures they wanted to use or thought were more appropriate in assessing adaptive behavior.

In February 1977 the Texas Regional Resource Center, at the request of the Texas Education Agency, initiated a comprehensive needs assessment of pupil appraisal practitioners concerning the concept and measure of adaptive behavior. The intent of the needs assessment was to determine the current status of policy implementation, to assess current measurement practices, and to determine needs for future planning, since only one of the two approved adaptive behavior measures was commercially available.

A needs assessment questionnaire (see Appendix) was developed which requested information regarding adaptive behavior from practitioners in pupil appraisal. Questions required either a yes/no answer, with expansion or specific descriptive information. This format was selected to allow for both quantitative (i.e., percentages) and qualitative (i.e., content analysis and verbatim comment) descriptions of the results. The questionnaire was divided into three basic information areas: (1) the concept and definition of adaptive behavior, (2) adaptive behavior instruments, and (3) the only available state-approved test of adaptive behavior.

In Part I opinions regarding the concept and definition of adaptive behavior were elicited with three questions. The first question elicited an opinion regarding the appropriateness of the concept for diagnosis regardless of the availability of any measures. The second asked for suggested changes in the current state definition of adaptive behavior. The third questioned the advisability of broadening the policy to include adaptive behavior measures in the diagnosis of other handicaps such as emotionally disturbed.

Part II of the questionnaire focused on tests used to measure adaptive behavior. The first question asked practitioners was if they were, in fact, measuring adaptive behavior. There was some speculation that practitioners were ignoring the policy, and this question was designed to elicit an estimate. The second question requested the names of tests used in three age ranges: 3 through 5 years, 6 through 12 years, and 13 through 21 years. Those age ranges conformed to the three areas of assessment (early childhood, elementary, and secondary school), and it was known that the approved instrument only fit the range of 6 through 12 years. The third question solicited information about practitioner needs regarding additional information, workshops, and other tests in the area of adaptive behavior measurement.

Part III dealt exclusively with the AAMD's Adaptive Behavior Scale—Public School Version (ABS—PS) (Lambert, Windmiller, Cole & Figueroa, 1974). The initial question asked practitioners how many protocols of this particular test they had administered. If the practitioner had not administered the ABS—PS, he/ she answered no additional questions in part three. If practitioners had administered the test, they were queried concerning the specific parts of the test used; difficulties with any aspects of the scale, such as administration, scoring, and interpretation; their thoughts on the appropriateness of the ABS—PS for use in their school setting; and their thoughts regarding spuriously high ratings in relation to IQ score if they were encountered when using the scale.

Demographic questions regarding the role or professional position of the informant, the number of years of experience in special education, the approximate average daily attendance of the population, and the education service center area were the only identifying characteristics asked of a person completing the questionnaire.

PROCEDURE

Two methods were used to collect data. First, 290 questionnaires with postage-free envelopes and a cover letter describing the questionnaire's intent were circulated to pupil appraisal practitioners via the 20 education service centers in Texas. Specific contact persons in each region were identified to assist in distributing questionnaires. Each practitioner completing the questionnaire was asked to return it as soon as possible. Second, a list of 56 pupil appraisal professionals located in all 20 education service centers was compiled and these professionals were contacted by phone to ensure full representation from the service center areas; the mailed questionnaires were used to assure a larger sampling of pupil appraisal practitioners. Both methods of data collection involved an effort to contact personnel who were actually involved in assessment, and avoided contacting administrators.

RESULTS

Rate of Questionnaire Return. From the total possible sample of 346 questionnaires, 249 were available when the compilation and analysis began; 206 questionnaires were returned by mail and 43 were completed by telephone, yielding a 71.9 percent rate of return for the total sample.

Participant Demographic Information. Of those participating in the survey, 58 percent were certified educational diagnosticians, and 16 percent were associated school psychologists or licensed psychologists. The remainder of the sample consisted of directors/supervisors, counselors, pupil appraisal consultants, or vocational adjustment coordinators. The median for years of experience in special education was 6 years, with 95 percent of the participants reporting less than 15 years. Participants in the study represented a broad range of small (0—5000) and large (5001 or more) school districts, as shown in Table 6–1.

Table 6–1
Representation within the Sample
by Size of School District

ADA	Frequency	Percent
0–3000	28	11
3001–5000	72	29
5001–10,000	38	15
10,000–20,000	25	10
20,000 or more	35	14
ESC Employees	22	9
Did not indicate	29	12
TOTAL	249	100

The detailed results of the participants' responses which follow reflect an extensive representation of practitioners throughout the state of Texas.

NEEDS ASSESSMENT ON ADAPTIVE BEHAVIOR

Part I. Concept and Definition

QUESTION 1:[1]

Do you think the concept of adaptive behavior is appropriate for inclusion in the definition of mental retardation?

As shown in Table 6–2, 83 percent of the survey respondents felt that the concept of adaptive behavior was appropriate for inclusion in the diagnosis of mental retardation. Of the 17 percent responding no, the most frequent reasons given were that adaptive behavior was not relevant to

[1] Questions cited in the results section have been paraphrased. For the complete questions, see the Appendix to this chapter.

Table 6–2
Answers to Part I, Question 1

	Frequency	Percent
Yes	206	83
No	43	17
TOTAL	249	100

the educational environment or that it was useful only for educational programming.

QUESTION 2:

Do you have any suggested changes in the current definition of adaptive behavior?

As shown in Table 6–3, 74 percent of the survey participants agreed with the present definition of adaptive behavior. The most frequently suggested modifications requested specific norms for age and cultural groups and inclusion of educational or academic skills as part of the definition.

Table 6–3
Answers to Part I, Question 2

	Frequency	Percent
Yes	64	26
No	185	74
TOTAL	249	100

QUESTION 3:

Should adaptive behavior be measured in the diagnosis of other handicaps?

Responses to the question of whether to include adaptive behavior measurement in the diagnosis of other handicaps were almost evenly split, with 53 percent indicating no and 43 percent indicating yes (Table 6–4). Of those answering yes, 90 percent thought adaptive behavior should be

Table 6–4
Answers to Part I, Question 3

	Frequency	Percent
Yes	116	47
No	132	53
TOTAL	248	100

included in the diagnosis of emotional disturbance (which is 41.9 percent of the total sample); 25 percent wanted it included in the definition of learning disabilities. In total, eight handicapping conditions were listed in addition to mental retardation. The most frequent reasons given for not including adaptive behavior measurement were that present procedures were adequate or that adaptive behavior was only useful in programming.

Part II: Tests Measuring Adaptive Behavior

QUESTION 1:

Are you currently attempting to measure adaptive behavior?

Almost the entire sample (96 percent) was currently attempting to measure adaptive behavior.

Table 6–5
Answers to Part II, Question 1

	Frequency	Percent
Yes	238	96
No	11	4
TOTAL	249	100

QUESTION 2:

What specific test are you using for the 3 to 5 year, 6 to 12 year, and 13 to 21 year ranges?

When asked what specific test was being used to measure adaptive behavior in the 3 through 5 year range, 37.5 percent reported the Vineland Social Maturity Scale (VSMS), and 14.3 percent reported the ABS—PS. In total, 247 responses were recorded, naming 27 tests. In the 6 through 12 year range 73.4 percent of the respondents listed the ABS—PS, with the VSMS the second most frequently mentioned, but only 13.2 percent of the respondents noted the scale. From a total of 282 responses to this question, 17 different tests were listed. In the 13 through 21 year range the ABS—PS was again most frequently noted (31.2 percent). The VSMS was also reported (29.2 percent) as well as 20 other tests in the 257 responses.

QUESTION 3:

What tests would you like added to the approved list?

When asked what tests should be added to the state approved list, 35 percent of the participants listed none or left the answer space blank; 14.7 percent noted the VSMS; and 12.8 percent the ABIC, one of the two

Table 6–6

Answers to Part II, Question 2

Tests/Scales	Frequency	Percent
3–5 years		
Vineland SMS	97	37.5
AAMD ABS—PS	37	14.3
Informal battery	21	8.1
AAMD—ABS	19	7.3
24 others (less		
than 5% each)	85	32.8
TOTAL	259	100.0
6–12 years		
ABS—PS	207	73.4
Vineland SMS	37	13.2
Informal battery	7	2.4
Camelot (Foster,		
1974)	6	2.2
13 others (less		
than 5% each)	25	8.8
TOTAL	282	100.0
13–21 years		
ABS—PS	80	31.2
Vineland SMS	75	29.2
AAMD-CV	27	10.5
20 others (less		
than 5% each)	75	29.1
TOTAL	257	100.0

Table 6–7

Answers to Part II, Question 3

Tests/Scales	Frequency	Percent
Vineland	38	14.7
ABIC of SOMPA	33	12.8
Camelot	11	4.3
34 others (less than		
5% each)	85	32.9
Nothing to add	91	35.3
TOTAL	258	100.0

scales currently on the list. In all, 37 different tests or special modifications were reported in 258 responses.

QUESTION 4:

Would you like to know more about procedures for submitting a test for approval?
Despite considerable effort to disseminate procedures for submitting a test for approval, 66 percent of the participants requested this information.

Table 6–8
Answers to Part II, Question 4

		Frequency	Percent
Yes		164	66
No		85	34
	TOTAL	249	100

QUESTION 5:

Would you like to know more about alternatives in gathering adaptive behavior information?
Despite the effort already mentioned to inform practitioners about the concept, when asked if they would like to know more about alternatives in gathering adaptive behavior information, 94 percent responded yes.

Table 6–9
Answers to Part II, Question 5

		Frequency	Percent
Yes		233	94
No		16	6
	TOTAL	249	100

QUESTION 6:

Would a workshop be helpful to you?
A total of 88 percent of the participants requested workshops regarding tests and/or procedures. More specifically, 79 percent of those answering yes requested a preview of available tests and 70 percent requested information on how to develop suitable local norms. Many participants requested workshops on test administration, scoring, and interpretation; 31 percent requested the ABIC; and 29 percent requested the ABS—PS.

Table 6–10
Answers to Part II, Question 6

	Frequency	Percent
Yes	219	88
No	30	12
TOTAL	249	100

QUESTION 7:

Do additional tests need to be developed?

There were 76 percent of the participants who indicated support for the development of additional tests of adaptive behavior.

Table 6–11
Answers to Part II, Question 7

	Frequency	Percent
Yes	190	76
No	59	24
TOTAL	249	100

Part III: AAMD Adaptive Behavior Scale—
Public School Version (ABS—PS)

QUESTION 1:

How many ABS—PS scales have you given?

A total of 220 participants[2] recorded that they administered one or more of the ABS—PS protocols and thus were asked subsequent questions in Part III. However, only 50 (19 percent) had given 20 or more protocols.

Table 6–12
Answers to Part III, Question 1

	Frequency	Percent
None	44	17
1–5	70	26
6–10	63	24
11–20	37	14
20 or more	50	19
TOTAL	264	100

QUESTION 2:

What parts of the ABS—PS do you routinely give?

In response to question 2, 62 percent reported using Part I of the scale only. No one reported using Part II exclusively, but 38 percent reported routinely administering both parts of the ABS—PS.

Table 6–13
Answers to Part III, Question 2

	Frequency	Percent
Part I	118	62
Part II	0	0
Both	72	38
TOTAL	190	100

QUESTION 3:

Do you feel the ABS—PS is appropriate for use in school?

Of the practitioners with experience, 60 percent felt that the ABS—PS was not appropriate for use in their school setting. Participants were asked to provide a rationale for answering no. Reasons for answering no appeared to cluster around 13 different factors (as determined via content analysis by two judges). Frequency for each factor is reported in Table 6–15.

Table 6–14
Answers to Part III, Question 3

	Frequency	Percent
Yes	80	40
No	118	60
TOTAL	198	100

QUESTION 4:

Do you have difficulties with any aspects of the ABS—PS?

Difficulties with administration were noted by 42 percent of the participants, problems with scoring were recorded by 20 percent, and 55 percent had problems with interpretation. Most frequently noted in the remarks was the ambiguity of guidelines for discriminating mentally retarded students form slow learners when attempting to interpret the ABS—PS.

Table 6–15

Frequency of Reasons for Responding No to
Appropriateness of ABS—PS

Comments	Frequency
1. Many items are *not* relevant to the adaptive skills in rural areas (i.e., AAMD—PS appears weighted toward urban and nonpublic school settings). Item content is inappropriate for rural areas: i.e., economic, vocational, leisure time.	35
2. Norms need improvement: (1) subscales do not differentiate EMR from TMR, (2) subscales do not differentiate the culturally/educationally deprived from "true" EMR, (3) norms need to extend below age 7 years and above 13 years, and, (4) there is *not* a normal distribution of scores in the tables.	53
3. Not one person available who can provide all information (i.e., parent, teacher).	18
4. Not an objective measure: (1) parents generally give inflated measures and (2) teachers sometimes give inflated/deflated measures.	16
5. Not a measure of academic adaptive skills.	12
6. Too time consuming.	8
7. Questionable validity/reliability; not adequate information for determining placement.	5
8. These questions are none of the school's business; the ABS—PS is harmful to the school/home relationship.	2
9. More a measure of school than home behaviors.	1
10. Needs more social/interpersonal questions.	1
11. Some questions do not relate to a public school setting.	2
12. Not appropriate for orthopedically handicapped.	1
13. Teachers do not use information.	1

Table 6–16
Answers to Part III, Question 4

	Frequency	Percent
Administration		
No	126	58
Yes	91	42
TOTAL	217	100
Scoring		
No	169	80
Yes	41	20
TOTAL	210	100
Interpretation		
No	86	45
Yes	105	55
TOTAL	191	100

QUESTION 5:

Do you think that the ABS—PS unfairly excludes students from placement as EMR because of spuriously high scores? If so, what percentage?

That the ABS—PS was erroneously excluding some students as mentally retarded as a function of spuriously high scores was the contention of 60 percent of the participants. Fifty-four percent, however, noted that this occurred less than 25 percent of the time, 25 percent noted that this occurred 26 to 50 percent of the time, and 10.5 percent noted that it occurred 51 percent or more of the time (10 percent of those answering yes did not indicate a frequency).

Table 6–17
Answers to Part III, Question 5

	Frequency	Percent
No	83	40
Yes	123	60
TOTAL	206	100
0–25%	66	54
25–50%	31	25
51% or over	13	10.5
Could not indicate	13	10.5
TOTAL	123	100.0

DISCUSSION

It is apparent that the majority of pupil appraisal practitioners participating in the needs assessment survey agree with the principle of broadening the appraisal process to include a measure of adaptive behavior for a diagnosis of mental retardation. Efforts to create an awareness of the inadequacies of traditional assessment (Nesbit, 1976) have been successful. Advocates of a least-biased assessment process (Mercer, 1973; Tucker, 1976) can now show broad-based support for a modification in traditional assessment. This support extends, to a lesser degree, to the diagnosis of emotional disturbance, where 41 percent of the practitioners included this handicapping condition. This may also reflect the current ambiguity regarding eligibility criteria of this handicapping condition (Long, Morse, & Newman, 1971; Phillips, Draguns, & Bartlett, 1975; Prugh, Engel, & Morse, 1975). Additional investigation of the feasibility of adaptive behavior measurement within the model of assessment for emotional disturbance is needed.

Most changes suggested in the definition of adaptive behavior reflect a misunderstanding of the concept because practitioners are looking for adaptive behavior in academic achievement or the academic environment rather than measuring aspects of a student's behavior outside the academic environment, which underlies the entire concept of adaptive behavior measurement (Mercer, 1977; see also Chapter 1). Additional explanation and in-service training with appraisal practitioners might articulate this concept.

Although many tests are currently being used as adaptive behavior measures, as noted in Part II of the results, general dissatisfaction is apparent. The high frequency of responses requesting more tests, alternative methods, and workshops depicts a need for better dissemination of available information as well as a need for additional research and product development. Most of the available tests are inappropriate for use in the diagnosis/placement phase of pupil appraisal (see Chapter 1). Existing tests noted in the survey may adequately yield information for designing an educational program, but they are relatively useless in discriminating between a mentally retarded and a slow learning student (see Chapter 8).

The one instrument (ABS—PS) used by many survey participants appears to present a number of problems. A majority felt that the instrument is inappropriate for use in their schools. The ambiguity of individual items, awkward phraseology for some settings (especially rural and low socioeconomic areas), and poorly developed norms (most subscales do not differentiate normals from EMR) are the most frequently cited reasons. Additionally, many practitioners report problems in administration and interpretation. The reported discrepancies in the normative structure are further highlighted by the suspicion that some students' spuriously high ABS—PS scores, when compared with IQ scores, result in inappropriate exclusion from special education on the basis that these students are no longer retarded. It may be that more specific in-service training on the ABS—PS would clarify many of these ambiguities. New information, however, indicates that the ABS—PS is not entirely functional as a diagnosis/placement appraisal instrument (Mastenbrook, 1977). Further investigation is necessary to determine the continued feasibility of the ABS—PS for this use.

The results of the entire survey illustrate the general state of confusion experienced by many professionals regarding adaptive behavior. Many fail to distinguish the two functions that an assessment of adaptive behavior can serve. Leland (1973) and the Parsons State Hospital Project, which developed the Adaptive Behavior Scale, established and validated the usefulness of developing programs to train the mentally retarded in adaptive skills. Conversely, Mercer (1973) and Tucker (1976) have shown the usefulness of adaptive behavior measurement in lessening the probability of a biased placement in special education. As mentioned previously, the Atlanta conference on nonbiased assessment led to statewide workshops in nonbiased assessment which disseminated the change in state board of education policy. Some confusion may be traced to the development of the actual policy on adaptive behavior, which was intended for nonbiased assessment of minority groups but was applied to all suspected mentally retarded students regardless of ethnicity. It may be that professionals confused the function of the assessment required by the policy because majority group (Anglo) students were included.

The results show at least three major needs:

1. All available information regarding the measurement of adaptive behavior should be widely disseminated through skill-training workshops and the professional media to practitioners responsible for conducting pupil appraisals.
2. Additional tests need to be developed which will assist the practitioner to discriminate the mentally retarded student from the slow learning student, especially in the adolescent age range (13 through 21).
3. The ABS—PS should be thoroughly scrutinized by both researchers and policy-level practitioners to determine the most appropriate use of the instrument.

While support for the measurement of adaptive behavior in the diagnosis of mental retardation is pervasive, the need for a more broadly developed technology to implement the measurement is obvious. Future efforts should focus on practical methods to aid appraisal practitioners in clarifying and implementing the concept.

REFERENCES

Laosa, L. M. Historical antecedents and current issues in nondiscriminatory assessment of children's abilities. In T. Oakland (Ed.), *With bias toward none: Non-biased assessment of minority group children.* Lexington, Ky.: Coordinating Office for Regional Resource Centers, 1976.

Lambert, N., Windmiller, M., Cole, L., & Figueroa, R. *AAMD Adaptive Behavior Scale: Public School Version* (1974 Rev.). Washington, D. C.: American Association on Mental Deficiency, 1974.

Leland, H. Adaptive behavior and mentally retarded behavior. In C. E. Meyers, R. K. Eyman, & G. Tarjan (Eds.), *Sociobehavioral studies in mental retardation: Papers in honor of Harvey Dingman.* Washington, D. C.: American Association on Mental Deficiency, 1973.

Long, N. J., Morse, W. C., & Newman, R. G. *Conflict in the classroom* (2d ed.). Belmont, Ca.: Wadsworth, 1971.

Mastenbrook, J. *Guidelines for using the AAMD norms for classification decisions.* Unpublished manuscript, 1977. (Available from Pluralistic Diagnostic Team, Corpus Christi Independent School District, 801 Leopard Street, Corpus Christi, Tx. 78403.)

Mercer, J. R. *Labeling the mentally retarded: Clinical and social system perspectives on mental retardation.* Berkeley: The Regents of the University of California, 1973.

Mercer, J. R. *System of Multicultural Pluralistic Assessment: Technical manual.* New York: The Psychological Corporation, 1977.

Mercer, J. R., & Lewis, J. F. *System of Multicultural Pluralistic Assessment: Parent interview manual and student assessment manual.* New York: The Psychological Corporation, 1977.

Mercer, J. R., & Ysseldyke, J. Designing diagnostic-intervention programs. In T. Oakland (Ed.), *With bias toward none: Non-biased assessment of minority group children.* Lexington: Coordinating Office for Regional Resource Centers, 1976.

Nesbit, M. J. *Final evaluation report: Institutes of nonbiased assessment.* Austin: Texas Regional Resource Center, 1976.

Phillips, L., Draguns, J. G., & Bartlett, D. P. Classification of behavior disorders. In N. Hobbs (Ed.), *Issues in the classification of children.* San Francisco: Jossey-Bass, 1975.

Prugh, D. G., Engel, M., & Morse, W. C. Emotional disturbance in children. In N. Hobbs (Ed.), *Issues in the classification of children.* San Francisco: Jossey-Bass, 1975.

Texas Education Agency. *Proposed revision 3572.5a, administrative procedure.* Austin: Author, Special Education Division, 1976.

Tucker, J. A. Operationalizing the diagnostic intervention process. In T. Oakland (Ed.), *With bias toward none: Non-biased assessment of minority group children.* Lexington, Ky: Coordinating Office for Regional Resource Centers, 1976.

Tucker, J. A. Personal communication. January 16, 1977.

APPENDIX: NEEDS ASSESSMENT ON ADAPTIVE BEHAVIOR (SURVEY FORM)

Part I: Concept and Definition

1. Presently, the measurement of adaptive behavior is required as part of a comprehensive individual assessment in considering a diagnosis of mental retardation for placement in special education. Disregarding the measurements currently available, do you feel the *concept* of adaptive behavior is appropriate for inclusion in the diagnosis of EMR and TMR? Yes _____ No _____
   If no, why?

   _____

   _____

   _____

2. The current definition of adaptive behavior as approved by the State Board of Education states, "Adaptive behavior is the effectiveness or degree with which the individual meets the standards of personal independence and social responsibility expected of the age and cultural group."
   Would you suggest any specific changes in the present definition? No _____ Yes _____
   If yes, what specific changes?

   _____

   _____

   _____

3. Do you think the measurement of adaptive behavior should be included in the diagnosis for eligibility of other handicaps? Yes _____ No _____ If no, why not?

   _____

   _____

   _____

If yes, include: Emotionally Disturbed _____
                  Learning Disabled _____
                  Other handicapping conditions (specify) _____

_____

If yes, please specify why you think any of the above should be included.

_____

_____

_____

Part II: Tests

1. Are you currently attempting to measure adaptive behavior?
    Yes _____ No _____

2. What tests, scales, etc., are you currently using to measure adaptive behavior in the following age range?

    3–5 yrs.: _____

    6–12 yrs.: _____

    13–21 yrs.: _____

3. Which existing tests would you like to see added to the approved list (specify):

    _____

    _____

    _____

4. Would you like to know more about procedures for submitting a test for approval? Yes _____ No _____

5. Would you like to know more about alternatives in gathering adaptive behavior information? Yes _____ No _____

6. Would a workshop regarding tests and/or procedures in measuring adaptive behavior be helpful to you? Yes _____ No _____
    If yes, check the specific areas you would want the workshop to address:

Preview of available tests _____
How to develop local norms _____
Specific test administration _____ Which test? _____
Specific test interpretation _____ Which test? _____

Others _____

_____

_____

7. Do you think additional tests need to be developed to measure adaptive behavior? Yes _____ No _____

**Part III: AAMD Adaptive Behavior Scale—
Public School Version (ABS—PS)**

1. How many ABS—PS scales have you administered? None* _____,
    1–5 _____, 6–10 _____, 11–20 _____, 20 or more _____
2. Which parts of the ABS—PS do you routinely administer?
    Part 1 _____ Part 2 _____ Both _____
3. Do you feel the ABS—PS is appropriate for use in your school
    setting? Yes _____ No _____
    If no, please specify why.

_____

_____

_____

4. Do you have difficulties with any of the following aspects of the
    ABS—PS?
    Administration? No _____ Yes _____
    If yes, specify.

_____

_____

_____

* If you have not administered the ABS—PS, disregard the remaining questions in this
section.

Scoring? No _____ Yes _____
If yes, specify.

_____

_____

Interpretation? No _____ Yes _____
If yes, specify.

_____

_____

5. Based on your experience with the ABS—PS, do you think some students who should be placed as MR are excluded because of spuriously high adaptive behavior score?
No _____ Yes _____
If yes, estimate what percentage of the students tested scored spuriously high? 0–25% _____, 26–50% _____, 51% or over _____

_____

Please complete the following background information:

1. Your role/position _____

_____

2. Number of years of experience in special education _____
3. Education Service Center region number _____
4. Approximate total ADA of the district(s) you serve.
   0–3000 _____, 3001–5000 _____, 5001–10,000 _____, 10,001–20,000 _____, 20,000 or more _____
   If you are an ESC* employee, question 4 is not applicable; so please check here _____

* ESC refers to Education Service Center, an intermediate education agency, of which there are 20 in Texas.

PART III

Measuring
Adaptive Behavior

When you starts measuring somebody, measure him right, child, measure him right. Make sure you done taken into account what hills and valleys he come through before he got to wherever he is. (Lena Younger admonishing her daughter in Lorraine Hansberry's play *Raisin in the Sun*.)

The selection, administration and interpretation of adaptive behavior measures encompass a major area of interest for pupil appraisal practitioners. Reliable and valid instruments are necessary in order to facilitate professional judgment. Chapter 7 presents a method and rating form to aid the practitioner in selecting adaptive behavior scales. The result of the selection process is a thorough knowledge of the strengths and weaknesses of each scale. Chapter 8 provides the professional with a collection of currently available measures of adaptive behavior, including the addresses of the respective test publishers.

Lambert in Chapter 9 describes the Public School Version of the Adaptive Behavior Scale (ABS—PSV). In addition to being the primary author of this scale, Lambert is a prominent school psychologist. In this chapter she carefully traces the development of the measure and provides the technical information regarding reliability and validity. There are guidelines for the use of data generated from the ABS—PSV in developing education plans.

In Chapter 10 Lewis and Mercer furnish a thorough description of the System of Multicultural Pluralistic Assessment (SOMPA), of which the Adaptive Behavior Inventory for Children (ABIC) is a part. The background for the original research and the subsequent models of assessment are presented as well as all of the measures that are now a part of SOMPA.

Henry W. Morrow,
W. Alan Coulter

7

A Practitioner's Approach to Selecting Adaptive Behavior Scales

A problem exists for professionals who conduct psychological assessments and who are aware of recent modifications in traditional assessment approaches. Adaptive behavior, a psychological entity and measurement concept, is being heralded as one method of approaching nonbiased assessment of clients (Lambert, Wilcox, & Gleason, 1974). The concept of adaptive behavior aids the school psychologist in examining students equitably within their own ethnic/socioeconomic groups (Tucker, 1976) and complies with current federal legislation and many individual state policies (see Chapter 5). Adaptive behavior is generally defined as the effectiveness or the degree to which the individual meets the standards of personal independence and social responsibility expected of his/her age and cultural group (Oakland, 1976).

Currently, several dimensions are recognized as independent components of a definition of adaptive behavior. Factorial studies of both children and adults (Lambert & Nicoll, 1976; Nihira, 1969a, 1969b, 1976) support at least two stable components within the definition, although single studies usually mention three or more. The first component, personal independence, is a term cited in most definitions and suggests skills and behaviors required to maintain independent functioning, such as self-care, language, physical development, and others. The second component, social responsibility, encompasses such social skills as cooperation, trust, acceptable manners, and absence of destructive or rebellious behavior. The two dimensions change in relative importance as a function of chronological age. That is, during early years (0 to 6) attaining personal independence is considered most important, while social responsibility emerges as the focus for measurement during middle childhood and early adolescence (Leland, 1973). An important point is that adaptive behavior has little empirical definition after the years of early adolescence.

An analysis of the chronology regarding the development of the concept of adaptive behavior reveals that the original purpose in studying it was to delineate behaviors desirable for acquisition by mentally retarded adults and children among institutional populations. Therefore, the original efforts to develop adaptive behavior scales were directed primarily toward this goal (Leland, 1973). Although it was recognized that adaptive behavior might also be an important component for an assessment of populations that exist in the mainstream community, funds and research efforts largely ignored the importance of this concept. Consequently, most of the available tests or scales purporting to measure adaptive behavior are oriented toward institutionalized populations (see Chapter 8; also Leland, 1973) and these tests emphasize a definition based upon the needs of institutional personnel for programming in adaptive behavior (see Chapter 1).

One recently developed scale is available for use with a school-based population and is designed to be administered by school personnel. Mercer & Lewis (1977) developed a broad-based appraisal technique called the System of Multicultural Pluralistic Assessment (SOMPA). SOMPA is designed through a series of different tests to provide a least-biased assessment of students from the three major ethnic groups— Caucasian, black, and Chicano. Part of the SOMPA is a measure of adaptive behavior called the Adaptive Behavior Inventory for Children (ABIC) (see Chapter 10). This scale was explicitly designed to be used to differentiate students who showed delayed development in adaptive behavior skills from those who were judged to be comparable to their peers. In this instance adaptive behavior has a different definition from that of an institutionally based scale in terms of its ideal use and the intent of its scores and norms.

The problem for the assessment professional is not the modification of traditional assessment; it is choosing how to define adaptive behavior and choosing a measure to define that hypothetical construct. A format or structured approach is needed to analyze systematically the appropriate definition applicable to a particular appraisal professional's needs. Following this analysis, the appropriate test could be selected based upon a comprehensive awareness of a number of adaptive behavior measures. This would represent an acceptable solution to the problem.

RATING FORM

Upon request of the National Association of State Consultants of School Psychological Services (NASCSP), the Texas Regional Resource Center developed a rating form for adaptive behavior scales which the center presented in a workshop at the association's annual conference in December 1976 in San Antonio, Texas. The intent of the form is to provide a format for evaluating different adaptive behavior scales on similar elements or dimensions. A facsimile of the rating form manual is included in Appendix A of this chapter. The rating form is divided into three major parts. Part I is composed of specific criteria mentioned in a state's definition of adaptive behavior; thus one is provided a guide to check each scale for inclusion of this needed information. For example, a state may want an acceptable adaptive behavior scale to have a norm group to which an individual's rating can be compared. Specific elements in Part I will vary as a function of the state's adaptive behavior definition and any other criteria the state wishes to consider. Part II is composed of elements concerned with scale content and psychometric considerations (norms, reliability, validity, specific item content). Part III consists of elements concerned with administrative aspects of adaptive behavior scales (cost, administration time, who administers the scale, and to whom the scale is given).

The rating form can be used both to gather information on a single adaptive behavior scale and to provide a format for comparing several scales on the same elements or dimensions. Multiple scale comparisons are made by writing the name of each scale on each comparison dimension, thus depicting the relative relationships to each other. The rating form is depicted in Tables 7–1, 7–2, and 7–3, and the complete revised form is included in the Appendix.

SIMULATION EXERCISE

To acquaint the workshop participants with the rating form and manual, a simulation exercise was developed. The exercise was divided into two parts. The first part consisted of an orientation to the manual and rating form, using the American Association for Mental Deficiency's Adaptive Behavior Scale—Public School Version. Any questions regarding the manual and rating form were clarified. The second part was initiated by dividing the group into four teams; each team was given a manual, rating form, general directions, and a copy of the Camelot Scale's Behavioral Checklist Manual. Each group's task was to rate the Camelot Scale on the rating form and report its results to the moderator for a reliability check between groups and for location of elements on the rating form in need of further explanation and additional clarification.

Each team was to consider itself a state-level school psychology consultant to the state department of special education in charge of answering questions regarding the state's policies and procedures for evaluating handicapped students. Along with general directions, the groups received a local district's request for approval to use the Camelot Scale as a measure of adaptive behavior.

Their task was twofold: (1) using the rating form manual, each group was to reach a consensus rating on each of the elements on the rating scale after reviewing the Camelot manual, and (2) each group was to make a decision regarding the state consultant's approval or disapproval to use the scale as an adaptive behavior measure by the local district.

Each group selected a moderator whose responsibility was to guide the group through the rating form manual and to reach a consensus rating about the Camelot Scale; then the moderator guided the group through the decision form regarding the Camelot Scale (a copy of the decision form is included in Appendix B at the end of this chapter). Each group was to select a recorder to write the group's consensus rating for the Camelot Scale on both the rating and decision forms. The recorder was also responsible for reporting these results to the simulation moderator. There were four groups of five participants, for a total of twenty. Individual evaluations of the scale were requested upon termination of the simulation exercise. Discussion of each element or domain focused on whether the element should remain in the rating form, the clarity of each element, and suggested changes for the element or rating form in general. A facsimile of the individual evaluation form is included in Appendix C.

RESULTS

The results of each group's ratings of the Camelot Behavioral Checklist on each element of the rating form are found in Tables 7–1, 7–2, and 7–3. Table 7–1 presents the results of the groups' criteria ratings of

Table 7–1
Criteria for Acceptance of Adaptive Behavior
Scales According to Individual State Policies

| | Group Rating Responses[a] | |
Policy Criteria	Yes	No
1. Are specific items related to the domain being measured?	4	0
2. Are out-of-school behaviors being measured?	4	0
3. Are norms provided for comparison of the individual's behavior?	3	1
4. Are items specific enough to be observed?	4	0

[a] $N = 4$

Part I of the Rating Form for Adaptive Behavior Scales (Appendix A). Table 7–2 presents the groups' rating results regarding instrument content (Part II of the form), and Table 7–3 provides the groups' rating results regarding administrative considerations (Part III of the form).

When interpreting these results, the authors considered whether there was less than 75 percent agreement among the four groups on a particular element. If there was less than 75 percent agreement, individual participant evaluations were examined to detect reasons for disagreement (i.e., a function of the rating form itself through such things as lack of clarity in the manual's directions, need for greater element specificity; a function of the adaptive behavior scale because of such things as lack of data in the scale's manual, lack of clarity).

Part I: Criteria for Acceptance

All four questions of Part I achieved a 75 percent or higher rating agreement among the four groups on the Camelot Scale (see Table 7–1). Only question 4—Are items specific enough to be observed?—received an unclear rating from more than 25 percent of the participants. Recommended changes focused on the need for finer gradations in rating rather than a yes/no format and the need for more examples to define the terms "clear" and "too general."

Part II: Instrument Content

Of the seven elements rated in Part II, only element 6, Norms, received less than 75 percent rating agreement among the four groups (see Table 7–2). The first part of element 6 deals with the nature of the sample population with which an individual's score will be compared. Two groups rated that no sample population was reported in the manual, and two groups rated that a sample of handicapped students was available in the manual. The second part of element 6, geographic area, asked for an indication of geographic size from which the comparison or norm group was drawn. Of the two groups that indicated a comparison group was available, one group rated the geographic area to be statewide, and the other rated it to be multistate.

Although 100 percent rating agreement among groups was achieved on element 11, Behavior Specificity of Items, more than 50 percent of the participants rated this item unclear. Recommended changes focused upon separating the "vague terms" aspect from "percent of items having examples" and the need to clarify further this element by providing examples. This element was subsequently omitted in the revised form found in the Appendix.

Table 7–2

Group Rating Results Regarding Instrument Content
Elements of the Camelot Behavioral Checklist

Element	Dimensions

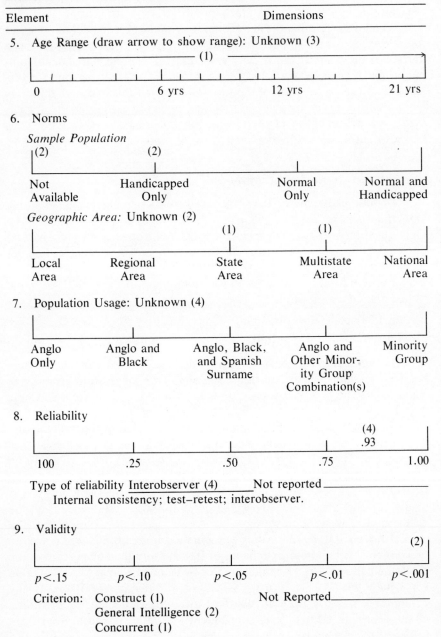

5. Age Range (draw arrow to show range): Unknown (3)

(1)

0   6 yrs   12 yrs   21 yrs

6. Norms

Sample Population

(2)   (2)

Not Available   Handicapped Only   Normal Only   Normal and Handicapped

Geographic Area: Unknown (2)

(1)   (1)

Local Area   Regional Area   State Area   Multistate Area   National Area

7. Population Usage: Unknown (4)

Anglo Only   Anglo and Black   Anglo, Black, and Spanish Surname   Anglo and Other Minority Group Combination(s)   Minority Group

8. Reliability

(4)
.93

100   .25   .50   .75   1.00

Type of reliability Interobserver (4)_____Not reported_____
    Internal consistency; test–retest; interobserver.

9. Validity

(2)

$p<.15$ $p<.10$ $p<.05$ $p<.01$ $p<.001$

Criterion: Construct (1)   Not Reported_____
          General Intelligence (2)
          Concurrent (1)

10. Specific Item Content

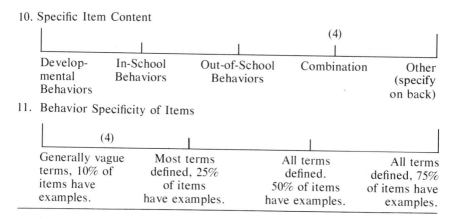

| Develop-mental Behaviors | In-School Behaviors | Out-of-School Behaviors | Combination (4) | Other (specify on back) |

11. Behavior Specificity of Items

| Generally vague terms, 10% of items have examples. (4) | Most terms defined, 25% of items have examples. | All terms defined. 50% of items have examples. | All terms defined, 75% of items have examples. |

Part III: Administrative Considerations

Element 14, Interpretation Time, of Table 7–3 was rated by 25 percent of the participants as needing further clarification regarding definition of this term.

Element 16, Who Administers Scale, and element 17, To Whom Is Scale Given, failed to achieve a 75 percent group rating agreement. Furthermore, element 17 was rated "unclear" by more than 50 percent of the participants. Major recommended changes on element 17 focused on need for clarity and need for additional possibilities listed regarding to whom the scale could be administered.

Element 18, Scale Utilization, was rated by 25 percent of the participants as needing additional clarification on the concept or intent of the element. Specifically, the last two areas dealing with educational programming were identified as confusing or not clear.

Elements 19, 20, and 21 were identified in the manual as highly subjective, and the results verified this statement. All three elements had less than 75 percent group rating agreement. Recommendations varied from a request for more specificity to suggesting that all three elements be combined. Several comments repeated the manual's caution about the high level of subjectivity and additionally suggested that they be eliminated from the form.

DISCUSSION

Part I: Criteria for Acceptance

It is apparent that any question answered no in this section may indicate that the scale is not acceptable for use in measuring adaptive behavior based on the state's criteria or definition of adaptive behavior. If

Table 7–3
Group Rating Results Regarding Administrative Consideration
Elements of the Camelot Behavioral Checklist

Elements	Dimensions

12. Cost per Child: Unknown (1)

```
      (3)
 |     |        |         |          |          |
10¢         50¢        75¢       $1.00      $2.00      above
```

13. Administration Time: Unknown (3)

```
 |    |         |         (1)        |        |         |
    30 min    1 hr              90 min    2 hrs    150 min   3 hrs
```

14. Interpretation Time: Unknown (3)

```
       (1)
 |     |        |         |          |          |
    30 min    1 hr      90 min     2 hrs      150 min     3 hrs
```

15. Total Time (Administration plus Interpretation Time): Unknown (3)

```
            (1)
 |    |         |         |          |          |
    2 hrs              4 hrs                 6 hrs
```

16. Who Administers Scale (may select more than one): Unknown (1)

(1)	(1)	(1)	(2)	( )
Parapro-fessional	Teacher	Diagnostic Personnel Only	Combination	Other (specify on back)

17. To Whom Is Scale Given (may select more than one): Unknown (1); All (1)

(2)	(2)			
Parent Interview	Teacher Interview	Parent Observation	Teacher Observation	Diagnostic Personnel Observation

18. Scale Utilization

| (2)   (4) |
| | | |

Determining	Several domains	Identifies general	Educational
eligibility—	measured; identifies	areas for edu-	programming
discriminates	general areas for	cational programming	—defines
between hand-	more detailed	(i.e., toilet training;	baselines,
icapped and	assessment.	fine-motor skills).	short- and
non-handi-			long-term be-
capped. Pro-			havioral objec-
vides only one			tives.
score.			

Degree of Effort to Attain Basic Competency

19. Administration

| (1)   (2)   (1) |
| | | | | |

Read step-	Read in-	Attend	Workshop	Workshop
by-step	structions	workshop	and	practice,
instructions	plus examples		practice	follow-up
in manual	in manual			workshop

20. Scoring

| (1)   (2)   (1) |
| | | | | |

Read	Carefully	Attend	Workshop	Workshop,
manual	study	workshop	and	practice,
once	manual		practice	follow-up
				workshop

21. Interpretation

| (1)   (1)   (2) |
| | | | | |

Read	Carefully	Attend	Workshop	Workshop,
manual	study	workshop	and	practice,
once	manual		practice	follow-up
				workshop

22. Is a non-English language version available?

Yes/No (Specify: ——————————————————————————————
     (4)

this is true, the rater may not want to pursue additional evaluation of the scale if the rater's intent is to locate a scale which will meet the state's administrative guidelines for evaluating handicapped students. Awareness of the difference between evaluation for diagnosis or placement in special education as opposed to educational programming, however, should also be considered in the decision to continue evaluting the scale. Participants requested more elaboration on the concept of evaluation for diagnosis as opposed to evaluation for programming when they evaluated element 16, Scale Utilization.

The majority of elements that received less than a 75 percent group rating agreement were evaluated as needing greater clarification in terms of being more specific on the rating form or by providing greater elaboration in the manual regarding the element's definition.

Part II: Instrument Content

On element 6, few participants rated either part unclear, which may reflect some ambiguity regarding normative information in the Camelot manual as the potential source of lack of group rating agreement.

Because of the high percentage of participant unclear ratings for element 11, Behavior Specificity, definite modifications are indicated for this element on the revised rating form. Possible modifications may be the separation of the element into two parts, the first part more specifically focusing upon degree of clarity of terms, which is related to degree of interobserver reliability, and the second part focusing upon how terms are clarified. However, since the major intent of the element was to alert the reader to the need for clear, exact terms facilitating agreement between raters on definitions of terms, perhaps only the first part of the modification should be included.

Part III: Administrative Considerations

Interpretation Time, element 14, was cited as needing further clarification and possible consideration as an element to be eliminated. The major problem with the element is its subjectivity and degree of variance as a function of the student and the individual examiner. Indeed, the revised form should eliminate both interpretation and total time elements, deferring to the best objective time dimension as that of administration.

Element 16, Who Administers Scale, was intended to provide differentiation between those scales which should only be administered by a professional and those scales which could be administered by a para-professional. Lack of agreement among group ratings was probably a function of lack of rating form and/or manual clarity and should be revised. Also, element 17 needs further clarification. The intent of this element was to alert the rater regarding the nature of data collected by direct observation, interview method, or possibly a third method not listed, questionnaire.

Element 18, Scale Utilization, may best be clarified by expanding the manual's explanation of the concepts "evaluation for eligibility" and "evaluation for educational planning," in addition to providing an operational definition of educational programming.

Elements 19, 20, and 21 were the only ones to receive ratings which indicated that they should be eliminated. Their high degree of subjectivity was the reason mentioned most often. The intent of these elements was to alert the rater to a need for various levels of training as a function of scale complexity before a scale should be recommended for dissemination.

In general, participants noted that the rating form concept should be pursued in a revised form and that such a rating form assists diagnostic personnel in organizing their thinking about adaptive behavior scales. Possibly it should be used with all other types of assessment instruments.

REFERENCES

Lambert, N. M., & Nicoll, R. C. Dimensions of adaptive behavior of retarded and nonretarded public school children. *American Journal of Mental Deficiency,* 1976, *81,* 135–146.

Lambert, N. M., Wilcox, M. R., & Gleason, W. P. *The educationally retarded child: Comprehensive assessment and planning for slow learners and the educationally mentally retarded.* New York: Grune & Stratton, 1974.

Leland, H. Adaptive behavior and mentally retarded behavior. In C. E. Meyers, R. K. Eyman, & G. Tarjon, (Eds.), *Sociobehavioral studies in mental retardation: Papers in honor of Harvey F. Dingman.* Washington, D. C.: American Association on Mental Deficiency, 1973.

Mercer, J. R. *System of Multicultural Pluralistic Assessment: Technical manual.* New York: The Psychological Corporation, 1977.

Nihira, K. Factorial dimensions of adaptive behavior in adult retardates. *American Journal of Mental Deficiency,* 1969, *73,* 868–878. (a)

Nihira, K. Factorial dimensions of adaptive behavior in mentally retarded children and adolescents. *American Journal of Mental Deficiency,* 1969, *74,* 130–141. (b)

Nihira, K. Dimensions of adaptive behavior in institutionalized mentally retarded children and adults: Developmental perspective. *American Journal of Mental Deficiency,* 1976, *81,* 215–226.

Oakland, T. (Ed.). *With bias toward none: Non-biased assessment of minority group children.* Lexington, Ky.: Coordinating Office for Regional Resource Centers, 1976.

Tucker, J. A. Operationalizing the diagnostic intervention process. In T. Oakland (Ed.), *With bias toward none: Non-biased assessment of minority group children.* Lexington, Ky.: Coordinating Office for Regional Resource Centers, 1976.

APPENDIX A: A RATING FORM FOR
ADAPTIVE BEHAVIOR SCALES
(REVISED FORM AND MANUAL)

INTRODUCTION

The intent of the Rating Form for Adaptive Behavior Scales is to provide a format for evaluating different adaptive behavior scales on similar elements or dimensions. The Rating Form is divided into three major parts. Part I is composed of specific areas mentioned in a state's definition of adaptive behavior and serves as a guide in checking each scale for inclusion of needed information covering specific adaptive behavior areas of concern. For example, a state may want an acceptable adaptive behavior scale to have a norm group to which an individual's rating can be compared. Specific elements in Part II will vary as a function of the state's adaptive behavior definition and whether other areas of concern would provide additional criteria for acceptance/rejection of an individual scale. Part III is composed of elements concerned primarily with administrative aspects of adaptive behavior scales (cost, administration time, who administers the scale, and to whom the scale is given).

The rating form can be used both to gather information on a single adaptive behavior scale and to provide a format for comparing several scales on the same elements or dimensions. Multiple scale comparisons are made by writing the name of each scale on each conparison dimension, thus depicting their relative relationships to each other.

Part I: Criteria for Acceptance

Questions developed for this section center upon a state's accepted definition of adaptive behavior. Questions are posed on the basis of specific areas mentioned in the definition. Additional specific areas can be added that are *not* covered in the adaptive behavior definition but reflect other measurement areas of concern determined by state level leadership.

Example of a state's definition: "The effectiveness or degree with which the individual meets the standards of personal independence and social responsibility expected of the age and cultural group." (Texas)

Example of additional area of concern: "Are norms provided for comparison of the individual's behavior?"

The provision of norms would be a specific area of concern not precisely reflected in a state's adaptive behavior definition but of sufficient concern to be requested as a part of state policy. In such a case,

127

the state would request that any adaptive behavior scale used according to state guidelines should have norms for comparing an individual's performance to a group. Such a stipulation would highlight the use of a normed scale as opposed to a behavior checklist or developmental scale.

Before practitioners can select a scale that will yield information consistent with state guidelines, they should know the state's intent in requiring a measure of adaptive behavior and the state's adaptive behavior definition.

In this rating form, the state uses the above-cited adaptive behavior definition but also has four other criteria to be considered in selecting a scale that would meet state guidelines.

1. Do specific items seem related to the domain being measured? In some instances, scales are developed where specific items do not seem related to the domain being measured. For example, the scale under consideration measures four general areas, one of which is social behavior. If many of the questions asked in this area do not seem related to the general domain, the practitioner may have some concern about the scale's face validity. The specific question, "Is the child's writing legible?" does not seem related to the domain of "social behavior."

    To elaborate further, if one general area is purportedly measured, such as adaptive behavior, check to see if the items are related to the area. In order to determine this, the author's definition of adaptive behavior should be stated in the manual. If it is not, then consider whether the items relate to the state's adaptive behavior definition.

    A very general estimate is requested as to percent of items related to domain(s) being measured. If all the items seem related to their respective domains, check 100% or 75%. If there is some serious question about the majority of items relating to their respective domains, check 50% or 25%. Also, if more than one domain seems to have a majority of items not related to it, note the number of domains within the scale having this problem.

2. Are out-of-school behaviors being measured? Usually implicit in a definition of adaptive behavior is that information will be gathered on how an individual functions in or adapts to as many situations or roles as possible. Therefore, the scale items should reflect an attempt to measure the individual's functioning outside the school environment. The practitioner would normally have multiple measures of the individual's functioning within the school environment (i.e., achievement and IQ tests, behavior ratings, teacher reports).

3. Are norms provided for comparison of the individual's behavior? The intent of this consideration is to focus upon an instrument that

would help the practitioner distinguish between normals and handicapped (specifically mentally retarded). Behavioral or developmental checklists normally do not provide the data necessary for such a distinction. They do provide a description of presence or absence of a particular behavior or skill. For the purposes of this rating form, circle Yes if any norms are present in the manual whether they are on the basis of age, sex, culture, handicapping condition, etc.

4. Are the majority of items objective enough to be observed by the informant?

The definition of adpative behavior refers to how well an individual functions in a variety of environments and roles. For the informant to make a decision regarding the individual's abilities, the items or questions asked should not be value loaded (i.e., Is this child a good child?) but should be directed more toward skills and abilities that could be observed by the informant (i.e., Can _____ prepare food for lunch?).

Rate the scale generally on item objectivity by circling one of the descriptions of poor, fair, or good. A rating of "good" implies that the majority of items were objective and avoided being value loaded.

Part II: Instrument Content

5. *Age Range:* Indicate the scale's age range by drawing an arrow between the two age extremes.

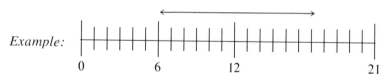

Example:

0	6	12	21

6. *Norms:* (a) Sample population: "Handicapped" implies that only a comparison group of handicapped students is available in the manual.

> *Example:* The TARC Assessment System was standardized on a population of 283 severely handicapped children.

"(M.R. _____ E.D. _____ All _____)" refers to the type of handicapped student in the norms. In the above example the M.R. _____ designation would be checked.

(b) *Geographic area:* Local, regional, state, multistate, and national refer to the size of the geographic area from which the norms were drawn. Local area would be a single school system or residential treatment center; a regional area would be considered any area larger than a single school system but not as large as an entire state, etc.

(c) *Other* refers to samples drawn from any group or area not described above.

7. *Ethnic Applicability:* The particular ethnic group(s) for which normative data have been collected.

8. *Reliability:* As defined by Guilford (1965) reliability is "some kind of self-correlation of a test" (p. 442). If this information is available, test manuals usually report test–retest reliability or some measure of internal consistency such as Kuder-Richardson or Spearman-Brown correlation. Interobserver reliability information may also be reported in the manual. An exception to this standard method of reporting and substantiating reliability may be noted for criterion-referenced tests (Carver, 1974; Popham, 1971).

9. *Validity:* Construct validity may be reported in terms of correlations with other adaptive behavior measures or with measures of general intelligence. Types of validity (Cronbach, 1960) that may be reported are:

Construct: How well a test relates to a theory or concept that could be used to interpret the test performance. In order to show that a theoretical construct is appropriate to the test, hypotheses must be generated from the theory and verified experimentally. Can scores on this test be explained by some psychological construct (anxiety, neurosis, etc.)?

Predictive: How well a test can predict performance on another criterion or future performance. Can scores on this test predict performance in school, on the job, entrance exams, etc.?

Content: How well the test items related to the actual content the examiner wishes to include. Does a math test include items or content covered in a math course?

Concurrent: How well the test relates to a similar measure of the same behavior. A math test may be compared with teachers' ratings of a student's classroom math skills.

10. *Specific Item Content:* The environment in which the behaviors are being observed. In-school behaviors refer to those behaviors associated with a structured work setting for the child such as a school

or work station. Items regarding in-school behaviors may not necessarily be observed in any other environment. Out-of-school behaviors refer to those behaviors associated with an unstructured or social setting (i.e., social behavior with peers, routine functioning in the home). Developmental behaviors refer to those behaviors learned as a function of increasing age or maturation, such as walking or talking. Age-level expectancies refer to the age at which the behavior would "normally" be mastered.

Part III: Administrative Considerations

11. *Cost per Answer Sheet:* Refers primarily to the price of a package of answer forms divided by the number of answer forms in one package. Such information is typically found in test catalogs. (Since the manual can be reused, its cost is not considered in computing cost.)

> *Examples:* (1) Camelot Behavioral Checklist and Manual checklists, package of 10—$2.50, or 25¢ per child.
>
> (2) AAMD Adaptive Behavior Scale (ABS) Public School Version Scale Booklet (scale, scoring sheet, profile summary)—$1.00, or $1.00 per child.

12. *Administrative Time:* The amount of time necessary to administer the scale to one child. This information is typically found in the scale manual.

> *Example:* (AAMD) The "interview method" is cited as taking 15 to 20 minutes for completion.

13. *Who Administers the Scale:* Compares scales on amount of professional time needed. The term "any of the above" means that *both* a professional (usually involved with interpretation) and someone else (a trained test administrator) is typically used rather than a single individual. Some scales may require a professional to both administer and interpret.

> *Example:* The Public School Version of ABS recommends that the teacher administer the scale.

If the interview method is used, typically a professional administers the scale.

14. *How Is Information Obtained:* Parent and teacher interview implies that the scale information is gathered from either of these people by directly interviewing them. Direct student observation implies that the scale items are completed *during* an actual observation of the child under natural or contrived conditions.

Example: The Public School Version of ABS recommends that the teacher act as informant under interview conditions rather than on-going child observation.

Nearly all adaptive behavior scales could be administered to the child by direct observation but the intent of this element is to record the typical or recommended way of gathering the information.

15. *Scale Utilization:*

   a. *Eligibility:* Can the scale be used to assist the practitioners in making a determination of special education eligibility? In order to accomplish this task, scores should discriminate between handicapped and nonhandicapped students. Norms are typically provided for this task.

   b. *Educational Programming:* Does the scale provide information useful in developing or modifying a student's instructional program? A more specific examination of this issue is required in item 16 below.

16. *Degree of Educational Programming: Several domains measured; identifies general areas for more detailed assessment*—tests which act as screening devices in order to select more precise measures in areas of deficit. (E.g., many rate the Vineland SMS here.)

   Many domains measured; baselines, short- and long-term behavioral objectives are identified for instructional planning: This would include tests and observation scales which allow the interpreter to describe specifically a student's current level of functioning (baselines) and the goals for short-term and long-term planning. (E.g., some practitioners place the Camelot Scale with its accompanying programming guide here.)

   Scores tied directly to curriculum—identifies next instructional task in sequence for each domain measured: This is a highly specific assessment which tells the teacher the next task the student is to perform in a sequence of activities which lead to a terminal objective such as "is totally independent in toileting skills for bladder." (E.g., the BCPC is roughly analogous to this rating.)

REFERENCES

Carver, R. P. Two dimensions of tests: Psychometric and edumetric. *American Psychologist*, 1074, *29,* 512–518.
Cronbach, L. J. *Essentials of psychological testing.* New York: Harper & Row, 1960. Pp. 103–110.

Guilford, J. P. *Fundamental statistics in psychology and education.* New York: McGraw-Hill, 1965.

Popham, W. J. *Criterion-referenced measurement: An introduction.* Englewood Cliffs, N. J.: Educational Technology Publications, 1971.

RATING FORM FOR ADAPTIVE BEHAVIOR SCALE(S) (REVISED EDITION)

Scale(s): _____

Part I: Criteria for Acceptance[1]

1. For each domain within the scale consider the following:

   a. Do the specific scale items seem related to the domain being measured? Check percent of items that *do* seem related to the domain being measured. (Note: The score you mark will be an average for all the domains in a scale.)

   0   25   50   75   100

   b. If more than one domain is included as part of the test, indicate how many domains have rated 50% or better on question 1a. (*Example:* 8 of 10 domains). _____

2. Are out-of-school behaviors being measured (circle one)? Yes / No

3. Are norms provided for comparison of the individual's behavior (circle one)? Yes / No

4. Are the majority of items within the entire scale objective enough to be observed by the informant (circle one)?

   poor   fair   good

Part II: Instrument Content

5. Age Range (draw arrow to show range)

   0   6 yrs   12 yrs   21 yrs

   Not given _____

[1] These criteria may vary as a function of the state's adaptive behavior definition.

6. Norms
   a. Sample

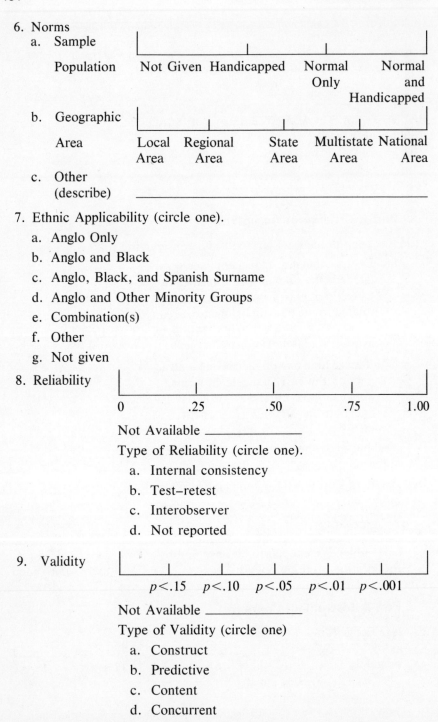

   Population   Not Given Handicapped   Normal   Normal
                                            Only   and
                                                          Handicapped

   b. Geographic

   Area   Local   Regional   State   Multistate National
                   Area   Area   Area   Area   Area

   c. Other
      (describe)   _____

7. Ethnic Applicability (circle one).
   a. Anglo Only
   b. Anglo and Black
   c. Anglo, Black, and Spanish Surname
   d. Anglo and Other Minority Groups
   e. Combination(s)
   f. Other
   g. Not given

8. Reliability

   0   .25   .50   .75   1.00

   Not Available _____
   Type of Reliability (circle one).
      a. Internal consistency
      b. Test–retest
      c. Interobserver
      d. Not reported

9. Validity

        $p<.15$ $p<.10$ $p<.05$ $p<.01$ $p<.001$

   Not Available _____
   Type of Validity (circle one)
      a. Construct
      b. Predictive
      c. Content
      d. Concurrent

10. Specific
Item
Content

Develop-mental Behaviors	In-School Behaviors	Out-of-School Behaviors	Combination	Other (specify on back)

Part III: Administrative Considerations

11. Cost (per
answer
sheet)

10¢	50¢	75¢	$1.00	$2.00	above

12. Adminis-
tration
Time

	30 mins.	1 hour	2 hours

Not given _____

13. Who Administers Scale (circle).
   a. Paraprofessional
   b. Teacher
   c. Diagnostic Personnel
   d. Any of the above
   e. Other _____

14. How is information obtained (circle).
   a. Parent Interview
   b. Teacher Interview
   c. Direct Student Observation
   d. Self-report Questionnaire
   e. Combination of the above
   f. Other _____

15. Scale Utilization (see instructions in Rating Form Manual)
   a. Can the scale be used to help determine eligibility
      for special education?   Yes / No
   b. Can the scale be used for educational program-
      ming?   Yes / No

16. Degree of Educational Programming

Several domains measured; identifies general areas for more detailed assessment (e.g., toilet training vs. feeding skills).	Many domains measured; baselines, short and long-term behavioral objectives are identified for instructional planning.	Scores tied directly to curriculum-identifies next instructional task in sequence for each domain measured.

17. Is there a non-English language version available?   Yes / No

        Specify language: ——————————

Any additional comments:

APPENDIX B: GROUP DECISION FORM

(RECORDER: *Please read the following description to your group*)

As the state's school psychology consultant, you have received a letter from a local school district's Pupil Appraisal Committee asking your approval to use the enclosed measures in assessing adaptive behavior as required as part of a diagnosis for mental retardation. Please make a group consensus decision regarding your approval of the scale in one of three ways and record the decision below.

Decision 1 = *Yes:* A "yes" indicator means that you give unconditional approval of the scale as a measure of adaptive behavior based on the Criteria for Acceptance (Part I) of the Rating Form for Adaptive Behavior Scales.

Decision 2 = *Yes-But:* A "yes-but" indicator means that you give conditional approval of the scale. The conditions to be met would probably be that local norms be developed because criteria 1, 2, and 4 would require further change of the scale necessitating another review before approval could be reconsidered.

Decision 3 = *No:* A "no" indicator means that the scale does not meet Criteria for Acceptance numbers 1, 2, or 4. The scale will have to be revised.

Record your group's approval decision on each enclosed scale by placing an X in the appropriate column.

Decision Regarding Approval

Scale:	Yes	Yes-But	No

APPENDIX C: EVALUATION FORM FOR DISCUSSION DRAFT

138

Part I: Criteria for Acceptance

Rate: Inclusion (I) or Exclusion (E)
Clarity of Dimensions
Rate: Clear (C) or Unclear (U)

Descriptors

Suggested Changes

1. Item Relationship to Domain

2. Out-of-School Behaviors

3. Norms

4. Item Specificity

Part II: Instrument Content

5. Age Range

6. Norms

   Sample Population

   Geographic Area

7. Population Usage

8. Reliability

9. Validity

10. Specific Item Content

Part III: *Administrative*
Considerations

12. Cost per Child
13. Administrative Time
14. Interpretation Time
15. Total Time
16. Who Administers Scale
17. To Whom Is Scale Given
18. Scale Utilization
19. Administration
20. Scoring
21. Interpretation
22. Non-English Version

Additional elements and dimension descriptors to consider:

1. _____

2. _____

General comments, please:

W. Alan Coulter,
Henry W. Morrow

8
A Collection of
Adaptive Behavior Measures

The most commonly accepted definition of adaptive behavior is Grossman's (1973), who defines it as "the effectiveness or degree with which the individual meets the standards of personal independence and social responsibility expected of his age or cultural group." When attempting to measure adaptive behavior as thus defined, the appraisal practitioner may be at a loss as to what particular instrument to use or how to obtain it. The results of a recent survey of pupil appraisal practitioners in one state (Chapter 6) indicated a need for a compiled list of available measures of adaptive behavior. This chapter is a collection of representative tests, scales, and forms that are used to measure adaptive behavior.

Two consistent elements which are present in most definitions of adaptive behavior are personal independence and social responsibility. The disadvantage of restricting the definition to only these two elements is that it allows for a plethora of known behavior rating scales and instruments to be considered as adaptive behavior measures which could number more than 100. A recent compilation of behavior checklists, which was not an all-inclusive list, counted 136 (Walls & Werner, 1976). To define the assessment of adaptive behavior simply as a measure of personal independence and social responsibility is confusing to the practitioner and does not encourage effective measurement practices. The authors feel that three additional prerequisites are needed to assist the practitioner and to compile a meaningful collection of adaptive behavior measures.

CONSIDERATIONS IN SELECTING A MEASURE

Function of the Assessment

First, a decision must be made regarding the *function* or purpose of the assessment being conducted (see Chapter 1). If adaptive behavior is being measured to assist in making an identification of mental retardation or a placement decision for special services or instructional arrangement (i.e., appraisal for identification/placement), the measurement should have norms that will discriminate among known groups (e.g., mentally retarded versus slow learning) and/or be representative of a normal distribution of the population (i.e., delineating two student deviations below the mean) capability to discriminate between the two profiles (i.e., mentally retarded versus slow learning) the data generated by the measure are not helpful in making the required decision. In fact, a position can be stipulated following an analysis of Grossman's definition that in addition to the two common elements noted (acquisition of expected skills and maintenance of responsible relationships) and the implied developmental trends (see Chapter 1), the definitions also imply a need for norms. With the requirement of a comparison of individuals with their age and/or cultural groups, more than just a criterion measurement of adaptive behavior is required. When the general definition (Grossman, 1973) is applied to a question of identification/placement, norms are needed to describe known groups (i.e., classes for mentally retarded, regular classroom, learning disabilities classes, etc., for majority and minority groups), which will enable the appraisal professional to make the required comparison. The purpose of including a measure of adaptive behavior in such an assessment is generally recognized as part of a least-biased assessment (see Chapter 5; also Mercer, 1977; Tucker, 1976).

One important but seldom articulated concern underlying nonbiased or least-biased assessment is the existing ethnic proportion of students in regular and special education classes (Tucker, 1977). A least-biased appraisal system should have identified proportions of ethnicity in special education that are comparable to the proportions found in regular education (e.g., resulting in 10 percent black in regular education and 10 percent black in special education). When norms are prepared for an appraisal for placement measure with the intent of developing a test for least-biased assessment, the norm population used should have the ethnic balance mentioned above. A significant criticism can be directed at norms for a measure which has existing student populations in special classes with no concern for balancing ethnic proportions. Unless regular and special education classes already have proportional minority group representation, norms developed on existing special education classes have an automatic built-in bias.

If the function of the assessment is to assist in planning or evaluating an instructional program for implementing an intervention (i.e., appraisal for intervention/programming), the measure should provide information which will assist in designating the specific scope, sequence, and content of what is to be conducted in the remedial or educational process of intervention (i.e., the individualized educational program). Norms may be helpful in this particular function of assessment for grouping individuals with similar instructional needs or in evaluating progress in an instructional program. Ideally, an adaptive behavior measure used in intervention/programming would compile baseline data specifically describing current performance and suggest subsequent steps for additional skill acquisition. It should not be automatically assumed that one measure or test can perform both functions of assessment (see Chapter 1).

Psychometric Prerequisites

Any measure used in adaptive behavior assessment should exhibit certain minimum psychometric prerequisites. Evidence of reliability and validity should be available and acceptable to the practitioner using a particular scale. Some attention has already been devoted to minimum standards for this type of measure (see Chapter 7; also Carver, 1974; Horrocks, 1964; Oakland & Matuszek, 1976; Walls & Werner, in press). Walls and Werner (in press) present the most comprehensive analysis of behavior rating scales. For the purpose of this chapter the assumption is made that practitioners will become aware of the psychometric characteristics of the measure they are considering.

Evaluation by Users of an Instrument

Practitioners involved in the assessment of adaptive behavior have the valuable perspective of having actually used individual tests or measures and of establishing a working knowledge of what measures best fit their needs. They are able to perform a consumer evaluation of the scales that does not always use the psychometric criteria noted. Factors such as administration time, cost per student, and facility of interpretation are important criteria and are most effectively evaluated by the professional judgment of actual users of the measure. For this reason the authors decided not to list all of the known developmental and behavior rating scales and checklists; instead, the measures included in this document are those which practitioners said they used to evaluate adaptive behavior.

Because a large number of practitioners from a wide geographic area were surveyed (see Chapters 5 and 6), only a small probability exists that a popularly used scale or test was omitted from the tables or lists noted here.[1] It is important to emphasize, however, that this is not an exhaustive list, but only a compilation of the more popularly used measures. For additional lists of scales, several resources are available: Buros (1965), Johnson, Marr, and Young (1976), and Walker, Tucker, Lauro, and Mirro (1975).

CATEGORIZING ADAPTIVE BEHAVIOR SCALES

To assist the reader in surveying the availability and characteristics of a large number of adaptive behavior measures, two tables—Table 8–1 and Table 8–2—have been constructed using the function or purpose of assessment (i.e., appraisal for identification/placement versus intervention/programming) as the primary descriptor. The tables do not provide a comprehensive analysis of each scale; the rating form mentioned below does a far better job in examing all of the variables.[2] Rather, the tables allow an appraisal practitioner to quickly scan and select several scales which fit the function of the assessment and age range necessary for an identified purpose. The tables also specify the publisher or clearing-house from which each scale may be obtained. The practitioner may then examine several scales, preferably using each in an actual trial assessment, and decide which is best. The applicability of that judgment for all professionals giving test is beyond the scope of any one author or practitioner.

Each table also includes the measurement reference[3] (normative or

---

[1] At the time of our surveys several scales were being field tested which were not included in our compilation due to their uncertain availability to the general readership.

[2] The additional dimension of severity of handicap could have been added to the tables. However, it is such an ambiguous dimension that definition is beyond the scope of this chapter or of our present technology. The authors recognize that some scales, due to specificity of measure, degree of detail, and comprehensiveness of areas covered, are best used only with students who exhibit severe and profound levels (regardless of variance in definitions) of handicap because of the time and expense involved in collecting the data. Indeed, many more dimensions are possible in reviewing available adaptive behavior measures. The reader may want to utilize the rating form for adaptive behavior scales (Appendix A, Chapter 7) as a guide to compare instruments which are under consideration for selection.

[3] A more explicit division can be hypothesized using both the dimension of function and the dimension of measurement reference. Due to the relatively recent emergence of adaptive behavior measures, however, there is an insufficient number of tests to make this more detailed division meaningful. The conceptual scheme is presented as an appendix to this chapter.

criterion) and the number of domains, chapters, or major sections of each test. For the purpose of this discussion, a normative test or scale is basically a standardized measure which allows a practitioner to determine a person's standing by comparing a score to that of the test's reference group. A student is compared to other students who comprised the external referent or population sample (Drew, 1973; Williams, 1975). In contrast, a criterion reference measure is dependent upon an absolute standard rather than a norm. A student is not compared to other students but rather to the standard or criterion, and the information derived from the test describes the level of skill mastered by the student. Livingston (1972) clarifies the distinction:

> When we use norm-referenced measures, we want to know how far a student's score deviates from the group mean. When we use criterion-referenced measures, we want to know how far his score deviates from a fixed standard, the criterion. (p. 15)

Identification/Placement Measures

Table 8–1 details the two available tests or scales which fit at least minimally the criteria discussed earlier for an appraisal for identification/placement measure. Mercer and Lewis (1977) have prepared the norms for SOMPA (System of Multicultural Pluralistic Assessment) from a sample of 2080 children from three ethnic groups (Anglo, black, and Spanish surname) as a representative sample of the state of California. The reader should note that the ABIC is designed to be used as a part of SOMPA and not as an independent measure (Mercer, 1977).

Lambert, Windmiller, Cole, and Figueroa (1975) also used a sample from the state of California which consisted of 2600 children. Johnson (1977) reports that the state of Florida has recently compiled representative norms on the ABS—PS for ages 3 to 15. Other tests or scales are no doubt being prepared which will allow identification/placement measure but were not known to the authors when this chapter was being written. We hope that at least one scale will be developed that will provide a measure for use with adolescents.

Intervention/Programming Measures

Adaptive behavior measures which assist in intervention/programming are more numerous and varied. The list in Table 8–2, as mentioned previously, represents only those scales nominated by practitioners participating in two surveys (see Chapter 5 and 6) and does not

Table 8–1
Adaptive Behavior Measures for Identfication/Placement

Test or Scale, Author(s), Publisher	Age Range	Measurement Reference[a]	Domains, Chapters, or Sections
Adaptive Behavior Inventory for Children (ABIC) (a part of SOMPA) Mercer & Lewis, 1977	5–0 to 11–11	N	7 subscales, 24 items (e.g., family role performance, peer-group role performance, student role performance)
The Psychological Corporation 757 Third Avenue New York, New York 10017			
Adaptive Behavior Scale— Public School Version (ABS—PS) Lambert, Windmiller, Cole, & Figueroa, 1974	7–3 to 13–2	N & C	2 parts, 21 subscales (e.g., independent functioning, physical development, responsibility, violent & destructive behavior)
Edmark Associates 13241 Northup Way Bellevue, Washington 98005			

[a] N = Normative, C = Criterion.

represent all of the available scales. It is interesting to note how few scales address those skills to be acquired during adolescence.

In summary, a variety of measures of adaptive behavior have been presented which perform either an appraisal for identification/placement or for intervention/programming. As for measures for identification/placement, the age range of adolescence appears largely neglected both in conceptual development (see Chapter 1) and construction of tests or scales. More scales need to be developed for the adolescent range and to fit the identification/placement prerequisites. These two needs depict the relative infancy of adaptive behavior measurement. No doubt the next five years will witness an expansion of the measurement technology to meet the need areas mentioned.

Table 8–2
Adaptive Behavior Measures for
Intervention/Programming

Test or Scale, Author(s), Publishers/ Clearinghouses	Age Range	Measurement Reference[a]	Domains, Chapters, or Sections
Adaptive Behavior Scale Nihira, Foster, Shell-haas, & Leland, 1975	3–0 to 69	N & C	2 parts, 24 subscales (e.g., independent functioning, physical development, domestic activity, un-trustworthy behavior)
Edmark Associates 1329 Northup Way Bellevue, Washington 98005			
Adaptive Behavior Scale—Public School Version Lambert, Windmiller, Cole, & Figueroa, 1974	7–3 to 13–2	N & C	2 parts, 21 subscales (see Table 8–1)
Edmark Associates 1329 Northup Way Bellevue, Washington 98005			
Balthazar Scales of Adaptive Behavior I. Scales of Functional In-dependence II. Scales of Social Adaptation	5 to 57	C	More than 8 major areas, 16+ subscales (e.g., toileting, eating, unadaptive self-directed behaviors, verbal communication, play activi-ties)
Balthazar, 1973			
Consulting Psycholo-gists Press, 577 College Ave. Palo Alto, California 94306			
Behavior Characteris-tics Progression Chart (BCP) Santa Cruz County Office of Education	o to adult	C	More than 50 domains or strands covering a wide range of development

Table 8–2 (continued)

Test or Scale, Author(s), Publishers/ Clearinghouses	Age Range	Measurement Reference[a]	Domains, Chapters, or Sections
Vort Corporation Box 11132 Palo Alto, California 94306			
Cain-Levine Social Competency Scale Cain, Levine, & Elzey, 1963	5–0 to 13–11	N	2 parts, 4 subscales (self-help, initiative, social skills, communication)
Consulting Psychologists Press 577 College Avenue Palo Alto, California 94306			
Callier-Azusa Scale Stillman (Ed.), 1975	0 to 8	N	5 subscales (perceptual abilities, daily living skills, language development, motor development, socialization)
Callier Center for Communication Disorders The University of Texas/Dallas 1966 Inwood Road Dallas, Texas 75235			
Cambridge Assessment, Developmental Rating & Evaluation Welch, O'Brien, & Ayers, 1974	0 to adult	C	16 domains (e.g., gross-motor development, dressing, fine-motor development, self-concept)
Cambridge Area Developmental Rehabilitation and Education Center Cambridge Independent School District Cambridge, Minnesota 55008			

Table 8–2 (continued)

Test or Scale, Author(s), Publishers/ Clearinghouses	Age Range	Measure-ment Reference[a]	Domains, Chapters, or Sections
Camelot Behavioral Checklist Foster, 1974 Edmark Associates 1329 Northup Way Bellevue, Washington 98005	not speci-fied	N & C	10 domains (e.g., self-help, physical development, home duties, vocational be-haviors, economic be-haviors, independent travel)
Developmental Evalutation Scale Dallas County MHMR Center, 1973 Dallas County MHMR Center 2710 Stemmons Freeway Dallas, Texas 75207	0 to adult	C	6 major domains, 16 subsections (e.g., physical, self-help, mal-adaptive behavior, communication, social independence)
Fairview Behavior Evaluation Battery Fairview State Hospital, 1970 Research Department 2501 Harbor Boulevard Costa Mesa, California 92626	0 to 10	C	5 scales (developmental, self-help, social skills, language evaluation, problem behavior record)
Learning Accomplishment Profile Sanford, 1974 Kapplan School Supply Corporation 600 Jonestown Road Winston-Salem, North Calolina, 27103	0 to 6	N	6 major areas (gross motor, fine motor, self-help, social cognitive, language)

Table 8–2 (continued)

Test or Scale, Author(s), Publishers/ Clearinghouses	Age Range	Measurement Reference[a]	Domains, Chapters, or Sections
Oakwood Resident Movement Scale and Curriculum Berdine, Murphy, & Roller, 1976 (In press) by Berdine	0 to adult	C	77 adaptive behavior areas, 8 subscales (e.g., independent functioning, physical development, economic activity)
Preschool Attainment Record American Guidance Services, 1966 American Guidance Services Publishers Building Circle Pines, Minnesota 55014	6 mos to 7 yrs	N	4 domains, 8 subtests (e.g., abulation, manipulation, rapport, creativity, communication, responsibility, information, ideation)
Social and Prevocational Information Battery Halpern, Raffeld, Irvin, & Link, 1975 CTB/McGraw-Hill Del Monte Research Park Monterey, California 93940	EMR adolescents	N	9 tests (e.g., purchasing habits, budgeting, job-related behavior, home management, hygiene, grooming)
The TARC Assessment System Sailor & Mix, 1975 H & H Enterprises P. O. Box 3342 Lawrence, Kansas 66044	3 to 16	N	Four major domains with specific subscales within each (self-help, motor, communication, social skills)
T.M.R. Performance Profile for the Severely and Moderately Retarded DiNola, Kaminsky, & Sternfield, 1968 (3rd ed.)	TMR	C	6 major domains subdivided into 4 areas each (e.g., social behavior, self-care, communication, basic knowledge)

Table 8–2 (continued)

Test or Scale, Author(s), Publishers/ Clearinghouses	Age Range	Measure- ment Reference[a]	Domains, Chapters, or Sections
Reporting Service for Children 563 Westview Avenue Ridgefield, New Jersey 07657			
Vineland Social Maturity Scale Doll, 1965	0 to 30	N	6 major areas (e.g., self-help, locomotion, communication)
American Guidance Service Publishers Building Circle Pines, Minnesota 55014			
Y.E.M.R. Performance Profile for the Young Moderately and Mildly Retarded DiNola, Kaminsky, & Sternfield, 1967	Pre- school EMR	C	10 domains with 10 sub- divided areas in each (e.g., social behavior, self-help, safety, motor, manipulative skills)
Reporting Service for Children 563 Westview Avenue Ridgefield, New Jersey 07567			

[a] N = Normative, C = Criterion.

REFERENCES

Buros, O. K. (Ed.) *The sixth mental measurement yearbook*. Highland Park, N. J.: Gryphon Press, 1965.

Carver, R. P. Two dimensions of tests: Psychometric versus edumetric. *American Psychologist*, 1974, *29*, 512–518.

Coulter, W. A. & Morrow, H. W. *A collection of definitions of adaptive behavior*. Austin: Texas Regional Resource Center, 1976.

Drew, C. J. Criterion-referenced and norm-referenced assessment of minority group children. *Journal of School Psychology*, 1973, *11*, 323–329.

Grossman, H. D. (Ed.). *Manual on terminology and classification in mental retardation* (Special Publication No. 2). Washington, D. C.: American Association on Mental Deficiency, 1973.

Horrocks, J. E. *Assessment of behavior: The methodology and content of psychological measurement.* Columbus, Ohio: Merrill, 1964.

Johnson, D. (Ed.). *Supplement user's guide: AAMD ABS—PSV.* Tallahassee: State Department of Education, 1977.

Johnson, W., Marr, J., & Young, E. *Preschool test matrix: Individual test descriptions.* Lexington, Ky.: Coordinating Office for Regional Resource Centers, 1976.

Lambert, N. M., Windmiller, M., Cole, L., & Figueroa, R. Standardization of a public school version of the AAMD Adaptive Behavior Scale. *Mental Retardation,* 1975, *13,* 3–7.

Livingston, S. A. Criterion-referenced applications of classical test theory. *Journal of Educational Measurement,* 1972, *9,* 13–26.

Mercer, J. R. Personal communication, April 28, 1977.

Mercer, J. R., & Lewis, J. F. *System of Multicultural Pluralistic Assessment: Parent interview manual and student assessment manual.* New York: The Psychological Corporation, 1977.

Oakland, T., & Matuszek, P. Using tests in nondiscriminatory assessment. In T. Oakland (Ed.), *With bias toward none: Non-biased assessment of minority group children.* Lexington, Ky.: Coordinating Office for Regional Resource Centers, 1976.

Tucker, J. A. Operationalizing the diagnostic intervention process. In T. Oakland (Ed.), *With bias toward none: Non-biased assessment of minority group children.* Lexington, Ky.: Coordinating Office for Regional Resource Centers, 1976.

Tucker, J. A. Personal communication, January 16, 1977.

Walker, J., Tucker, J. A., Lauro, C., & Mirro, M. *Individualized programming for the severely multiply handicapped: 1975.* Austin: Texas Regional Resource Center, 1975.

Walls, R. T., Werner, T. J., Bacon, A. Behavioral checklists. In J. D. Cone & R. P. Hawkings (Eds.), *Behavioral assessment: New directions in clinical psychology.* New York: Brunner/Mazel, 1977. In press.

Williams, R. L. The bitch-100: A culture-specific test. *Journal of Afro-American Issues,* 1975, *3,* 103–116.

APPENDIX: A CONCEPTUAL SCHEME OF PSYCHOLOGICAL ASSESSMENT TO ASSIST IN CLASSIFYING ADAPTIVE BEHAVIOR MEASURES

To reiterate, the term *psychological assessment* will be functionally defined as the psychological assessment of students directed toward either or both an identification/placement (e.g., educable mentally retarded, emotionally disturbed) and/or an intervention/programming (e.g., remediate vowel confusion, building paragraph comprehension) (see, Chapter 1). Additionally, the structural characteristics of tests selected for the assessment may be thought of as either norm-referenced (measuring differences between individuals) or as criterion-referenced (measuring differences within an individual). This two-dimensional distinction (i.e., identification/placement versus intervention/programming and norm-referenced versus criterion-referenced) is important in the planning of assessment procedures and the selection of tests or measures to be used at various points in the assessment process.

Although the functional dimension of identification/placement versus intervention/programming has been explained at several previous points see (Chapters 1 and 7), the structural characteristics dimension needs additional explanation. Traditional psychometric technology has been oriented toward certain values in the structural characteristics of a test (i.e., reliability, validity, and item selection). A test is typically evaluated in terms of norm-referenced properties (Horrocks, 1964), i.e., measuring differences between individuals. However, increased sophistication in testing technology and an expanded function of testing (i.e., for intervention as well as for identification), especially in the public schools, has produced an additional and contrasting set of properties by which tests may be constructed, evaluated, and selected. Criterion-referenced properties of a test are the extent to which they reflect gain or growth within individual differences. Using the contrasting criteria of function or purpose (identification/placement versus intervention/programming) and structural characteristics (norm-referenced versus criterion-referenced), one can thoroughly scrutinize a test's reliability, validity, item selection, etc.

For example, reliability is concerned with the consistency of a test in measuring differences. For norm-referenced properties reliability is synonymous with consistent measurement of differences between individuals. Criterion-referenced reliability focuses on consistent measurement of an individual when compared to an absolute criterion.

By combining the two dimensions of psychological assessment (function and structural characteristics),[1] it is possible to describe four types of outcomes or products of assessment (see Table 8–3).

Contemporary appraisal processes usually focus upon two of the outcomes listed in Table 8–3: appraisal for identification/placement using norm-referenced tests and appraisal for intervention/programming using criterion-referenced tests. This method results in appropriate eligibility determination and the construction of detailed individual educational plans. There has been criticism (Faur, 1975) of appraisal practitioners who have used more traditional appraisal tests or procedures (such as norm-referenced tests) for both functions (i.e., intervention as well as identification). The criticism generated by Faur and others deserves more discussion and empirical examination in the professional literature.

By considering the four possible outcomes of assessment noted in the table, tests can be selected which will yield the information desired by the appraisal practitioner. These four outcomes of assessment, though compatible in meeting the needs of a referral, are not necessarily accomplished by using the same tests, as has been reported in the literature concerning nonbiased assessment models (Tucker, 1976). One major contention of the authors is that the selection of tests measuring adaptive behavior will be significantly influenced by the desired outcome(s) or intent of the assessment, which may cause each pupil appraisal professional to use different measures (see Chapters 7 and 8).[2] Carver (1974) expresses a similar position in commenting on the intervention/programming dimensions of assessment described by the table: "All tests, to a certain extent, reflect both between individual differences and within individual growth. Because of their design and development, however, most tests will do a better job in one area than the other" (p. 512). Test selection, given this two-dimensional conception, is yet to be thoroughly explicated for the total array of measures in psychological assessment. For the purposes of this appendix Table 8–3 is presented again, but with a sample of adaptive behavior measures in each cell rather than the outcomes or products of the assessment (see Table 8–4).

The most obvious observation in scanning the four cells of Table 8–4 is the paucity of norm-referenced measures used in identification/placement. This further substantiates the need (as also depicted in Chapter 8) for a greater variety of instruments used in identification of handicaps.

[1] The concept of two dimensions is similar to Carver's (1974) distinction between "psychometric" and "edumetric" tests and their contrasting qualities.

[2] When one is selecting which particular tests or procedures are best for identification/placement versus intervention/programming, the correct selection is usually never precise, as some tests may have relative value for both types of functions. The efficacy of a dual function test has not been thoroughly investigated at this point. In general, though, a test is seldom designed for a dual purpose.

Table 8–3
Outcomes or Products of Assessment

Structural Characteristics	Functions of Assessment	
	Identification/Placement	Intervention/Programming
Norm-referenced (between individuals)	Identifies presence of a handicap Determines eligibility for placement in special education Allows for political accounting of funds	Specifies strengths and weaknesses in comparison to the norm group Can demonstrate degree of educational need in comparison to others Can identify areas for further detailed testing
Criterion-referenced (within individuals)	Groups students by skill level or stage of development (e.g., low reading group, etc.) for instruction and resource allocation	Specifies skill level of student in relation to the scope and sequence of the criterion (criteria) Identifies next step(s) in the intervention sequence for the individual educational plan (IEP)

Table 8–4
Classification of Adaptive Measures

Structural Characteristics	Functions of Assessment	
	Identification/Placement	Intervention/Programming
Norm-referenced	ABIC in SOMPA ABS—PSV	Camelot Behavior Rating Scale ABS Cain-Levine Social Competency Scale Social & Prevocational Information Battery Vineland Social Maturity Scale
Criterion-referenced	Camelot Behavior Rating Scale Behavior Characteristics Progression Chart Balthazar Scales of Adaptive Behavior	Developmental Evaluation Scale Balthazar Scales of Adaptive Behavior Behavior Characteristics Progression Chart Oakwood Resident Movement Scale & Curriculum

Note: Only a sample of the available measures is used because of limitations of space.

155

In summary, a two-dimensional conceptualization of psychological assessment (function or purpose and structural characteristics) has been presented to assist the reader in classifying a sample of the available measures of adaptive behavior.

REFERENCES

Carver, R. P. Two dimensions of tests: Psychometric versus edumetric. *American Psychologist,* 1974, *29,* 512–518.
Faur, P. *Train, don't test.* Champaign, Il.: Children's Research Center, 1975.
Horrocks, J. E. *Assessment of behavior: The methodology and content of psychological measurement.* Columbus, Ohio: Merrill, 1964.
Tucker, J. A. Operationalizing the diagnostic intervention process. In T. Oakland (Ed.), *With bias toward none: Non-biased assessment of minority group children.* Lexington, Ky.: Coordinating Office for Regional Resource Centers, 1976.

Nadine M. Lambert

9
The Adaptive Behavior Scale—
Public School Version: An Overview

The methods developed in the early 1970s for the assessment of adaptive behavior in a public school population were motivated by the need to respond to legislative mandates. These mandates required that eligibility decisions for special education programs be based on multiple rather than single assessments of children's functioning. The concept of adaptive behavior did not develop as a consequence of increasing concern over the procedures used for evaluating the functioning of children who were vulnerable to school failure, for it has a long, philosophical, literary, and medical history in the field of mental retardation (Kagin, 1967). In the nineteenth century, for example, the medical definition of retardation incorporated those functions that we now call adaptive behavior. Itard and Haslow in 1819, Sequin in 1837, Voisin in 1843, Horne in 1858, and Goddard in 1912 spoke essentially about adaptive behavior, using such terms as social competency, skills training, social norms, the power of fending for oneself in life, and adaptability to environment (Horton, 1966).

The later approach to defining mental retardation, which relied heavily on individual tests of intelligence, is, by contrast, a relatively new occurrence. It began with Binet's work in 1905 for the Paris schools and was extended in 1959 when the American Association on Mental Deficiency continued to define mental retardation, in part, on the basis of measured intelligence (Grossman, 1973). The distinction between the

This work was completed in part under the support of California State Department of Education Grant No. 76-62-G.

157

information about individual differences obtained from the assessment of adaptive behavior and the assessment of intelligence is considerable. Assessment of adaptive behavior provides information about the community's judgment of an individual's degree of independence. The assessment of intelligence depends on a person's ability to perform a sample of cognitive, verbal, reasoning, and performance tasks.

Many of those involved in the education of mentally handicapped children incorrectly believe that until landmark litigation (*Charles S.* v. *Board of Education, San Francisco; Larry P.* v. *Riles; Diana* v. *California State Board of Education*) challenged procedures for placement of mildly mentally retarded children in special classes, recommended practice was to use only intelligence tests to determine eligibility. Handbooks for assessment of children to determine eligibility for placement in special programs, however, were available to assist psychologists in the diagnostic process shortly after the passage of enabling legislation in California (1947–1948) that permitted school districts to recover the excess costs of educating mildly retarded children. In addition, guidelines, such as those published by the California State Department of Education (Daly & Henderson, 1959), detailed a wide variety of information which was to be integrated into the case study, such as psychometric examination, educational examination, social history, developmental history, family history, and physical examination.

While the assessment of social development, social history, or social functioning was intended to appraise aspects of the child's independence, social maturity, and interpersonal skills that we now refer to as adaptive behavior, the term adaptive behavior was not used until the publication of the 1961 "AAMD Manual on Terminology" (Heber, 1961). Adaptive behavior was defined there as (1) the degree to which individuals are able to function and maintain themselves independently, and (2) the degree to which they meet satisfactorily the culturally imposed demands of personal and social responsibility.

Once adaptive behavior was explicitly defined, the task of developing reliable and valid tools for assessing this area of social functioning was undertaken by a team working for the American Association on Mental Deficiency in Kansas. The item development and validation procedures (Nihira & Shellhaas, 1970) consisted of analyzing the relationship between ratings of independently derived estimates of adaptive behavior and selected items while controlling for the contribution of intelligence. Initially, many of the several hundred items which were tried out were eliminated because they did not correlate with adaptive behavior assessment or because they were simply proxies for intelligence. As new items were written, evaluated, and contrasted with one another, a scale measuring adaptive behavior as independent as possible from measured intelligence began to emerge. Part I of the first edition of the scale consisted of

10 domains assessing adaptive behavior in areas such as economic activity, self-direction, responsibility, and independent functioning.

As the scale development proceeded, Nihira and his co-workers realized that another aspect of adaptive behavior had been ignored in the item development of Part I. This aspect of adaptive behavior reflected the degree to which an individual could meet the demands for appropriate behavior in the school and community setting. The items for development of Part II of the scale came from a study of critical incidents produced by teachers and community and residential workers and reflected behaviors which, if present to a great extent, would make it impossible for the individual to remain in the environment. Item analysis proceeded in a similar fashion as for Part I and resulted in the creation of 14 behavior domains useful in appraising social-emotional adaptational problems. The 1969 edition of the scale (Nihira, Foster, Shellhaas, & Leland, 1969) provided a comprehensive assessment of adaptive behavior, which included items measuring self-reliance and social development (Part I), with appraisal of social adaptation relying on the nature of the individual's affective characteristics (Part II).

DEVELOPMENT OF THE PUBLIC SCHOOL VERSION

Early in the 1970s, in response to concern over appropriateness of measures employed to assess intellectual development and adaptive behavior, a team at the University of California, Berkeley, which included this author, investigated the appropriateness and validity of a wide variety of procedures for diagnosing mild mental retardation. The results of our extensive review of the literature and our recommendations for assessment practice (Lambert, Wilcox, & Gleason, 1974) included a review of methods for assessing adaptive behavior. Our inquiry determined that the AAMD Adaptive Behavior Scale was the most carefully developed tool for assessing behavior associated with the standard definition of adaptive behavior and the best available for use with school-age children. The scale, however, had not been evaluated for its appropriateness in a public school setting, and before recommending its use, we conducted pilot, feasibility, and standardization studies of the scale with normal and handicapped pupils attending public school.

The first step was to evaluate the range of item values obtained in a public school population and to determine whether parents or teachers would be the most appropriate reporters of children's adaptive behavior. We studied item scores and determined that the score ranges were adequate for an elementary school population. We gathered reports from parents and teachers and could find no significant differences between their ratings whether the population was normal children or mildly retarded children. We examined score differences attributable to sex and ethnic status and found that any systematic effects attributable to these factors were minimal. The consequences of the pilot phase led us to proceed with a broader-based feasibility study and to use teachers as reporters of the adaptive behavior functioning of school children in a standardization project.

TEACHERS OR PARENTS AS REPORTERS OF ADAPTIVE BEHAVIOR

The decision to use teacher judgments of adaptive behavior rather than those of parents in the standardization rested on (1) the desire to involve teachers in the assessment process because ultimately they will be relied upon to provide educational programs for exceptional children, (2) the relative economy of teacher-supplied data because parents are often difficult to reach, and (3) the potential reliability of teacher reports.

To study further any potential discrepancy between teacher and parent reports, we obtained independently a sample of 200 mildly and moderately retarded children from white Anglo and Spanish-speaking backgrounds. The results of this substudy have been completed, and Cole (1976) showed that there were no significant differences between parent and teacher ratings regardless of the sex or ethnic status of the child. Thus, though the standardization data were collected from teachers, the scale is applicable as well for use in interviewing parents about the adaptive behavior status of their children or in training parent groups about adaptive behavior concepts, after which they can complete a rating of the child independently just as the teacher does. Ratings from both parents and teachers provide a good basis for comparing the child's functioning in these two environments and, in turn, produce an excellent set of data for planning home and school activities to promote development.

We realized that for some items and for some children teachers might not know their pupils well enough to provide accurate evaluations of their adaptive behavior and would need parental assistance.

APPROPRIATENESS OF THE ADAPTIVE BEHAVIOR SCALE IN PUBLIC SCHOOLS

In the early phase of our work educators and psychologists expressed concern about the appropriateness of items reflecting social incompetence in the appraisal of children's functioning in the school setting. To assess the range of adaptive behavior functioning over the entire spectrum from incompetence to competence, and from total dependency to independence, requires items reflecting a wide range of social functioning. Two types of information provided evidence on the appropriateness of the item content for ratings of school behavior.

The first test of school appropriateness centered on determining whether teachers had enough information to rate children on the items. In our instructions to teachers we asked them to indicate whether they had an opportunity to observe the behavior of the child who was being rated. If the teacher had not observed exactly the same behavior but had observed similar behavior, we asked the teacher to infer the appropriate rating and to put an "I" opposite the rating. When teachers had not had an opportunity to observe similar behavior and had to make a guess based on their general knowledge of the pupil, they placed a "G" opposite the rating. From counts of the frequencies of "I"'s or "G"'s for each item, we had an empirical test of the degree to which teachers considered the item to be appropriate.

The second feasibility test came from data provided by special education, pupil personnel, and research staffs of participating school districts. Each staff member reviewed the scale and indicated those items which he or she believed were impossible for teachers to rate or which were inappropriate to the school setting.

The combination of information from teachers and staff specialists provided a basis for deciding whether to retain items for the Public School Version. The Domestic Activity domain was deleted from Part I of the scale and the nine remaining domains were retained. On Part II the domains of Self-abusive Behavior and Sexually Aberrant Behavior were deleted, but the remaining 12 domains were judged to be appropriate.

VALIDITY AND RELIABILITY OF THE PUBLIC SCHOOL VERSION

The Standardization Population

The elementary school population which served as subjects in the feasibility and standardization studies of the Public School Version of the Adaptive Behavior Scale (Lambert, Windmiller, & Cole, 1975; Lambert, Windmiller, Cole, & Figueroa, 1975a, 1975b) was defined on the basis of six school and demographic variables. These were (1) class placement: regular, EMR (educable mentally retarded), TMR (trainable mentally retarded), and EH (educationally handicapped); (2) age: children enrolled in second through sixth grade; (3) sex; (4) population density of residence;

(5) socioeconomic status: census tract data on percentage of unemployment and average education level; and (6) ethnic status: black, white, Asian, and Spanish-speaking background. The proportion of pupils with the above characteristics in each school district in the state were evaluated using statewide school census information, and schools representative of the state's population characteristics were identified.

A population of 2800 children was selected, with the objective of sampling approximately equal numbers of regular and EMR subjects and smaller representative samples of TMR pupils and those assigned to programs for the educationally handicapped.[1] We also sampled equal numbers of males and females and an equivalent distribution of subjects in the major ethnic groups. The objective of the sampling procedure was to produce representative groups of male and female children from different ethnic backgrounds in the selected age range in the several classification groups rather than to identify a representative school population in which children in the special education categories were selected as a proportion of the total school population which these classifications represent.

We also examined the appropriateness of the placements of the EMR pupils in our standardization population. The data for the California study were collected in 1972, several years after the *Diana v. California State Board of Education* consent decree required school district reports of the ethnic representation in special education programs and a year after the state legislature required a reevaluation of all pupils in programs for the EMR. These actions supported our confidence in the appropriateness of the placements of the EMR subjects. To affirm, additionally, the status of the EMR pupils, we analyzed the IQ distributions of these pupils at the conclusion of the data collection. These analyses showed that only 4, 3, and 3 percent, respectively, of the white, black, and Spanish-background subjects had an IQ score higher than two standard deviations below the mean and that they would have met the eligibility criteria which were defined in the California Education Code Statutes then in effect.

Item Validities of the Public School Version

The manual (Lambert et al., 1975a) of the Public School Version of the scale (pp. 41–42) presents the findings of the item validities (for all items including those deleted from the public school version) for predicting adaptive behavior as inferred from school classification status controlling for sex and ethnic status. We determined the significance level of the partial correlations of item score, with classification status defined as

[1] We included a small representative sample of pupils assigned to programs for EH children. The requirement for classification into this program was that the child have serious learning deficiencies and be within the normal range of intelligence.

regular or EMR school placement. We considered the relationship of item values to EMR and regular class status to be a more definitive test of item validity than the correlation of scores with regular and TMR status or with EMR and TMR status. In general, these analyses showed that 80 to 90 percent of the Part I items were significantly related ($p < .01$) to classification status from ages 7 through 12, and that 20 to 75 percent of the items on Part II were equally as valid. We expected to achieve a greater degree of relationship between level of adaptive behavior (inferred from school classification) and items on Part I than those on Part II. Part I assesses independence and responsibility functions associated with adaptive behavior while Part II assesses problems in social-emotional functioning which are not restricted to individuals with evidence of mental retardation. In general, however, the number of valid items increased with age on Part II, suggesting a greater extent of behavior disorders as EMR children grow older.

Domain Validities of the Public School Version

Our analysis of the validity of the domain scores (Lambert, in press) included simultaneously an analysis of the unique contribution of school classification, sex, and ethnic status to the scores. We conducted identical analyses for 9 domains of Part I and 11 domains of Part II for all age groups in the sample. We did not include the educationally handicapped sample in these analyses but centered our efforts on determining whether differences in domain scores were associated with regular and EMR status.

Multiple-regression procedures (Cohen, 1968; Darlington, 1968) make possible inferences regarding the significance of variance attributable to a variable when the effects of other variables of interest are accounted for. We analyzed (1) the unique variance attributable to adaptive behavior level as inferred from classification status when the variance attributable to sex and ethnic status were accounted for, (2) the unique variance attributable to sex accounting for the variance attributable to ethnic status and classification, and (3) the unique variance attributable to ethnic status accounting for the variance attributable to classification and sex.

Details of the results of these extensive multiple-regression analyses are presented in Lambert (in press); hence, only a summary of the analyses will follow. Classification status was significantly associated with Part I domain scores for ages 7 through 12 for all domains with the exception of a nonsignificant contribution at age 8 to 9 on Vocational Activity. Thus, in 45 analyses of the predictive validity of the scale, only one failed to reach an alpha level of $<.01$. Similarly, on Part II domains the .01 level of significance was not obtained in only 10 of 60 analyses. The findings extended those from the item analyses and demonstrated that differences in domain scores based on the Public School Version are very highly associated with the classification of regular and EMR pupils and can be considered valid for differentiating regular class pupils from those assigned to EMR programs.

The multiple-regression analyses of the unique contribution of sex to domain score showed that sex made no significant contributions at any ages on the Physical Development, Economic Activity, and Language Development domains. On the domains of Independent Functioning, Numbers and Time, Vocational Activity, Self-direction, and Socialization, sex contributed significantly at one age level only, either for ages 8 to 9 or 9 to 10. Where sex differences occurred on the Responsibility domain, one can tentatively account for them as differences in sex role demands made on boys and girls.

Differences in socialization practices for boys and girls most likely explain the somewhat greater influence of sex on Part II domain scores. After accounting for the variance in scores associated with classification and ethnic status, sex was significantly associated with Part II domain scores in 19 of 60 analyses. Girls, for example, were judged to be less destructive and nonconforming than boys. Girls were also considered to be less hyperactive than boys at all age levels. In order to provide sufficient reference material for appropriate interpretation of the domain scores, the manual provides norms for boys and girls as well as the total sample in each age and classification group for the Part II domains. One cannot generalize from these findings, however, and state that there is an unwarranted sex bias in the scores. The domains on which there were differences attributable to sex reflect behaviors which boys and girls acquire differentially as a result of different standards for socialization; therefore, the results can be assumed to reflect the behavioral expectancies of families and community rather than inherent differences between males and females.

The increment of variance associated with ethnic status on Part I on the scale was significant in only 1 of 45 analyses. The inference follows that ethnic status does not contribute to domain scores when the effects of classification are accounted for on Part I of the scale. Similarly, on the Part II domains ethnic status contributed significant, unique variance to the scores in 12 of 60 analyses and only at two or three of five age levels on the Rebellious Behavior, Untrustworthy Behavior, and Antisocial Behavior domains. We interpreted these few significant contributions to be a reflection of different cultural demands which are reflected in maladaptive interpersonal behavior, which in turn influenced ratings assigned to the items of the Antisocial and Untrustworthy Behavior domains. Similarly, rebellious behavior manifest in response to authority, diligence in following instructions, and punctuality are functions of the pupil's classification status as well as the ethnic group to which the pupil belongs.

Even though the contribution of ethnic status to Part II domain scores was significant for only 3 of 12 domains, we considered these results important enough to prepare additional norms by ethnic status for the public school version. These norms, along with the norms for the total sample and those by sex, provide the user with reference groups sufficient for adequate and fair interpretation of the results.

The remaining variables by which subjects were identified in the study were population density and socioeconomic status. When each of these measures was correlated with domain scores, controlling for the effects of class placement, sex, and ethnic status, there were, in a practical sense, no significant results. There were only two correlations which were significant at the .01 level on Part I of the scale, and no correlations which were significant at this level of Part II over all of the analyses of the contributions of these demographic and social status variables.

On the basis of the data reported in the study, we concluded that the scale was valid for differentiating between pupils assigned to regular and EMR classes from ages 7 through 12. These analyses did not answer an additional important question as to whether the mean scores for children within a classification group at each age level were the same. Accordingly, Cole (1976) undertook a multivariate analysis of variance of the data collected for the regular, EMR, and TMR subjects. As one would expect from the multiple-regression analyses which were reported, mean scores for the three classification groups at each age level were very significantly different. The variance in scores explained by age and classification status ranged from 8 to 39 percent for the Part I domains and from 2 to 10 percent on the Part II domains. The mean scores for regular class subjects on Part I domains were always higher than those for EMR pupils, which, in turn, were always higher for children in TMR classes. For Part II domains children in regular classes always had lower scores, indicating better adaptation for all domains. The mean scores of EMR subjects on Part II domains, however, were not always indicative of more adaptability than those of TMR subjects. For example, EMR subjects manifested a greater extent of maladaption on the domains of Antisocial Behavior, Rebellious Behavior, Untrustworthy Behavior, Hyperactivity, and Psychological Distubances. TMR subjects, on the other hand, had higher, more negative scores on Withdrawal, Stereotyped Behavior, Inappropriate Manners, Unacceptable Vocal Habits, and Unacceptable or Eccentric Habits. Additional study of the interaction of level of intellectual functioning and manifestations of emotional disturbance of these several types can shed light on the diagnostic significance of these findings.

The findings from the multiple-regression analysis showed that there was essentially no contribution of sex and ethnic status to Part I domains when we controlled for classification status. Similarly, Cole's data showed that there was neither a significant sex nor ethnic status effect within the groups of EMR and TMR subjects. There were, however, small though significant differences in means (ranging from 1.3 to .07 raw score points) between ethnic groups on six of nine domains. Even though small differences can be significant in large samples such as those used in these studies, only 1 to 2 percent of variance was explained by cultural factors. The contribution of ethnic status to scores of regular class pupils is minimal. There were no differences among ethnic groups on Independent Functioning, Physical Development, or Vocational Activity. An examination of the mean scores over all subjects showed, for example, that the differences benefited no particular ethnic group. For example, the Spanish-background subjects had higher scores on Responsibility, Socialization, and Economic Activity; the black subjects scored higher on Independent Functioning; and the white subjects were rated higher on Language Development, Number and Time Concepts, Vocational Activity, and Self-direction. While cultural factors may be a factor in adaptive behavior functioning represented by the Part I domains, we can conclude from the data reported here that there is no systematic bias in the scores which would favor one or another ethnic group.

There were significant differences between means for classification groups on all domains of Part II of the scale. The variance explained by classification status and age varied from 2 to 10 percent. Differences between means of ethnic status groups were significant for 6 out of 12 domains for regular class subjects, for 4 of 12 domains for EMR subjects, and for 3 of 12 domains for the TMR pupils. The variance explained for the ethnic status variables ranged from 1 to 2 percent. Since norms for different ethnic groups within classification and age are available in the manual, psychologists and others who use the scale have appropriate reference material to interpret results, taking into account, when appropriate, differences in functioning which might be attributable to cultural factors.

Mean differences between domain scores for boys and girls were not significant for pupils assigned to EMR and TMR classes. There were, however, four domains on Part I where regular class boys and girls were judged to have significantly different levels of adaptive behavior. The difference in means was about one raw score point, and the explained variance was from 1 (three domains) to 3 percent (Responsibility domain). Sex was only 1 percent. The Responsibility domain was the only one to which sex made a significant contribution after controlling for classification status in the mutiple-regression analyses, indicating that EMR and regular class females function at a slightly, but significantly, higher level than their male peers on the items assessing Responsibility.

On the basis of the findings summarized from these studies, we concluded that the scale was valid for differentiating among pupils assigned to regular, EMR, and TMR classes from ages 7 through 12. Even though our data show that the scale provides a valid measure of adaptive behavior, we do not mean to imply that all children with scores in a critical range necessarily should be classified as retarded. The obtained scores must be compared with other information, contrasted with reports from parents and other observers of the child, and integrated into and evaluated as part of a comprehensive case study.

Our research supports the assumption that Part I domains reflect behaviors which are acquired by both boys and girls similarly across the three major California ethnic groups which were represented in the study. The small differences between means within the regular class population indicate that the user of the scale must always exercise caution in interpreting the results of adaptive behavior assessment, just as care would be required in interpreting the results of other tests. One must always be sure that the child has had sufficient opportunity to acquire the skills or competencies being measured in the preparation of an interpretation of test findings. Our data show further that children who were assigned to EMR and TMR programs were significantly different with respect to adaptive behavior and that within these classifications boys and girls from different ethnic groups had, on the average, similar levels of adaptive behavior. One can infer from such a result that the groups of EMR subjects from the school districts which contributed to these studies were eligible to be classified as mentally retarded based on the criteria of retarded intellectual and adaptive behavior functioning.

Reliability of the Scale

Information to assess the internal consistency reliabilities of the domain scores was available from the data collected in the standardization studies. We determined that the reliabilities of Part I domain scores varied from .70 to .92, with a mean of .88. Reliabilities of the Part II domains varied from .80 to .92, with a mean of .87. These reliability estimates can be contrasted with the interrater reliabilities reported in the 1974 revision of the scale (Nihira, Foster, Shellhaas, & Leland, 1974). The range of interrater reliabilities for Part I domains was from .71 to .93, with a mean reliability of .86. For the Part II domains the manual reported the reliabilities to range from .44 to .77, with a mean reliability of .57. Unless two raters have equal opportunity to observe an individual, which is rarely the case, raters observe subjects under different environmental circumstances. Differences in environmental demands, in part, explain the somewhat lower average interrater reliabilities reported when compared with the internal consistency estimates.

Relationship of Domain Scores to IQ

A logical question to raise about the data from administrations of the Adaptive Behavior Scale is whether domain scores are simply proxies for intelligence. The subjects for these studies were selected on the basis of their school classification, but not necessarily on the basis of meeting a specified measured intelligence criterion. We combined the regular and special education subjects and computed the correlation between domain scores and reported IQs. The findings showed that on Part I domains over the age range of subjects, the magnitude of the relationship ranges from about .10 (Vocational Activity, Self-direction, and Responsibility) to about .60 (Number and Time Concepts, Economic Activity, and Language Development). The correlation between IQ and Part II domains ranged from −.01 (Destructive, Nonconforming) to −.21 (Withdrawal, Stereotyped Behavior). There was considerable variation in the relationship of IQ to specific domain scores over the age range of of subjects, suggesting differing patterns of development of these social and intellectual attributes. Nevertheless, the magnitude of these correlations informs us that this measure of adaptive behavior and measured intelligence share a low to moderate amount of variance attributable to a common underlying factor which we infer to be level of general development.

In concluding this discussion of the validity and reliability of the Public School Version it is important to point out that the item development phase (Nihira & Shellhaas, 1970) made no attempt to eliminate items on which males and females or individuals of different socioeconomic or ethnic status groups performed differently. The outcomes of our studies of the contribution of sex and ethnic status to item and domain scores illustrate variations in adaptive behavior functioning of subjects grouped by sex and ethnic status as measured by items selected to assess an independently derived adaptive behavior criterion. The fact that the results of our studies show no consistent ethnic status or sex contributions to domain scores on Part I of the ABS make it possible to infer that differences in adaptive behavior assessment on this scale reflect real differences in adaptive behavior functioning and provide assessment of adaptive behavior that can be applied fairly to boys and girls and to children of different ethnic groups. The provision of additional norms by sex and ethnic status for Part II of the scale ensures that users of the scale will have reference material to make fair and appropriate interpretation of the child's level of functioning on domains to which sex or ethnic status made occasional significant contributions.

APPLICATION OF THE RESULTS OF THE PUBLIC SCHOOL VERSION OF THE ADAPTIVE BEHAVIOR SCALE TO EDUCATIONAL PROGRAMMING

The validity and reliability data from our studies of the adaptive behavior of public school children support the fact that the Adaptive Behavior Scale measures a wide range of levels of adaptive behavior of normal and handicapped children who are attending school. It seems reasonable to conclude that domain scores can provide essential information both for determining eligibility of children for placement in programs for mentally retarded pupils and for developing educational plans to promote children's development.

Federal and state guidelines for programs for handicapped children require that children be assigned to the least restrictive environment for learning. In the near future it is likely that the requirement of a diagnosis of mild retardation such as now required to identify a a child for programs for the educable mentally retarded will be replaced by descriptive statements of individual differences of children which specify the degree of need for special education attention and which can be used as the basis for development of educational plans.

Whether or not diagnoses of mental retardation will continue to be required as a condition of delivery of special education services to educable mentally retarded children, it is instructive to note that children who are eligible under existing California Education Code provisions for EMR programs are children who are defined as academically retarded, and evidence of clinical factors associated with the condition is not required for diagnosis. In the medical history of those diagnosed as moderately or severely retarded, such as individuals in TMR programs, one would expect to find relevant clinical factors which account for the condition, such as those resulting from infections, metabolic disorders, trauma, gross brain disease, unknown prenatal influences, chromosomal abnormalities, or gestational disorders (Grossman, 1973). The California Education Code defines mildly mentally retarded pupils as ones who "because of retarded intellectual development as determined by individual psychological examinations are incapable of being educated profitably and efficiently through ordinary classroom instruction." The evidence of the child's handicap is failure in school, which is a result of differences in rate of development. Children who are eligible for placement in EMR programs, therefore, would not necessarily be children whose functioning would be judged to be retarded in the community or home environment. The code presently states that a child's eligibility for such programs be determined by a case study that includes a measure of his/her intellectual functioning and adaptive behavior. Psychologists who are required to determine the eligibility of children for programs for the educable mentally retarded know full well that they can never state with finality that such a child *is* "mentally retarded." On the basis of individual psychological examination the psychologist can state only that a child is "eligible" for the special education program and provide some indication of the probability that the child's performance will remain within specified limits suggested by the errors of measurement of the measures of intelligence, adaptive behavior, and other assessment methods that the psychologist employs. The cause of the academic retardation of educable mentally retarded children is likely to be unknown, may have a clinical basis, but in all probability can best be understood as a manifestation of individual differences in rate of cognitive and social development. The task for the psychologist is to assess the present intellectual and social developmental status of the child, contrast his/her findings with supportive or contradictory evidence in the case history, and determine whether the child, at the time of referral and appraisal, needs and is eligible for special education assistance, and if eligible, what types of educational experiences will be most beneficial.

The shift away from diagnoses of etiologies of handicapping conditions toward educational planning is a major positive trend in school psychology and special education. We have always known that simply categorizing or labeling children and assigning them to special programs would not guarantee continued developmental progress. We may have found ourselves spending more of our energies on diagnosing and placing than on developing educational plans because the evidence provided from most diagnostic tools is not easily adapted to educational recommendations. Even though competent psychologists never assume that the totality of an individual's intellectual potential can be represented by a single score, some have become trapped in a single score mentality when they have employed the IQ measure as the locus of individual functioning. Similarly, if we reduce the wide variety of individual differences in adaptive behavior functioning to a single score, we encourage the same kind of simplistic assumptions about adaptive behavior as we have encouraged in summing up a child's intellectual functioning in the IQ.

The Dimensions of Adaptive Behavior

The available data from several studies (Lambert & Nicoll, 1976; Nihira, 1969a; Nihira, 1969b) provide no basis to conclude that adaptive behavior is a single, unitary characteristic of individual functioning. Rather, the dimensionality of adaptive behavior as measured by the items and domains of the scale can be defined by four clusters of domains describing (1) Functional Autonomy (Independent Functioning, Language Development, Economic Activity, Number and Time Concepts, and

Vocational Activity), (2) Social Responsibility (Self-direction, Responsibility, and Socialization), (3) Interpersonal Adjustment (Destructive Behavior, Antisocial Behavior, Rebellious Behavior, Untrustworthy Behavior, and Psychological Disturbances), and (4) Intrapersonal Adjustment (Stereotyped Behavior, Inappropriate Manners, and Unacceptable Vocal Habits). The first two dimensions closely parallel the definition of adaptive behavior as comprised of those attributes necessary for maintaining oneself independently and functioning in a personally and socially responsible manner. The second two dimensions are associated with sociobehavioral adjustment factors which indicate the degree to which the individual will be able to meet the environmental demands of the school environments.

The Public School Version of the Adaptive Behavior Scale provides data expressed as an individual's percentile rank compared with age and classification peers. The results are valuable for the dual purposes of (1) determining the child's level of adaptive behavior as inferred from performance on the domains associated with the functional autonomy and social responsibility dimensions and (2) evaluating the potential for successfully meeting environmental demands of regular and special education classrooms based on evidence of social-emotional maladaptation.

Determining the Level of Adaptive Behavior

The manual for the Public School Version of the Adaptive Behavior Scale provides norms for regular, EMR, TMR, and EH subjects from ages 7 through 13 and additional norms for sex and ethnic status for Part II of the scale. Data collected in a large scale field study conducted by the Florida State Department of Education (1970a, 1970b) provide additional norms for subjects from ages 3 through 16. The Florida data will be compared with data presently being studied on groups from ages 3 to 7 and from 13 to 16 and within a year, normative data on the Public School Version will include norms from ages 3 through 16 based on the combined data.

After teachers have been trained to use the scale (Windmiller, 1977) and have completed their ratings, domain scores are computed for each child and checked for accuracy before an individual profile of adaptive behavior is developed. Figure 9–1 illustrates an adaptive behavior profile for a child who was referred for special education. The raw scores earned on each Part I domain are listed at the bottom of each column for the domain scores. Because the question being asked was whether the child's level of adaptive behavior was low enough to warrant consideration for special education placement, his/her profile of percentile ranks was drawn to reflect his/her position with respect to peers of the same age in regular

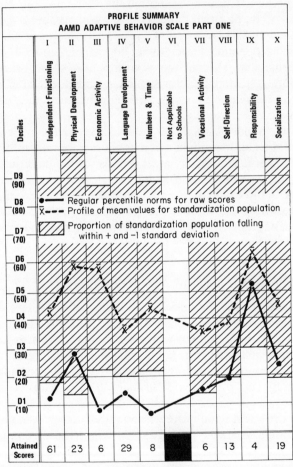

Fig. 9-1

class programs. Percentile ranks for regular-class subjects for each raw score were plotted on the profile, and they were at or lower than the fifteenth percentile for all domains associated with the functional autonomy dimension described above with the exception of Physical Development.

The shaded area on the profile outlines the proportion of subjects in the reference group who fall between ± one standard deviation from the mean domain score of the group. Some distributions of raw score on the Adaptive Behavior Scale such as that for Physical Development and those on Part II are skewed; therefore, percentile distributions were selected in favor of standard score distributions because such reference data retain the features of the domain distribution.

Physical Development provides a rough indication of whether a child's sensory and motor functioning are within normal limits. The manual suggests that a useful rule of thumb for interpreting this score is to use a raw score of 20 as an indicator of normal physical development. Raw scores on this domain indicate whether the presence of physical handicaps should be taken into consideration when interpreting a profile. Raw scores of 20 or higher usually mean a normal to perfect range of physical development. Approximately 90 percent of regular class pupils and 70 percent of EMR children fall in this category. A raw score of 10 or lower indicates the presence of one or more serious physical handicaps and referral to specialists for evaluation of these problems would be mandatory. Scores between 10 and 20 suggest possible physical handicaps and the items on the Physical Development domain should be examined to identify areas of sensory or motor functioning which should be considered in the interpretation of other domain scores. The Physical Development domain score (percentile), as presented on the profile in Figure 9–1, indicates that EFG's sensory and motor development is normal for his age.

To facilitate interpretation of the percentiles, the shaded area outlines a range of functioning that is clearly within average limits for the group. Individual scores within this range can be compared to the mean of the reference group in percentile ranks (the heavy dash line), and one can estimate the relative standing of the child with age peers as a percentile value below or above the norm and within or without a critical score range.

Pupil EFG's scores on the Functional Autonomy domains fall below the critical range indicated by the shaded area. This child does not have, however, any physical problems which would interfere with his ability to acquire higher levels of adaptive behavior on these domains. The low level of his functioning on these domains indicates that he may be eligible for special education placement. His performance is at a somewhat higher, though still borderline level on the domains associated with social responsibility. A report summarizing his adaptive behavior functioning on Part I of the Scale would indicate that with respect to independence skills, his behavior is seriously below that of regular class pupils of his age, but his ability to initiate and carry out tasks and get along well socially with peers, while also at a low level, is within an acceptable range of functioning for regular class pupils. His performance also can be compared with

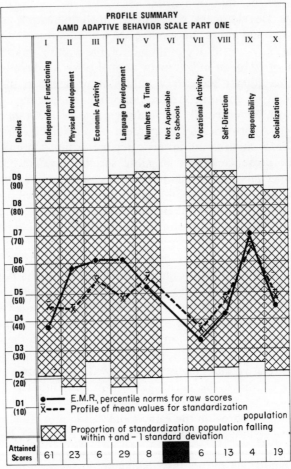

Identification E. F. G. using EMR norms

Age 9 years 6 months

Sex Male

Date of Administration 1-25-77

PROFILE SUMMARY
AAMD ADAPTIVE BEHAVIOR SCALE PART ONE

Deciles	I	II	III	IV	V	VI	VII	VIII	IX	X
	Independent Functioning	Physical Development	Economic Activity	Language Development	Numbers & Time	Not Applicable to Schools	Vocational Activity	Self-Direction	Responsibility	Socialization

●—— E.M.R., percentile norms for raw scores
X̄--- Profile of mean values for standardization population
▨ Proportion of standardization population falling within + and − 1 standard deviation

Attained Scores	61	23	6	29	8	■	6	13	4	19

Fig. 9-2

pupils in EMR programs. Figure 9-2 shows EFG's profile with respect to the EMR reference group. As one can see, his performance varies around the domain means for the EMR pupils of his age. His adaptive behavior is typical of those pupils who were assigned to EMR classes in the standardization population, 96 or 97 percent of whom were eligible on the basis of the measured intelligence criterion. What decisions should be made? On the average, 9 out of 10 regular class pupils have acquired

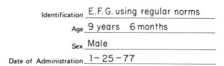

Identification __E.F.G. using regular norms__

Age __9 years   6 months__

Sex __Male__

Date of Administration __1- 25 - 77__

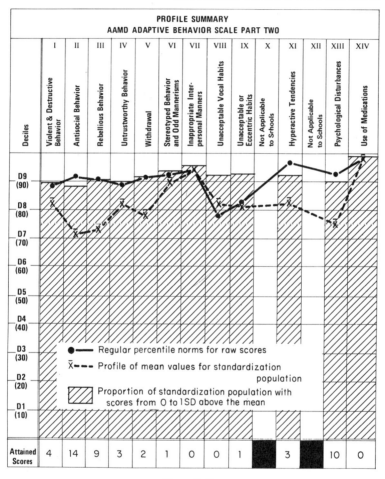

Fig. 9–3

higher level adaptive behavior skills than EFG on all areas except those related to social and personal responsibility. EFG's performance in some areas indicates that he needs special education assistance to improve his functional independence skills and the acquisition of knowledge necessary to perform independently. He is responsible and probably would carry out assignments given to him as well as some other children in a regular class. If his measured intellectual functioning is also marginal,

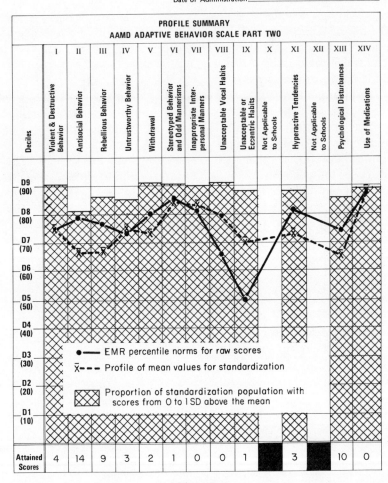

PROFILE SUMMARY
AAMD ADAPTIVE BEHAVIOR SCALE PART TWO

Deciles	I Violent & Destructive Behavior	II Antisocial Behavior	III Rebellious Behavior	IV Untrustworthy Behavior	V Withdrawal	VI Stereotyped Behavior and Odd Mannerisms	VII Inappropriate Inter-personal Manners	VIII Unacceptable Vocal Habits	IX Unacceptable or Eccentric Habits	X Not Applicable to Schools	XI Hyperactive Tendencies	XII Not Applicable to Schools	XIII Psychological Disturbances	XIV Use of Medications

- ●—— EMR percentile norms for raw scores
- X̄--- Profile of mean values for standardization
- ▨ Proportion of standardization population with scores from 0 to 1 SD above the mean

Attained Scores	4	14	9	3	2	1	0	0	1		3		10	0

Fig. 9-4

consideration should be given to continuing him in a regular class assignment with special instruction either within the regular class or in a resource room.

The degree to which a child can succeed in a regular class program can be inferred from information provided by domain score percentiles on Part II of the scale. Figure 9-3 shows EFG's profile with respect to the regular class norms. From this chart one can determine that EFG is in a critical range (outside the shaded area) with respect to Antisocial Behavior, Hyperactive Tendencies, and Psychological Disturbances. One now can predict that his behavior in a regular classroom would be judged by the teacher to be hyperactive and antisocial and that even though he demands lots of teacher attention, when criticized he responds defensively and feels persecuted. EFG's interpersonal problems exceed the average for children in the EMR norms (see Figure 9–4), so that even in a special education class group he would have more than the average degree of difficulties in these areas.

The information from an analysis of adaptive behavior profiles should never be used as a single source of information for determining eligibility for special education assistance. Parents can be interviewed and complete a complementary adaptive behavior rating. Consistencies between perceptions of the child at school and at home, and evidence from other areas in the case study can be sought for confirmation of the adaptive behavior assessment. In the case of EFG, parents, teachers, and psychologist will have to collaborate to determine where the child will learn most efficiently and what combination of regular and special education program will provide the best set of opportunities for improving his level of functioning. Once the pattern of regular and special instructional settings has been determined, the next and most crucial step is the development of an education plan.

DEVELOPING INDIVIDUAL EDUCATIONAL PLANS FROM THE ASSESSMENT OF ADAPTIVE BEHAVIOR

In the previous section it was pointed out that there is no rule that will permit the psychologist to state with assurance that below a particular cutoff point a child conclusively can be considered to have retarded adaptive behavior. Psychologists, however, can specify the probability that a true measure will lie between a range of obtained scores. Since studies have shown that the comprehensive set of items associated with adaptive behavior is not measuring a single unitary trait, use of one overall measure of adaptive behavior is not warranted. The Adaptive Behavior Scale, therefore, provides measures of different types of social functioning rather than a summative score. Integrating the results of the Scale into a diagnostic perspective requires professional judgment in the interpretation of the child's social functioning in the context of his school, home, and cultural environment. As the AAMD Manual on Terminology and Classification in Mental Retardation points out, "neither IQ nor adaptive behavior are sufficient for individual diagnosis or classification purposes." Applied as part of a comprehensive assessment procedure and supplemented with clinical judgment and interdisciplinary and parental collaboration, the use of the Adaptive Behavior Scale will enable the educator to appraise the relative social functioning of the child and to make a determination of the appropriateness of educational placement options.

The author believes that finding the program where the child can learn best is infinitely more important than programming the child through a labeling ritual. Even if we could all agree on what evidence warrants the conclusion that a child who functions as a mildly retarded child is truly mentally retarded, what help have we given the child when all our energies are expended in the labeling effort? And if we discover that a large number of youngsters who are functioning as mildly retarded children do not qualify for the label, how have we helped them by concluding that the label does not apply?

Many who are involved in the assessment, placement, and programming processes for handicapped children are turning attention away from labeling toward planning. If we can be sure that the child's and parents' rights to due process are ensured, that to the best of our knowledge and skills a child demonstrates that he or she is eligible for special education placement, and that we make provision for regular evaluation of the child's status, then our professional objectives should turn toward the educational planning process.

One of the main strengths of the Adaptive Behavior Scale is that it gives an individualized profile which can be used to develop an appropriate educational program for the pupil. The profile of a child's various adaptive behaviors describes his/her status on several domains, such as Independent Functioning, Language Development, and Responsibility. Because educational goals for all handicapped children always include the development of independent functioning and personal and social responsibility, the profile provides the basis from which a program of remediation can be developed. This is a crucial enterprise because children in some public school classes for the mildly retarded may not have been taught or helped to develop beyond their assessed deficiencies. Consequently, in such instances, the degree to which an extensive program of individualized behavioral instruction would alter a child's abilities and expectations for personal and vocational success can never be known. As teachers, parents, and psychologists collaborate to develop educational plans, it is important to keep in mind that educational plans must be individualized, that is, children with similar profiles may require quite different educational programs. Moreover, the nature of a child's adaptive behavior must be considered with respect to expectancies of both the school and environment and prior opportunities to acquire particular aspects of adaptive behavior functioning.

As the teacher and psychologist refer to the child's profile and consider its educational implications, they can view the results as specifying an individualized set of possible educational objectives. The items within each domain specify a set of adaptive behaviors which can be acquired by normal and most retarded children during their developing years. The score received on a domain, when compared with norm group, indicates how well individual children are functioning with respect to age-level peers of similar educational status. When a score on a domain is lower than would be desirable for a particular child, reference to his/her ratings on each of the individual items comprising that domain suggests a set of instructional or learning objectives which can form the basis of an individual educational plan.

Educational Planning Considerations Regarding Part I Domains

The Part I domains are Independent Functioning, Physical Development, Economic Activity, Language Development, Number and Time Concepts, Domestic Activity (which is not included in the Public School Version), Vocational Activity, Self-direction, Responsibility, and Socialization. Several of these domains such as Independent Functioning, Vocational Activity, and Self-direction focus on the acquisition of skills which promote independence, responsibility, or autonomy. To increase competence in these areas, children should be provided with opportunities to be exposed to new experiences that enhance growth and to make choices and decisions consistent with their capabilities. In all cases the activities which are provided should be concrete, well defined, and have clearly specified reinforcement contingencies.

Children can be exposed to activities and information in which they have the opportunity to attempt and to succeed on tasks requiring new levels of competence for performing regular and routine operations well. Continued responsibility for the performance of newly learned behaviors increases independence and feelings of success.

To achieve competence on other activities within the domains of Independent Functioning, Vocational Activity, and Self-direction involves the need to provide children with opportunities to make choices and decisions among several equivalent alternatives consistent with their capabilities. In these instances cause and effect for each alternative should be demonstrated where possible. The choice to be made can be limited initially to presentation of two options, such as, "Would you like to play on the bars outside with the other children?" or "Would you rather stay inside with me and work on your project?" Both should be carefully delineated and have their consequences illustrated. As the child learns to choose and follow through from these experiences, the chances for making more decisions with more complex options and opportunities for responsibility can be increased.

Other domains focus on concepts or activities which require learning specific knowledge or information, like the domains of Number and Time Concepts and Economic Activity. By introducing concepts, activities, and materials related to these domains in a concrete way, the child can learn the concept and experience the process. Actually going to a store and buying something and paying for it is a useful, concrete way of teaching concepts and procedures to children who are unable to deal with abstractions. The experience may have to be repeated many times for children to be able to incorporate it successfully in their behavior repertoire. In many of these types of activities it is important for teachers to consider the value of their own behavior as a model for the children to emulate.

Still other domains such as Language Development and Socialization involve both learning and developmental considerations. In establishing an educational plan for children in these behavioral domains, teachers and psychologists should appraise the child's current level of development, making assessments of his/her cognitive, language, and social development, if necessary, before establishing an appropriate set of educational goals for the child. Then, by offering a wide variety of opportunities for self-expression or social interaction, the teacher can observe evidence of new levels of maturation and can determine when the readiness of the child to make the next step in learning has occurred.

Matching Educational Planning Recommendations on Part I Domains to Available Curricula

The Texas State Learning Resource Center (1976) provided an excellent example of the curriculum materials available to assist the teacher in carrying out educational planning recommendations. It has catalogued instructional packages with the items from Part I domains. With these materials at hand, those collaborating to provide and evaluate instruction for handicapped children can select from the most appropriate resources from those which are identified. The instructional guidelines suggested by the Texas document should encourage others who use the scale to create similar curriculum packages based on local needs and resources.

Educational Planning Considerations Regarding Part II Domains

The behaviors which are assessed on Part II of the Adaptive Behavior Scale are related to social and emotional development and, as noted earlier, the more frequent the behaviors and the higher the child's score, the more likely the child is to be perceived as a problem or as a disturbance and the greater the probability that he/she is experiencing serious emotional distress. When evidence exists to assume a child's adjustment reflects a severely disrupted system and that the child is a threat to his/herself or others, the teacher should review the case with the psychologist and they should consider a referral to an appropriate source for further evaluation and treatment.

Some of the behaviors described within the domains on Part II lend themselves to improvement through a well-structured program of classroom management where improved performance is monitored and consistently rewarded. An educational program such as the one proposed by Hewett (Hewett, 1968; Hewett & Forness, 1974) is an excellent regimen for assisting educationally retarded and emotionally handicapped pupils to function effectively in a classroom setting while providing them with academic learning experiences within their capabilities.

Evaluation of Individual Educational Plans

At the conclusion of the review of the information provided by the Profile Summary Sheet, the teacher, in collaboration with the psychologist, will have developed a set of learning and behavioral objectives for the individual child. These objectives will vary from child to child since they are dependent on individual pupils' development levels, their current level of academic and social functioning, and the appropriateness of the objectives for their particular educational program. A procedure for evaluation of the educational plan should be developed concomitantly with a time schedule for conducting it. Readministration of the Adaptive Behavior Scale may be considered as the most appropriate method for appraising the child's progress. Requesting adaptive behavior ratings from other adults in the school who have contact with the child, getting a third-party assessment, or conducting an interview with both parents of the child provide additional information by which to evaluate the effectiveness of the child's program.

CONCLUSION

We undertook the study of adaptive behavior of normal and handicapped public school children to determine whether a modification of the AAMD Adaptive Behavior Scale could provide a valid and reliable measure of adaptive behavior functioning. The summary of our research presented here provides ample evidence of the usefulness of the scale for obtaining an evaluation of the child's adaptive behavior functioning, and the validity and reliability of its measures. Our belief is that the scale will be an indispensable adjunct to the assessment of intellectual functioning and, as part of a comprehensive case study, the scale can provide invaluable information in developing educational plans to improve the adaptive behavior skills of the child at school and at home.

REFERENCES

Cohen, J. Multiple regression as a general data-analytic system. *Psychological Bulletin*, 1968, *69*, 426–433.

Cole, L. J. *Adaptive behavior of the educable mentally retarded child in the home and school environment*. Unpublished doctoral dissertation, University of California, Berkeley, 1976.

Daly, F. M., & Henderson, R. A. Education of mentally retarded minors in the public schools of California. *Bulletin of the California State Department of Education*, 1959, *28* (8).

Darlington, R. Multiple regression in psychological research and practice. *Psychological Bulletin*, 1968, *69*, 161–182.

Florida State Department of Education. *Guide to adaptive behavior assessment*. Tallahassee: Bureau of Education for Exceptional Students, 1977. (a)

Florida State Department of Education. *Supplement, user's guide AAMD Adaptive Behavior Scale, Public School Version*. Tallahassee: Bureau of Education for Exceptional Students, 1977. (b)

Grossman, H. J. (Ed.). *Manual on terminology and classification in mental retardation* (Special Publication No. 2). Washington, D. C.: American Association on Mental Deficiency, 1973.

Hewett, F. *Emotionally disturbed child in the classroom*. Boston: Allyn & Bacon, 1968.

Hewett, F., & Forness, S. *Education of exceptional learners*. Boston: Allyn & Bacon, 1974.

Horton, L. *The historical development of the concept of adaptive behavior*. Paper presented at the annual meeting of the Kansas Psychiatric Association, Wichita, Kansas, May 1966.

Kagin, E. The literary and philosophic antecedents of the concept of adaptive behavior. *Project News*, 1967, 1–9.

Lambert, N. M. Contributions of school classification, sex, and ethnic status to adaptive behavior assessment. *Journal of School Psychology* (in press).

Lambert, N. M., & Nicoll, R. C. Dimensions of adaptive behavior of retarded and nonretarded public school children. *American Journal of Mental Deficiency*, 1976, *81*, 135–146.

Lambert, N. M., Wilcox, M. R., & Gleason, W. P. *The educationally retarded child*. New York: Grune & Stratton, 1974.

Lambert, N. M., Windmiller, M. B., & Cole, L. J. *AAMD Adaptive Behavior Scale, Public School Version*. Washington, D. C.: American Association on Mental Deficiency, 1975.

Lambert, N. M., Windmiller, M. B., Cole, L. J., & Figueroa, R. A. *Manual for the Public School Version of the Adaptive Behavior Scale*. Washington, D. C.: American Association on Mental Deficiency, 1975. (a)

Lambert, N. M., Windmiller, M. B., Cole, L. J., & Figueroa, R. A. Standardization of a public school version of the AAMD Adaptive Behavior Scale. *Mental Retardation*, 1975, *13*, 3–7. (b)

Nihira, K. Factorial dimensions of adaptive behavior in adult retardates. *American Journal of Mental Deficiency*, 1969, *73*, 868–878. (a)

Nihira, K. Factorial dimensions of adaptive behavior in mentally retarded children and adolescents. *American Journal of Mental Deficiency*, 1969, *74*, 130–141. (b)

Nihira, K., Foster, R., Shellhaas, M., & Leland, H. *AAMD Adaptive Behavior Scale*. Washington, D. C.: American Association on Mental Deficiency, 1969.

Nihira, K., Foster, R., Shellhaas, M., & Leland, H. *AAMD Adaptive Behavior Scale, 1974 Revision*. Washington, D. C.: American Association on Mental Deficiency, 1974.

Nihira, K., & Shellhaas, M. Study of adaptive behavior: Its rationale, method, and implication in rehabilitation programs. *Mental Retardation*, 1970, *8*, 11–16.

Texas State Learning Resource Center. *Instructional media and materials suggested for use to ameliorate deficiencies identified through the AAMD Adaptive Behavior Scales*. Austin, Tx.: Author, 1976.

Windmiller, M. B. An effective use of the Public School Version of the AAMD Adaptive Behavior Scale. *Mental Retardation*, 1977, *15* (3), 42–45.

June F. Lewis,
Jane R. Mercer

10

The System of Multicultural Pluralistic Assessment: SOMPA

The System of Multicultural Pluralistic Assessment (SOMPA)[1] consists of nine sets of measures, each appropriate to one of three assessment models: the medical model, the social-system model, and the pluralistic model. Medical model measures are the Physical Dexterity Tasks, the Bender Visual Motor Gestalt Test (Bender, 1946) the Health History Inventories, and Measures of Vision, Hearing, and Weight/Height. Social-system measures are the Adaptive Behavior Inventory for Children (ABIC) and a measure of School Functioning Level (SFL) as well as the Wechsler Intelligence Scale for Children—Revised (WISC—R) (Wechsler, 1974) or the Wechsler Preschool and Primary Scale of Intelligence (WPPSI) (Wechsler, 1969). The pluralistic model yields the Estimated Learning Potential (ELP) based on pluralistic norms for the WISC—R and WPPSI. Complete instructions for administering, recording, scoring, and profiling each of the SOMPA measures are contained in the *Parent Interview Manual* (Mercer & Lewis 1977a), the *Student Assessment Manual* (Mercer & Lewis, 1977b), and the *SOMPA Profile Folder*. Detailed information on the conceptual background of SOMPA and the statistical analyses of the standardization sample appear in the *SOMPA Technical Manual* (Mercer, 1977).

The SOMPA is conceptualized as a *system* of assessment. Its measures are most effective when used as a system, looking at the child as a multidimensional human being. It is not recommended that the system be

[1] The SOMPA is composed of the Parent Interview Manual and Record Form, the Student Assessment Manual and Record Form, and the SOMPA Profile Folder.

dismembered by using its measures separately. SOMPA is especially valuable in those situations in which the child being assessed is from a racial or ethnic heritage that differs from the majority Anglo-American cultural tradition and/or is of an economically disadvantaged or socially isolated background. Multiple measures operating from varying assumptions are most likely to yield the variety of valuable information so essential in the assessment of such children.

DEVELOPMENT OF THE SOMPA

The development of a system of multicultural pluralistic assessment which would utilize three assessment models simultaneously in the evaluation process has emerged from a series of basic research studies on mental retardation conducted between 1963 and 1965 in Riverside, California (Mercer, 1973). Three major conclusions emerged that were central to the development of the SOMPA.

1. A *two-dimensional definition* of mental retardation should be established.
2. A *3 percent criterion* should be used as the cutoff for defining subnormality.
3. *Pluralistic norms* should be the basis for test comparison standards.

It was concluded from the studies that a two-dimensional definition of mental retardation, incorporating a measure of adaptive behavior *and* intellectual functioning, should be operationalized. The measure of adaptive behavior should cover a broad range of social-role performance in depth, be long enough and sufficiently reliable to be useful in the assessment of individual children, have a sufficiently high ceiling to measure superlative performance, be normed on a representative sample of the general population so that it can be used in noninstitutional and/or public school settings, and faithfully represent the norms of the social system in which the role is imbedded and the expectations of those participating in the system.

In order to standardize clinical practice, the traditional 3 percent criterion should be universally adopted as the cutoff defining subnormality. This criterion is least likely to lead to disproportionate labeling as subnormal of lower socioeconomic and/or ethnic minorities who are likely to fill a normal complement of social roles in their own milieu or as adults. On the other hand, the 3 percent criterion best identifies those who need nurturance and supervision because they are not able to manage their own affairs.

It was concluded that it is feasible, and a method should be devised, to distinguish the socioculturally nonmodal individual from the modal so that a child's performance on a standardized test would be compared only with the performance of other persons from similar sociocultural backgrounds who, presumably, have had similar opportunities to acquire the knowledge and skills needed to respond to the test. In other words, there should be pluralistic norms.

The importance of these three basic conclusions from the Riverside study to the development of SOMPA was matched in importance by a series of historical events occurring between 1965 and 1975. Six interrelated issues surfaced during the decade which relate to defining appropriate procedures for assessing, classifying, and placing children in special education programs in the public schools: (1) the requirement that testing take into account the linguistic and sociocultural origins of the child and be racially and culturally nondiscriminatory; (2) the requirement that a child's adaptive behavior be evaluated in making placement decisions and planning educational interventions; (3) the child's right to "least restrictive treatment," sometimes called "mainstreaming"; (4) the child's right to be tested in his or her primary language when other than English; (5) the issue of the appropriate cutoff level for defining subnormality; (6) the right of a child to the safeguards of due process procedures when decisions concerning placement or other major educational interventions are being made.

The social and intellectual concerns of the decade 1965–1975 provide the nontraditional models and values on which the SOMPA is based. Central to the development of SOMPA is the conclusion that American society is pluralistic, both culturally and structurally. SOMPA views contemporary America as a multicultural society organized around an Anglo core culture. It postulates that there are many racial and ethnic groups, that each group has its own unique relationship to the Anglo core culture, and that each individual occupies a position in American society which can be described by his or her ethclass.[2] The SOMPA assumes that there are ethnic groups that will remain identifiable and culturally distinct from the Anglo core culture for the foreseeable future. Some are being continually augmented by new migrants; some choose to maintain the integrity of their own culture and institutions. The SOMPA presumes

[2] Ethclass is a term coined by Gordon (1964) to refer to "the portion of social space created by the intersection of the ethnic group with the social class" (p. 51). Ethnic groups are seldom socioeconomically homogeneous but are internally differentiated into socioeconomic levels. The subsociety of the ethclass describes relatively precisely the location of an individual in American society. The measures of sociocultural modality which are central to the notion of pluralistic assessment, can be regarded as a set of measures to determine the ethclass of the family of an individual child.

that all languages and cultures are of equivalent value and that linguistic and cultural differences must be taken into account when interpreting individual performance. The SOMPA assumes that the dominant Anglo core culture will continue to be perpetuated through the public schools as a matter of public policy and will continue to dominate the major economic and political institutions of American society. Hence, one of the primary responsibilities of public education is to assist every child to master the language, skills, knowledge, and behavioral styles of the core culture, so that he or she will have an equal opportunity to participate fully in the economic and political life of American society, sharing equally in its benefits and responsibilities. Thus, it becomes necessary for the schools to identify those children who are likely to have problems coping with the common core culture so that they can be given whatever assistance they need in order to participate, if they wish to do so.

ASSESSMENT MODELS OF SOMPA

The SOMPA is based on three assessment models—the medical model, the social-system model, and the pluralistic model. Each has a different definition of normal and abnormal and is based on a different set of assumptions. Thus, each has characteristics that clearly distinguish it from the other models. These characteristics require measures of a particular type, and they place limits on the interpretations of scores from those measures. A potential user of SOMPA needs to understand the assumptions, characteristics, and limitations of each of the models in order to use the system to the best advantage.

The Medical Model

The medical model, which also has been called the pathological model, the deficit model, the disease model, and the clinical model, was developed in medical research to understand and combat disease processes. It has provided a very powerful tool for comprehending and controlling diseases and other organic pathologies.

"Abnormal," in the medical model, is defined as any organic condition that interferes with the physiological functions of the organism. Severe malfunctions may lead to death, but less extreme conditions are identifiable as biological malfunctions which interfere with the most effective functioning of the organism, i.e., visual or auditory impairments, spastic or palsied conditions, and so forth. Pathological conditions are defined by their symptoms, and symptoms are regarded as signs of a biological state. Some symptoms are clearly physiological, but others are primarily behavioral. "Normal," in the medical model, is treated as a residual category consisting of those persons who do not have pathological symptoms. The medical model focuses on describing the symptoms of pathology, i.e., the deficits, and organizes the symptoms into sets which characterize particular diagnostic syndromes.

When the medical model is used to interpret behaviors as evidence of pathology, the assumption is that biological processes are causing the behavior. However, the justification for the use of the medical model when there are no observable organic malfunctions rests on those who use the model to make organic inferences. In such situations the medical model may or may not be appropriate, depending on whether the symptomatic behaviors are, in fact, biologically determined or whether they are the result of learning.

The medical model assumes that the sociocultural background of the person is not relevant to diagnosis, since biological concepts and technology are applicable across cultural boundaries and transcend social systems. Therefore, cross-societal comparisons or prevalence and incidence rates for organic pathologies are appropriate. Sociocultural characteristics are relevant *only* if they have produced biologic effects which are, in turn, producing pathological conditions. For example, if the poor nutrition and poor prenatal care associated with low socioeconomic status are producing biological pathologies in the child that, in turn, are producing the symptomatic behavior, then the medical model is appropriate. When there is no basis for assuming a physiological change in the organism as a result of the effects of the sociocultural environment, then the medical model is not appropriate.

Measures of the medical model differentiate among those who have different levels of pathology. Persons may be ranged along a continuum by the severity of their pathology, determined by the number and gravity of their symptoms. Most of the population will be classified in a large, undifferentiated category of "normals." Typically, measures do not distinguish the above-average and superior from the average. The value consensus that a nonsymptomatic condition is better than having the symptoms of pathology is taken for granted. Persons are studied in terms of their abnormalities and are labeled in terms of their disabilities. Typically, measures count the number of "errors" in performing a task because measures are designed to assess the amount of pathology. The "normals" are those who make few, if any, "errors."

The medical model perceives pathology as existing in the person. A person *is* mentally ill or *is* mentally retarded in much the same sense as we would say a person *is* tubercular or *has* rheumatic fever. The focus for intervention is on "curing"; the burden of change is on the individual; the perferred method of treatment is medical intervention. Etiological questions are automatically raised by the medical model. What has caused the symptoms? Causal chains are traced back to the organism. There is a strong tendency to explore physiological and genetic hypotheses. Social and cultural factors are discounted, unless it can be demonstrated that such factors have produced organic damage which, in turn, has produced the symptoms of pathology. Biological malfunctioning is often posited, even if not clearly demonstrated. Such is the case in many marginal diagnoses—for example, minimal brain dysfunction, learning disorders, and hyperactivity. On the other hand, a pathological condition can exist unrecognized. Individuals may have a pathology even though no one around them is aware of it; hence, when one operates from a medical model, it is appropriate to do epidemiologic studies in which a population is screened for undiagnosed or undetected pathologies.

The statistical distributions of scores of measures based on the medical model tend to have a low ceiling, with the majority of persons rated as nonpathological. Distributions of scores are negatively skewed, with a long negative tail which makes it possible to differentiate levels of pathology. Those who are "normal" tend to be lumped together. For example, if a person achieves 20/20 vision, no attempt is made to differentiate among those with visual acuity above that level, but there is careful measurement of lower levels of acuity. There is a single norm for visual acuity which can be used equally appropriately in the United States, for instance, or in India or South Africa, with no differentiation among superior, above-average, and average performers. Consequently, the SOMPA profiles for plotting scores on measures based on the medical model are truncated. They allow for plotting scores below the fiftieth percentile only, with the exception of a measure of weight by height.

Measures of the medical model focus on deficits. The higher the number of "errors," the more the deficit. For example, the raw score for ambulation, one of the SOMPA Physical Dexterity Tasks, consists of the number of errors the child makes while attempting to walk a line on the floor. Scores on measures correlate with other measures of the biological state of the organism gained from a health history, direct physical examination, or other medical sources. Thus, validity of an instrument is determined by the extent to which it predicts scores on other biologic measures, and scores on measures within the model are directly comparable. On the other hand, because the medical model is not culture bound, scores should not be highly correlated with the sociocultural characteristics of the person being measured. Modest correlations will exist in those cases in which economic and medical deprivation are producing pathologies. However, these correlations will disappear when the intervening variable, the biological status of the organism, is controlled.

There is a pervasive code in medical decison making which holds that it is much worse for a physician to dismiss an ill patient than to retain a well patient (Scheff, 1966). This set of diagnostic values stems from the fundamental assumption of the medical model that pathological signs are produced by biological malfunctions which, if untreated, may endanger life itself. There is little harm in suspecting pathology in a person who later proves to have no pathology. Consequently, a person conducting screening procedures would conform to the diagnostic values of the medical model and use a relatively high cutoff level for defining abnormality. In the SOMPA it is suggested that persóns scoring more than one standard deviation unit below the mean on the medical model measures be referred for an in-depth examination by a medical doctor.

The Social-System Model

The social-system model is derived from the social-deviance perspective of sociology. It has its own definition of normal and carries a set of assumptions with it which differ from those of the medical model. Since its relevance is implicit in most present-day psychological assessment procedures, the user who has been schooled in the tradition of the medical model may experience some difficulty in thinking in terms of the social-system perspective. In SOMPA both models are operationalized and treated as two different ways of perceiving the same child.

The social-system definition of "normal/abnormal" is concerned with the interlocking social systems in which the child is participating and the child's role performance within these social structures. Associated with each social system are sets of social statuses, or social positions. Associated with each status is a role which consists of the behaviors of persons occupying the position. Behavior is quite different if a child is playing the role of student, or first baseman, or son in his family, or leader of the neighborhood gang. Each role is located in a different social system, and persons participating in each system share common expectations as to how others should play their roles. Group expectations differ from one group to another and from one role to another within the group. These shared behavior expectations are the *norms* of the social system. In the social-system model, then, "normal" behavior is role performance that conforms to the expectations of other members of the group. "Abnormal" (deviant) behavior is that which does not meet group expectations. Knowledge of the norms of a group is obtained by asking group members to describe the behaviors of persons filling different roles, and it is essentially the approach used to develop items for the SOMPA Adaptive Behavior Inventory for Children (ABIC). When the ABIC is used in assessment, the mother or principal caretaker serves as informant. Consequently, the responses to ABIC questions represent the viewpoint of an insider who sees the child from the perspective of his or her own family, neighborhood, and sociocultural group.

Information about the norms of a social system is obtained also by observing the operation of the sanctioning mechanisms of the system. Role performance which meets group expectations is rewarded through praise, prizes, or promotions to more esteemed statuses or simply by permitting the person to continue playing the role. On the other hand, negative sanctions, such as scolding, fines, being demoted to a less esteemed status, or being removed from the group entirely are used against those whose role performance does not meet expectations. By observing which behaviors are positively sanctioned and which behaviors are negatively sanctioned, the observer can infer the nature of the basic rules that relate to that particular role. Thus, achievement tests, aptitude tests, intelligence tests, and so forth, developed to evaluate academic role performance in the school are used in SOMPA as social-system measures of the norms governing the academic student role.

Norms of a particular social system result from a political definitional process and are constantly being modified. Groups and organizations continually examine their values, develop new norms, and modify or abandon old norms. Those who have the greatest power in a social system impose their definition of normal on less powerful groups and make their definition binding on those who wish to continue to participate in the system. Therefore, there is no universal value framework within the social-system model. Unlike the medical model in which "health" can be assumed as a universal value, values differ from social system to social system. Values of the school may differ from those of the home or peer group. Social-system measures, therefore, are culture bound, system bound, and role bound. Interpretations or behavior which cross these boundaries are not appropriate when using a social-system model.

The social-system model is both a deficit and an asset model. Members of social systems make the full range of evaluations concerning the behavior of other members. Thus a full range of measurement is possible, and scores form a normal distribution curve and are not truncated as in the medical model. A child's performance can be evaluated against any set of role expectations and be judged subnormal, normal, or supranormal. Deviance is not viewed as a trait of the individual but as a characteristic of behavior. Thus, deviation from system norms does *not* imply pathological or biological deficits *in* the person who deviates. The focus of attention is on learning, motivation, and socialization to a particular set of role behaviors valued by persons in a particular sociocultural milieu. Since behavior cannot be judged as "normal" or "subnormal" unless observed and evaluated by others in the particular system, the notion of undefined, unrecognized, or hidden "deviance" is inconsistent within the social-system model, a contradiction in terms.

Social-system measures may have multiple distributions of scores, with each distribution relating to a particular role. For example, in SOMPA the ABIC has a separate distribution of scores for family roles, peer group roles, community roles, and so on. Since the social-system model identifies supranormal as well as subnormal performance, appropriate measures include questions that identify role competencies and role deficits. Appropriate measures embody the viewpoint and evaluations of persons in the system, and questions are generated by system participants, not outsiders. Hence, the "validity" of a social system measure cannot be determined by the extent to which scores on the measure correlate with judgments of outsiders. Individual scores on measures of role performance in one system cannot be generalized to performance in another system. For example, one cannot assume that a child who is a good pitcher on the baseball team will be a successful student in spelling class or a good trumpet player in the band.

Diagnostic values within a social-system model differ markedly from diagnostic values operating within a medical model. Within a social-system model it is more serious to label or diagnose behavior as deviant than to label behavior as nondeviant. A diagnosis of deviancy may initiate movement on the part of the labeled individual toward a deviant career which may be difficult to reverse. On the other hand, the nonlabeling of behavior as deviant may deprive a child of certain services provided to children occupying deviant statuses. The diagnostician must weigh carefully which course of action will most benefit and least damage the child. Since precipitating a deviant career through labeling behavior as deviant has more negative consequences for the child than does nonlabeling, the SOMPA incorporates lower cutoff levels for defining subnormality within the social-system model than within the medical model, i.e., a score *two* or more deviation units below the mean.

The Pluralistic Model

The pluralistic model differs substantially from the medical and social-system models in its assumptions, characteristics, and interpretations. It is a supplementary rather than a competing model and provides additional insights into the child's performance from a third perspective. The pluralistic model assumes that if learning opportunities and all other social, cultural, and emotional factors are equal, those persons who learn the most and who perform the best probably have greater learning potential than those who learn least and perform most poorly. The major difficulty in applying the logic based on this assumption is that in actual test situations, especially situations which involve children from very different sociocultural backgrounds, all other factors are never equal. The pluralistic model assumes that the WISC—R and similar tests are achievement tests, that they measure learning, that they are culture bound and can be used to make inferences about a child's aptitude only if his or her performance is compared with the performance of others who have come from a similar socio cultural setting and who have had equal opportunity to learn, equal motivation to learn, and equal test-taking experience. The model requires an identification of the appropriate normative framework within which to interpret each child's performance so that he or she is compared only to others who have come from a similar ethnic and cultural background.

In American society identifying an appropriate normative group must go beyond simply categorizing children by ethnic group because ethnic groups within themselves are culturally and socioeconomically heterogeneous. To deal with this heterogeneity, the pluralistic model is operationalized in SOMPA by using multiple-regression equations to determine which sociocultural characteristics of children in the three ethnic groups are most related to performance on the WISC—R, to establish the appropriate weight to be given to each characteristic in predicting performance on the WISC—R, and to determine the average score which would be predicted for a child from precisely the same sociocultural background as the child being evaluated. The score of the child being evaluated can then be compared with this average score to determine whether he or she is above, below, or near the average for his or her sociocultural group. Therefore, in the pluralistic model whether a child is evaluated as normal, subnormal, or supranormal depends on the location of his or her score in the distribution of scores for other children of the same age from similar sociocultural backgrounds.

Implicit in the model is the assumption that the average learning potential, biological intellectual capacity, aptitude, or "intelligence" of persons from various ethnic heritages is essentially the same and that observed differences in the average scores of persons of different ethnic groups on culture-specific tests reflect differences in exposure to the materials in the test, reinforcement for learning the material in the test, and test-taking experience. The pluralistic model does assume that there are differences in learning potential *within* groups when individual children are compared with each other but that seeming differences *between* groups are mainly produced by the cultural specificty of the test.

The model is based on multiple normal distributions of scores, one for each of the possible combinations of the child's sociocultural characteristics as measured on the SOMPA sociocultural scales. It is evaluative in that it assumes high learning potential is more desirable than low learning potential. The pluralistic model is both a deficit and an asset model. It identifies those who have a relatively low Estimated Learning Potential (ELP) and those who have a relatively high Estimated Learning Potential. In actual practice it operates as an asset model, adjusting most scores for non-Anglo children upward. Its primary value lies in its ability to uncover the assets of children from minority groups whose learning potential may not have been recognized because of sociocultural differences between the family and the school. Unlike the medical model, which views sociocultural background as irrelevant in interpreting medical symptoms, the pluralistic model treats sociocultural background as the *central* factor in interpreting measures of learning and achievement as estimates of learning potential. The pluralistic model views learning potential as an attribute of the person and assumes that learning potential can exist unrecognized.

Although SOMPA has developed pluralistic norms for the WISC—R only, there is no reason why pluralistic norms could not be developed for other measures of learned behavior if they would be useful in making inferences about a child's learning potential. Rather than modifying the test, the procedure modifies the normative framework within which scores are interpreted. Test items, test administration, and test scoring schemes remain intact. Because the idea of pluralistic norms based on scores predicted from sociocultural characteristics is a new approach in assessment, the predictive validity of the ELP remains to be tested. The face validity of the measure, on the basis of individual case studies, is encouraging (Mercer, 1977). It seems reasonable to argue that the fundamental test for the predictive validity of the ELP will be determined by following two groups of children who have been matched on SFL (WISC—R score on the standard norms) but who differ significantly on ELP, e.g., by 15 points or more. If ELP is identifying potential which has been masked by cultural differences, we would hypothesize that those children with the higher ELP will, on an average, perform significantly better in their school roles than children having the same SFL but a lower ELP. We are in the process of selecting samples from our standardization populations to test the above hypothesis.

SOMPA MEASURING INSTRUMENTS

The Sociocultural Scales

In the SOMPA the sociocultural scales serve three primary purposes. First, the scales serve as descriptors of the sociocultural setting in which the child is being reared. They measure the extent to which the child's family background differs from the American core culture and indicate the socioeconomic status of the family. Information provided by the items in the scales can assist the school in designing individualized programs for the child in those cases in which the cultural distance between home and school is a significant factor influencing the child's performance. The SOMPA profiles for the scales provide a means by which the child can be compared in relation to other children from his or her same ethnic group and in relation to the core culture of the school. The latter profile provides insight into the extent to which a child may be experiencing cultural shock and possible culture conflict as a consequence of divergence between the culture of the home and that of the school. Second, the sociocultural scales provide information about the family characteristics of the child in the form of scores that are inserted into appropriate multiple-regression equations to secure the child's Estimated Learning Potential (ELP). Thus, the scales are central to the operationalization of the pluralistic model. Third, the scales provide information that can be used to determine the amount of variance in any measure that can be explained by sociocultural factors. This determination is critical in deciding whether a particular measure best meets the assumptions of the medical model or those of the social-system model.

The scales are the end product of a series of data reduction procedures applied to the standardization data which are fully described in the *SOMPA Technical Manual* (Mercer, 1977). Nine factors resulted from the analysis: (1) *marital status,* based on the sex of the head of the household, the marital status of the mother or mother substitute, and whether the child is living with both biological parents; (2) *anglicization,* based on the highest grade completed by the head of the household, the highest grade completed by the mother or mother substitute, where the head was reared, where the mother or mother substitute was reared, and an interviewer rating of English language usage; (3) *occupation of the head of the household,* based on a description of the work or occupation of the head of the household; (4) *family size,* based on the number of full brothers and sisters of the child and the total number of persons living in the household at the time of the interview; (5) *parent–child relationship,* based on the biological relationship between the child and the head of the household and the biological relationship between the child and the respondent; (6) *sense of efficacy,* based on questions which dealt with the respondent's sense of powerlessness; (7) *source of income,* based on whether the head provides most of the family income and a rating of the sources of financial support for the family; (8) *urbanization,* based on the size of the place where the head was reared, the size of the place where the mother or mother substitute was reared, and whether the family moved constantly; (9) *community participation,* based on the respondent's report of frequency of attendance at meetings with groups at school, with church or religious groups, with community groups, and with social groups.

These nine factors were combined into the four sociocultural scales by factor analysis and were assigned the best weight for each of the initial factors when these were combined with the other factors from the factor loadings.

1. *Urban acculturation* consists of anglicization, sense of efficacy, community participation, and urbanization. Anglicization is the most important factor, with a weight of 6.
2. *Socioeconomic status* consists of occupation of the head of the household and source of income, which are equally weighted.
3. *Family structure* consists of marital status and the relationship of the child to the head and to the mother or mother substitute, with marital status having a slightly greater weight.
4. *Family size* consists of a single factor. The raw score for family size is negatively correlated with the raw scores of the other three scales.

Statistical comparisons of raw scores from the standardization sample established that there were significant differences in scores between the three ethnic groups, both on individual items and on the average raw scores for the four scales. From this analysis it was concluded that the sociocultural scales measure sociocultural characteristics which differ sufficiently so that Anglo, black, and Hispanic children *cannot* be treated as a single population with a common life-style and a homogeneous cultural heritage.

Medical Model Measures

There are six measures included in SOMPA which are appropriately interpreted within the medical model. The Physical Dexterity Tasks and the Health History Inventories are measures developed especially for the SOMPA. The Bender Visual Motor Gestalt Test is included as a measure of motor performance. Vision, hearing, and weight standardized by height are included because these three organic characteristics are basic to any decision made about educational programming for a child.

The SOMPA medical model measures are intended as a set of screening procedures which can be administered by trained personnel within the school setting and in a home interview. Scores are standardized so that they can be entered on a profile and interpreted by an evaluator. Children who score more than one standard deviation unit below the mean should be considered "at risk" and referred for a more complete screening and medical examination.

For all six measures the degree of abnormality is defined by the extent to which there are pathological symptoms, and the assumption is made that symptoms are caused by biological conditions in the organism. The definition of abnormality is transcultural, and knowledge about sociocultural background is regarded as irrelevant to diagnosis. Norms for the measures are transcultural. Pathological signs that may have been undiagnosed may be revealed, and all pathological signs are regarded as attributes of the organism. Most children will perform the required tasks with few errors—the higher the number of errors, the poorer the performance. The measures do not differentiate between normal and supranormal performance.

A complete discussion of the standardization procedures and statistical analyses employed in the development of the SOMPA medical model measures is found in the *SOMPA Technical Manual* (Mercer, 1977). The *Student Assessment Manual* (Mercer & Lewis, 1977b) contains directions for administering, recording, and scoring each measure.

THE PHYSICAL DEXTERITY TASKS

A series of standardized tests of the intactness and capability of the motor and sensory pathways that are involved in the performance of each task are provided by the Physical Dexterity Tasks Measure. In combination with other measures they may be used as a procedure for screening for possible biological anomalies. The tasks can be administered by a school nurse or other trained school personnel. They take about 20 minutes. There are six sets of tasks: placement, ambulation, involuntary movement, motor sequencing, equilibrium, and finger–tongue dexterity. Placement consists of finger-to-nose and heel-to-shin exercises; ambulation, tiptoe and heel walking, hopping, and tandem walking; involuntary movement, standing arms extended, standing eyes open or closed on one or both feet; motor sequencing, finger and foot tapping; equilibrium, standing, and counting; finger–tongue dexterity, finger exercises, tongue movement.

Raw scores on the Physical Dexterity Tasks are calculated by counting errors. Performance on the tasks is significantly related to the age of the child: the older the child, the fewer the errors. Since the range of raw scores decreases as age increases, there is significantly less variability in the scores of older children. Scaled scores having a mean of 50 and a standard deviation of 15 were derived for each subtest from the individual z-scores of the standardization sample children. With scaled scores performance on one task can be compared directly with performance on the other tasks. Scaled scores are presented in conversion tables that appear in the *Student Assessment Manual* (Mercer & Lewis, 1977b). A large number of errors receives a low scaled score and a low percentile.

Correlations between the Physical Dexterity Tasks and sociocultural background characteristics are so low that interpreting scores on tasks within the medical model and without reference to sociocultural background is appropriate. Although the Physical Dexterity Tasks are related to each other, the strength of the relationship is, statistically, quite weak, and the tasks appear to identify relatively independent factors in sensorimotor function.

THE BENDER VISUAL MOTOR GESTALT TEST

In the Bender Visual Motor Gestalt Test nine figures are presented to the child, one at a time. The child is given a blank sheet of paper, and as each figure is presented, he or she is asked to copy the figure. Koppitz (1963, 1975) developed an objective scoring system for the Bender which is now generally used by clinicians. The system produces an "overall" score based on an assessment of distortion of shape, rotation, integration, and perseveration in the drawings of the nine figures and was used for the SOMPA standardization sample. The form for recording and scoring the Bender responses which appears in the Student Assessment Record Form is designed for use with the Koppitz system. Like the Physical Dexterity Tasks, raw scores are calculated by counting errors, and performance on the Bender is significantly related to the age of the child: the older the child, the fewer the errors. Since the range of raw scores decreases as age increases, there is significantly less variability in the scores of older children. Therefore, the procedures for producing scaled scores having a mean of 50 and a standard deviation of 15 are the same as those followed in developing scaled scores for the Physical Dexterity Tasks. Similarly, in the conversion tables for the Bender, high raw scores were converted to low scaled scores, making it possible to compare the child's performance on the Bender directly with his or her performance on other measures or with the performance of other children regardless of age.

Although correlations between scores on the Bender and the sociocultural characteristics of the child are positive and statistically significant, the largest correlation explains only 2 percent of the variance in Bender scores. Therefore, Bender scores can be interpreted without reference to the child's sociocultural background and meet the transcultural assumptions of the medical model.

MEASURES OF HEIGHT/WEIGHT, VISION, AND HEARING

Each child's height and weight are measured in SOMPA during the student assessment session. It is suggested that a school nurse test the vision of each child and provide the child's Snellen scores for the SOMPA record form. Although SOMPA does not have standardization data on auditory acuity, the SOMPA profiles provide a place for recording test results, and it is recommended that the hearing of all children be routinely tested as part of any comprehensive assessment.

In SOMPA children are weighed using a physician's scale, with shoes and heavy outer garments removed. The rod attached to the scale is used for measuring height. The *Student Assessment Manual* presents the instructions to be followed in making these measurements. Standardization procedures for the weight/height measures combined the measurements of children 5 through 11 years of age but separated the measurement data on boys from that on girls. Measurement data is grouped into categories by height, using 2-inch intervals beginning at 42–43 inches and continuing through 62–63 inches. In the procedures for producing scaled scores the mean weight category of the standardization sample was calculated and then set at 50, with a standard deviation of 15. The manual contains conversion tables for both sexes from which the scaled score for each height/weight category is obtained. When plotted on the SOMPA profiles, the height/weight scaled score indicates whether the child is overweight or underweight in relation to other children of the same sex and height.

In SOMPA the Snellen Test is used as the measure of visual acuity, with the standard Snellen notation: 20/20, 20/25, 20/30, 20/40, and so on. The Snellen score for better monocular acuity (i.e., the score for the child's best eye) is plotted directly onto the SOMPA profile and indicates whether the child's visual acuity is better than 20/40 or poorer that 20/40.

Sociocultural correlates of weight by height are very small, indicating that these measures fit the assumptions of the medical model. Correlations of weight by height and vision with the Physical Dexterity Tasks and the Bender are small, indicating that the two measures are assessing dimensions not encompassed by either.

THE HEALTH HISTORY INVENTORIES

The purpose of the Health History Inventories is to provide systematic, scorable information on the health history of individual children. It consists of a set of structured, precoded questions which are asked of the mother during the parent interview session. Each question is designed to be individually coded and scored. Responses to the separate items are combined into sets of scales that are standardized for presentation on the SOMPA profiles. The Health History Inventories is a preliminary screening instrument and should not be construed as a medical index. Since it deals with historical data and rests entirely on the report of the mother or mother substitute, there will be problems of recall and other types of error found in retrospective reports. For this reason questions deal mainly with major illnesses, operations, accidents, and medical problems, which are less likely to be forgotten. Questions do not ask for detailed descriptions of medical events and do not include a detailed inquiry into current physical impairments. Most of the items used are adaptions of questions in the series of questionnaires developed by the U.S. Public Health Service for the National Health Surveys and Health Examination Surveys of children 6 through 11 and youths 12 through 17 years of age.[3]

The Prenatal/Postnatal Inventory questions complications during pregnancy, length of pregnancy, birth problems, length of hospitalization, weight of child at birth, and problems of the infant at birth and during the first year of life. The Trauma Inventory concerns high temperatures, accidents resulting in unconsciousness or coma, accidents or injuries, and operations. The Disease and Illness Inventory contains questions on current medication; chronic illnesses such as heart trouble, kidney trouble, diabetes, and cerebral palsy; acute illnesses such as red measles, scarlet fever, rheumatic fever, polio, diphtheria, meningitis, whooping cough, and pneumonia; and seizures. The fourth inventory, Visual Acuity, asks about eye operations and specific problems with the eyes. A fifth inventory deals with Auditory Acuity. It is concerned with ear operations, use of a hearing aid, and ability to locate sounds.

The Health History Inventories is based on the assumption that the greater the number of biological insults suffered by the child and the more severe the episodes, the higher is the probability that the child may suffer from biological dysfunctions that will interfere with his/her academic performance and social-role performance in various social systems. Consequently, the inventories included are weighted, additive measures. For example, an accident or injury is weighted for severity depending on whether a doctor was seen, what the doctor said about the injury, whether the child went to the hospital, how long the child remained in the hospital, and how long it took the child to recover.

There are three types of questions in the inventories: structured, precoded questions; precoded questions with probes; and funnel questions. Structured, precoded questions ask for some specific piece of information or require either a yes or no response. Structured questions with probes require a second question or probe when the respondent answers in the affirmative. The response to the question and the probe are

---

[3] The pre-/postnatal complications questions and the questions concerning serious acute illness were adapted from the U.S. Public Health Series, Publication No. 1000, Series 1, No. 8, *Health Examination Survey of U. S. Youth 12–17 Years of Age*, Appendix 1-B, p. 41; questions on chronic conditions, major operations, and injuries from Public Health Series, Publication No. 1000, Series 10, No. 48, *Prevalence of Selected Impairments*, July 1963–June 1965, Card A, pp. 78 and 67–69, and from Public Health Series, Publication No. 1000, Series 1, No. 8, *Health Examination Survey of U. S. Youth 12–17 Years of Age*, Appendix 1-B, p. 40; and the questions on vision from Public Health Series, Publication No. 1000, No. 46, *Characteristics of Visually Impaired Persons in the United States*, July 1963–June 1964, pp. 4–5 (Washington, D. C., U. S. Government Printing Office).

scored as a single question. Funnel questions consist of a series of interrelated, sequential questions which begin with a general question and then move to more specific questions if those that precede are answered in the affirmative. Responses in the sequence are added together to score for the overall question.

The raw scores on the Health History Inventories conform to the pathological model and are interpreted within the pathological model. As for the Physical Dexterity Tasks and the Bender Gestalt, a high raw scores indicates that the child has experienced a large number of health hazards. The focus is on estimating the possibility of pathology, and the child's scores reflects his/her probable health deficits. "Normal" is a residual category for those who have experienced few medical pathologies. Correlations between raw scores and the sociocultural scales for the children in the standardization sample are very small. The largest correlation accounts for only 1 percent of the variance. Hence, the family background of the child need not be taken into account in interpreting his or her scores. Correlational analyses also indicate that the inventories are relatively independent measures, and a child's score on one inventory cannot be generalized beyond that inventory, although scores on the inventories do relate to one another in a meaningful and statistically reliable manner.

Social-System Measures

There are seven measures included in SOMPA which are appropriately interpreted within the social-system model: the six scales of the Adaptive Behavior Inventory for Children (ABIC) and the Wechsler Intelligence Scale for Children—Revised (WISC—R). The ABIC, using the mother as informant and representative of the family and community social systems, measures the child's role performance in six social systems: the family, the peer group, the community, nonacademic school roles, earner/consumer roles, and self-maintenance roles. The WISC—R in the SOMPA is a measure of academic performance in the public school. Using the published norms for the test, SOMPA interprets the full-scale, verbal, and performance scaled scores as measures of the child's School Functioning Level (SFL).

A complete discussion of the statistical analyses and standardization procedures employed in the development of the ABIC and WISC—R as measures appropriate to the social-system model is available in the *SOMPA Technical Manual* (Mercer, 1977). Complete directions for administering, recording, and scoring the ABIC are contained in the *Parent Interview Manual* (Mercer & Lewis, 1977a).

ADAPTIVE BEHAVIOR INVENTORY FOR CHILDREN
(ABIC)

The ABIC is based on a particular set of concepts and premises concerning the nature of human adaptation. Adaptation or "adaptive fitting" (Cassel, 1976) is a dynamic, continuous process by which the individual modifies behavior to fit the demands of the social system *and* other participants in the system modify their behavior and expectations when confronted with the unique characteristics of each individual. To achieve an adaptive fit within a particular social system, a child must acquire two types of role competencies: (1) the child must develop skill in creating and maintaining interpersonal ties with other members of the system, generating affective attachments which will support his or her continued participation in the system; (2) the child must learn the skills expected of a person in his or her status so that he or she can negotiate entry into a social system and can participate at a level considered appropriate for his or her age and sex in the achievement of group tasks and goals.

Negotiating successful entry to any social system is made easier by the presence of a secure base, the presence of a transition agent and/or system, and anticipatory socialization. Cassel (1976) uses the term *secure base* to describe a condition in which the child has developed an attachment relationship in an ongoing system, usually the family, which provides support for the child to explore new social situations and assures the child that the new environment is both physically and psychologically safe. Having a secure base also supports the child in acquiring new social statuses and roles; its lack is likely to inhibit the child from even negotiating entry. A *transition agent,* a person who already has an established status in the system, introduces the child to other participants, legitimates his or her presence, and supports his or her initial efforts to function in the system. *Anticipatory socialization* occurs when a child has the opportunity to practice a new role in a familiar setting, to acquire some of the technical skills needed to perform the role successfully, and to develop interpersonal ties with persons similar to those who will participate in the new group. Experience in a transitional system, such as preschool, Head Start, or kindergarten, also allows the child an opportunity to practice new role behaviors.

Ideally, a child should be assisted through major transitions by transition agents who can provide a secure emotional base for the new experience as well as anticipatory socialization. Whenever possible, transition systems should provide gradual movement into the new status and role. Analysis of critical transitions will provide valuable information in understanding the child's current functioning as well as provide useful avenues for intervention when the child is experiencing difficulties in negotiating an adaptive fit in a particular social system.

The optimal way to measure adaptive behavior would be to develop a longitudinal chart, an adaptive "trajectory," of the child's movement through the social systems which make up his or her social experience. The analysis would encompass the nature of the statuses, roles, and normative structures of each social system; problem encountered in negotiating entry to each system and maintaining adaptive fit; the presence or absence of a secure base, a transition agent, anticipatory socialization, and so on. The ABIC is not designed for such an in-depth analysis but focuses, instead, on securing a cross-sectional view of the child's adaptive behavior in a variety of social systems at a single point in time. Although a cross-sectional view provides relatively little information on the trajectory which produced the current adaptation, it does make it possible to assess the child's current functioning and work backward to try to establish the nature of his or her adaptation behind the present profile. To develop a profile of a child's adaptive fitting, SOMPA establishes a baseline for purposes of measuring individual variation with standardization data from responses given by the parents of the 2100 children in the standardization sample.

The ABIC serves three primary functions in a system of pluralistic assessment. (1) It provides a multidimensional view of the child's performance in several social systems other than the school. (2) It provides systematic information about the child from the perspective of the family and its norms, measuring the child's performance in relation to the normative expectations for the statuses he or she occupies and the roles which he or she plays in the family, community, peer group, nonacademic school roles, and economic and self-maintenance roles. (3) It operationalizes the two-dimensional definition of mental retardation advanced by the American Association on Mental Deficiency, which calls for a measure of adaptive behavior as well as "general intellectual functioning" (Grossman, 1973).

Questions in the ABIC for younger children are concerned mainly with roles in the family, the immediate neighborhood, and peer group. As the child moves into the social system of the school, there are questions about performance in nonacademic school roles and interaction with peers at school. Questions for older children are concerned with performance of the child as he or she assumes more community roles, learns to function in earner and consumer roles, and assumes greater responsibility for protection of his or her own health and welfare. This developmental sequencing is reflected in placement and content of the ABIC items.

The questions which make up the ABIC as presented in SOMPA

came from a pool of items derived from three major sources: adaptations of questions developed for the Riverside epidemiology (Mercer, 1973); questions based on information secured from interviews of mothers of 230 children who had been labeled as mentally retarded by the public school; and, the most important source, questions based on information from a series of in-depth interviews with Anglo, black, and Hispanic mothers of differing social class levels with children, 5 through 11, attending regular public school classes. In so far as possible, items were developed which would apply equally to both sexes, to all socioeconomic levels, and to all ethnic groups. These interviews took approximately three months and resulted in a pool of 480 questions. All of these items were then organized into a series of questionnaires that were presented to black, Hispanic, and Anglo parents during a six-month pretest. Over the period of the pretest, 1259 questionnaires were completed by 214 black, 230 Hispanic, and 815 Anglo mothers and fathers.

Analysis of the pretest items provided the information needed to develop the standardization version of the ABIC. Questions which parents found redundant were eliminated or consolidated; ambiguous questions were reworded; questions inapplicable for many students were dropped. The remaining questions were reworked so that they conformed to a format in which response choices were organized into three basic categories: latent, emergent, and mastered. In general, the latent response indicates that the child has never demonstrated a particular role competency; the emergent response indicates that the child performs the role occasionally and/or under the supervision or direction of an adult; the mastered response indicates that the child regularly demonstrates competency in the role without supervision or adult assistance. Information from the pretest also provided a firmer basis for determining the appropriate age placement for each item. A subset of items proved to be appropriate for children of all the age levels. These were clustered into a nonage-graded section for the standardization questionnaire. All other items were placed in approximate chronological order from simplest to most difficut, based on the average age of the children for whom the role was emergent. Finally, a Spanish translation was prepared, and the standardization version of ABIC was administered to the 2100 mothers of the children in the standardization sample.

Extensive analysis of the standardization version of the ABIC produced 242 items, 35 nonage-graded, 207 age-graded, organized into six scales. Questions in each scale reflect the adaptation process within the social system: providing a secure base for exploration of new systems, transition agents for support, and a setting in which the child may experiment with materials and tools and master complex skills. The ABIC scales cover the following types of role performance:

1. *Family role performance:* Behavior in which the child plays the role of son or daughter, brother or sister. In addition to items relating to the child's interpersonal skills, such as the responsibilities which the child has around the house, the following were included: the child's activities in preparing food for himself or herself and for other family members; the child's activities in playing with, helping, and teaching younger siblings; the child's participation in repairing and caring for family possessions and the family dwelling.

2. *Community role performance:* The roles of neighbor, citizen, and participator in community groups. Role skills include the child's ability to move about the community independently in visiting friends, neighbors, and relatives; the child's knowledge of the families, pets, and neighborhood personalities; the child's participation in social, political, religious, and recreational activities; the child's use of community facilities. Interpersonal items describe the manner in which the child relates to adults and authority figures in the community.
   community.

3. *Peer group role performance:* Behavior and interaction with other children of approximately the same age who are not family members. Behaviors include the kinds of games and activities in which the child participates with his/her peers, the nature of their social group, and the extent to which the child meets and plays with a group of friends. There are questions about the interpersonal ties the child has established with peers, the extent to which they include him or her in their activities, the manner in which the child handles disputes with peers, and the extent to which the child initiates interaction and assumes the leadership role in peer groups.

4. *Nonacademic school role performance:* Behavior of the child in relation to teachers and peers at school and interaction with classmates. Nonacademic aspects of the school role are included, such as holding class offices; serving as monitor or other type of helper in the classroom, office, or cafeteria; behavior on the playground; participation in social affairs and athletic activities at school; and participating in school competitions and projects.

5. *Earner/consumer role performance:* The child's economic behavior. Specifically, the questions ask about the child's understanding of money, knowledge of monetary values, shopping skills, and activities in which money is earned. Questions cover behavior in carrying, handling, borrowing, and spending money; knowledge of brand names and values of products; ability to accumulate money for desired purchases; and uses made of money in paying expenses.

6. *Self-maintenance role performance:* A range of behaviors that facilitate adaptation in most social systems. Questions ask about the

child's knowledge and skill in caring for his or her physical needs, health, body, and safety and ability to cope with unfamiliar social situations and to maintain control under stress or distraction. Specific questions deal with skills in making needs known; ability to dress and to fix food; skills, in recognizing dangerous situations; ability to cross busy streets, schedule time, and manage appointments.

In order to have some method for making an internal check on the probable veracity of the responses given by each respondent and estimating the extent to which a total score might have been inflated by a respondent routinely selecting the mastered response for each query, a *veracity scale measure* is included in the ABIC items. Twenty-four questions designed for children 11 years of age, having the highest difficulty level and not needed to maintain the ceiling, make up the veracity scale. These items are interspersed at frequent intervals among the other ABIC questions in the final version of the measure.

Raw scores are obtained for the child on each of the six subtests of the ABIC. The percentage of the variance in adaptive behavior scores of children in the standardization sample explained by scores on the sociocultural scales is substantively quite small. Consequently, the child's raw score is converted to a scaled score and plotted on the SOMPA profiles without reference to the child's sociocultural background. Conversion tables appear in the appendix of the *Parent Interview Manual*. The mean for each age group on each subtest is set at 50, the standard deviation at 15. Thus, it is possible to compare the performance of a child directly with a child of his or her own age and to plot profiles for the individual child so that scores on the various subtests can be compared with each other. Analysis of the scaled scores of the standardization sample indicate that the social roles played by 5-through-11-year-old children of different ages and ethnic backgrounds appear to be quite similar when viewed as a scaled score. However, there are internal differences among items of the subtests, so it is important for the assessor to look at responses to individual items as well.

THE WECHSLER INTELLIGENCE SCALE FOR CHILDREN—REVISED (WISC—R)

There are those who argue that all standardized tests should be abandoned, especially those which purport to measure "intelligence." A standardized test is included as part of the SOMPA for several reasons. A method is needed to identify children who have a high probability of failing in the public schools so that educational programs can be developed to help them acquire the interpersonal and technical skills needed to survive in the role of student. When used for the purpose of educating children (not for the purpose of labeling and placing them), the individually administered standardized test is the most reliable approach that is currently available for this purpose. Second, a standardized test is included in the SOMPA to circumvent, as much as possible, the use of more questionable methods in the assessment of children. Educational decisions will be made with or without tests. If the carefully administered individual test is eliminated, educators are likely to turn to ad hoc techniques for making decisions. Since ad hoc instruments are not standardized, it is impossible to take cultural loading into account when interpreting scores of individual children. Third, scores from a standardized test provide the basis for developing pluralistic norms, as in the SOMPA, to identify children who have learning potential that is not apparent when their performance is evaluated against the standard norms for the test.

The WISC—R was selected for use in the SOMPA rather than some other standardized instrument because it is an individually administered measure which avoids problems of group testing, such as misunderstanding directions, inability to read the questions, and poor motivation. It can be administered successfully to young children. The WPPSI is applicable to 5 year olds and younger, the WISC—R to those 6 years and over. The norm for the WISC—R, published in 1974, is more recent than the norm for any other individually administered test. Finally, the test itself is more widely used by school psychologists and educational diagnosticians than any other individually administered measure. For these reasons the SOMPA includes the WISC—R among its assessment instruments and treats it as a social-system measure. Scores on the WISC—R are referred to as measures of School Functioning Level (SFL). The rationale for including the test rests on the argument that it meets the assumptions of the social-system model and has all the characteristics of measures appropriate for the model that were discussed earlier.

Analyses of the data from the standardization sample do establish that the statistical distributions of the WISC—R have all of the characteristics of the social-system model. Scores form a normal distribution and have a high ceiling so that low, average, and superior performers can be distinguished. Correlations of WISC—R scores with the sociocultural scale scores were statistically significant. With a large percentage of variance in WISC—R scores accounted for by sociocultural factors, the WISC—R is clearly a social-system measure.

Pluralistic Model Measures

ESTIMATED LEARNING POTENTIAL (ELP)

The SOMPA system of pluralistic norms for the WISC—R should *not* be used to arrive at a child's Estimated Learning Potential (ELP) until the examiner is certain that the child is not emotionally disturbed, has no physical disabilities which might interfere with learning, and is being compared with other children from the same sociocultural group. Information from the Physical Dexterity Tasks, Health History Inventories, and ABIC will assist in identifying children who may have physical disabilities and/or may be emotionally disturbed. The pluralistic norms are focused on the *other* three assumptions of the inferential model for estimating learning potential: similar opportunity to learn the materials in the test, similar motivation to learn the material, and similar experience in taking tests. These characteristics are directly related to the child's sociocultural background. Pluralistic norms assume that children from similar sociocultural backgrounds are roughly similar on these experiential dimensions.

A full discussion of the standardization procedures and statistical analyses relevant to ELP is contained in the *SOMPA Technical Manual* (Mercer, 1977). Directions for calculating ELP are contained in the *Student Assessment Manual* (Mercer & Lewis, 1977b).

Nine multiple-regression equations for predicting WISC—R scores from the four sociocultural scales were developed from the standardization data, three for each ethnic group. One equation predicts full-scale score, another predicts the verbal score, and the third predicts the performance score. The estimated score produced by each equation is the mean score predicted for persons having a particular combination of sociocultural characteristics, in other words, the norm for that group. Because each configuration of sociocultural scores has a different predicted mean and the standard errors vary slightly from one equation to another, a worksheet for calculating ELP is included in the Student Record Form. Conversion tables of scaled scores having a mean of 100 and a standard deviation of 15 were developed from data from the standardization sample and are included in the *Student Assessment Manual*.

SOMPA recommends that a young child should not be tested with the WISC—R if the predicted mean on the verbal score is below 75 for his or her sociocultural group. The SOMPA system of pluralistic norms cannot adequately adjust for the mismatch between the culture of the school and the culture of the child's family when the child is completely nonanglicized. For this reason the conversion tables for Estimated Learning Potential do not provide a score value for children whose predicted verbal scores are below 75.

SOMPA regards any child who comes from a sociocultural background for which the predicted mean score on the WISC—R is 100 or higher to be a child who fits the assumptions of the standard norms for the test. For these children the standard score is regarded as a measure of School Functioning Level and as a gauge of Estimated Learning Potential. Because ELP is calculated by using regression equations based on the responses of children in three California public school samples

(California State Department of Education, 1967), persons who use these equations to derive predicted WISC—R scores for other children and then calculate an estimate of the children's learning potential based on those predictions will be assuming that the children they are assessing can be regarded as members of the population from which the sample was selected. Specifically, they are assuming that a Spanish-surname child in Texas or in Colorado comes from the same population as the Spanish-surname child in California, that the black child in Tennessee or New York comes from the same population as the black child in California, that the English-speaking Caucasian child in Iowa or Pennsylvania comes from the same population as the Anglo sample in California. Given the large migration of Anglo, black, and Spanish-surname families to California from all over the United States and Latin America in the past quarter century, the California public school population is possibly more representative of all sections of the United States than the public school population of any other single state. It is important, however, for the user to be acutely aware that the SOMPA samples are from a single state and that the user is assuming that the child being tested is adequately represented in the California sample by children from similar backgrounds.

A related issue concerns the stability of the WISC—R predictions when the SOMPA equations are used on various student populations. Will the WISC—R scores predicted from a given set of sociocultural characteristics vary greatly from one sample to another? If the study had been done in another state or region, how similar would the predictions be to those found in California? Beta weights and constant terms in multiple-regression equations can change dramatically from one sample to another. Internal shifts in beta weights and constant terms, per se, are not, however, the critical concern for the user. The important concern is whether the predicted scores for a particular set of sociocultural characteristics are similar from one sample equation to another.

Further research will be needed on randomly selected samples of other student populations in other states and regions to determine, empirically, how stable the predictions are from a given set of sociocultural scale scores. To date, data are limited to that from the SOMPA sample.

CONCLUSION

Statistical analysis of the standardization data shows conclusively that the SOMPA measures do form an interrelated system of assessment. Relationships tend to be statistically significant and are in the appropriate directions. The child's physical dexterity is related to sensorimotor functioning, to the child's health history, to adaptive behavior, and to scholastic functioning level.

The sociocultural scales make a significant unique contribution to the variance in WISC—R scores over and above the variance which can be explained by the medical model measures and the ABIC. Medical model measures explain 15.2 percent of the variance in verbal score for the total sample. The percentage increases to 17.2 percent of the variance when the ABIC total score is added to the equation and then jumps to 36.2 percent of the variance when the sociocultural scales are added. Thus, sociocultural factors uniquely account for 18.8 percent of the variance in Scholastic Functioning Level. The unique contributions of the sociocultural scales to performance score is 6.0 percent and to full-scale score 14.1 percent. It is clear that cultural factors have the greatest effect on verbal scores. We interpret this finding to mean that sociocultural factors make a sizable independent contribution to WISC—R scores, a contribution not correlated with the SOMPA medical model measures or the ABIC.

Although statistically significant, all of the intercorrelations among the SOMPA measures are relatively low, indicating that there is still a sizable residual variance in each of the measures which is not accounted for by other instruments in the system. In short, there is minimal redundancy in the system. Each measure contributes some information not provided by other measures in the system.

To interpret the SOMPA profile for the individual child, the psychologist triangulates the assessment process by looking at the child's performance from the perspective of each of the conceptual models. A wide variety of patterns of scores is possible and can be utilized to gain an assessment of the child that is not racially or culturally discriminatory.

The SOMPA functions primarily as an assessment tool for making administrative decisions about the child's educational placement, decisions about the allocation of resources, and assignment to programs. This function has been called the "psychometric" function by Carver (1974). He differentiates it from the "edumetric" function. The latter is concerned primarily with measures that can be used in the teaching-learning process to chart progress toward prespecified educational goals.

The SOMPA is most useful in laying the broad diagnostic foundation on which specific interventions can be built. It is most enlightening in those situations in which there are large sociocultural differences between the family background of the child and the culture of the school.

REFERENCES

Bender, L. *Bender Visual Motor Gestalt Test: Cards and manual of instructions.* New York: The American Orthopsychiatrist Association, 1946.

California State Department of Education. *Racial and ethnic survey of California public schools: Distribution of pupils, fall 1966.* Sacramento: Author, 1967.

Carver, R. Two dimensions of tests: Psychometric and edumetric. *American Psychologist,* 1974, *29,* 512–518.

Cassel, T. Z. A social-ecological model of adaptive functioning: A contextual developmental perspective. In N. A. Carlson (Ed.), *Final report: The contexts of life: A socio-ecological model of adaptive behavior and functioning.* East Lansing: Institute for Family and Child Study, Michigan State University, 1976.

Gordon, M. M. *Assimilation in American life: The role of race, religion, and national origins.* New York: Oxford University Press, 1964.

Grossman, H. J. (Ed.). *Manual on terminology and classification in mental retardation* (Special Publication, No. 2). Washington, D. C.: American Association on Mental Deficiency, 1973.

Koppitz, E. M. *The Bender Gestalt Test for Young Children.* New York: Grune & Stratton, 1963.

Koppitz, E. M. *The Bender Gestalt Test for Young Children, volume 2: Research and application, 1963–1973.* New York: Grune & Stratton, 1975.

Mercer, J. R. *Labeling the mentally retarded: Clinical and social system perspectives on mental retardation.* Berkeley: University of California Press, 1973.

Mercer, J. R. *Identifying the gifted Chicano child.* Paper presented at the First Symposium on Chicano Psychology, University of California, Irvine, May 1976.

Mercer, J. R. *System of Multicultural Pluralistic Assessment: Technical manual.* New York: The Psychological Corporation, 1977.

Mercer, J. R., & Lewis, J. R. *System of Multicultural Pluralistic Assessment. Parent interview manual.* New York: The Psychological Corporation, 1977. (a)

Mercer, J. R. & Lewis, J. F. *System of Multicultural Pluralistic Assessment: Student assessment manual.* New York: The Psychological Corporation, 1977. (b)

Scheff, T. J. *Being mentally ill: A sociological theory.* Chicago: Aldine, 1966.

Wechsler, D. *Wechsler Preschool and Primary Scale of Intelligence (WPPSI).* New York: The Psychological Corporation, 1969.

Wechsler, D. *Wechsler Intelligence Scale for Children–Revised (WISC—R)* New York: The Psychological Corporation, 1974.

PART IV

Research Considerations in the Study of Adaptive Behavior

The current status of the concept and measurement of adaptive behavior as presented in this technical report has provoked many questions. In Chapter 11 many questions are posed regarding the future development of adaptive behavior and its measurement. These questions form a number of directions for future research.

Integral to any future discussions about the concept and measurement of adaptive behavior is the knowledge accumulated to date. Chapter 12 is a concerted effort to list as many references as possible. No doubt some have been overlooked; nonetheless, this chapter will assist the reader in surveying the store of present knowledge. To further aid the reader, each reference cited is briefly detailed and critiqued.

W. Alan Coulter
Henry W. Morrow

11
The Future of Adaptive Behavior: Issues Surrounding the Refinement of the Concept and Its Measurement

The historical roots of the concept of adaptive behavior, given the general definition (Grossman, 1973), can be traced to Aristotle. The first formal measure is generally credited to Felix Voisin, a French psychiatrist, in 1843. Adaptive behavior is not new, but because the concept has been so generally defined and broadly used, only recently have social scientists learned enough to ask the right (critical) questions. Before such questions can be posed, it is important to consider the context or environment in which they are being presented. Mannheim (1936), a theorist in the sociology of knowledge, proposed that all knowledge is accumulated through a social process and therefore is only fully understood within a specific, concrete sociohistorical environment. In Chapter 1 a context was presented for the development of two adaptive behavior scales which originated from the same definition but resulted in different intents or purposes and therefore different products. The particular environment in which each adaptive behavior scale was developed is integral to understand how it could best be used and to determine which questions about adaptive behavior are to be asked. These questions will require the careful deliberation of many professionals before the concept is better clarified and the confusion resolved.

Questions posed in this chapter are derived from a conception of psychological assessment which has two purposes or functions: identification/placement and/or intervention/programming (Chapter 1). The current social and political environment no doubt influences both these conceptions of psychological assessment and the particular attention directed toward adaptive behavior. Baumeister and Muma (1975) realized the environmental context of their own discussions regarding the definition of mental retardation when they stated, "The present decade seems to be characterized more by heightened responsiveness to political, legal, and ethical implications that derive from our conceptions of deviancy" (p. 294).

The political-social context of the discussion in this chapter is best reflected in a recent statement by the President's Committee on Mental Retardation (1976):

> Application of present knowledge makes it possible to improve the level of functioning and reduce the dependency of *every* retarded person regardless of the degree of disability. Increased knowledge of learning and of *adaptive development*, together with the discovery and application of new supportive technologies will vastly increase the independence and social adequacy of people with limited intellectual and *adaptive capacity* (p. 8).

This statement can be interpreted to mean that the onus clearly lies with the profession either to produce the results mentioned above or to produce an explanation for not meeting the needs of the mentally retarded. It is within this political-social context that the questions concerning adaptive behavior have been posed.

After evaluating the material presented in this volume, it is clear that the term "adaptive behavior" actually encompasses more than one concept. As noted in Chapter 1, different authors speak of adaptive behavior and use the same general definition, but the products of their efforts (the measures produced) vary widely. The generally accepted definition (Grossman, 1973) of adaptive behavior is, in part, responsible for the often confusing differences in authors' points of view and measures. In a recent critique of this definition, Baumeister and Muma (1975) comment, "It is so general as to miss the major point of what human adaptation is all about" (p. 304). The definition, however, is a product of complex influences and professional discussions and is not likely to change significantly in the near future. As these authors admit, "Challenges to definitions are, in effect, attacks upon the institutions and value systems that promulgate and sustain the definitions" (p. 305). Additionally, the definition is not solely responsible for the confusion. As contended in Chapter 1, not knowing the function or purpose for measuring adaptive behavior may be the greatest cause for the confusion surrounding its measurement.

ADAPTIVE BEHAVIOR AND IDENTIFICATION/PLACEMENT: IS ADAPTIVE BEHAVIOR ENOUGH?

When the function of psychological assessment is directed toward the identification of a handicap (e.g., educable mentally retarded, learning disabled), the focus of adaptive behavior is to differentiate individuals in an almost strictly statistical sense. For example, the use of standard deviations in the interpretations of adaptive behavior scores to discriminate between slow learning students and those eligible as educable mentally retarded has been advocted (Texas Education Agency, 1977). It is this function of adaptive behavior (both concept and measurement) that will receive the most comment from professionals in the near future.

The concept of adaptive behavior, when used in the identification of handicaps and the determination of eligibility for special services, raises several questions. First, the inclusion of adaptive behavior as a second dimension in the definition of mental retardation was advocated as a method to reduce the bias toward minority groups incorporated in most traditional measures of intelligence (Mercer, 1973; Tucker, 1976). Is the inclusion of adaptive behavior sufficient to eliminate this bias? Little or no evidence exists to fully answer this question, but it raises at least two issues. If bias is defined as disproportionate placement of minority groups in special education, then the effects of the inclusion of adaptive behavior in the definition of mental retardation should be easy to estimate.[1] Where disproportionate populations existed in special education before the two-dimensional definition, those proportions should change to represent a similar ratio to that existing in regular education classes of the same school district. Some preliminary evidence and informal reports (Mastenbrook, 1977; Mercer, 1972, 1977b) indicate that adaptive behavior may be functioning as a sufficient gatekeeper to prevent disproportionate placements. This, however, is an issue that will require thorough examination of the results of special education placements in future years.

Conversely, if bias is defined as the unfair and inaccurate estimate of a student's learning potential because of unequal opportunity to be exposed to the material covered by the test, then including the measurement of adaptive behavior will be found insufficient to estimate learning potential. The addition of another type of measure cannot correct the bias in an existing measure. Adaptive behavior may, however, facilitate multidimensional assessment now required in federal legislation (Public Law 94-142) because it is an important out-of-school measure. The issue of a least-biased measure of learning capacity or potential is only beginning to produce salient discussion (see Chapter 10).

A related issue that must be thoroughly examined concerns the pseudoretarded. The pseudoretarded are those individuals who score significantly low on a measure of intelligence and average on a measure of adaptive behavior (Mercer, 1972). They are not eligible for special educa-

---

[1] An important assumption in requiring equal proportions of minority groups in special education when compared to regular education is that incidence of handicapping conditions is also proportionally distributed. This is largely untested, but none the less an important pluralistic value to advocates of this principal (Mercer, 1977a).

tion services under new federal legislation (Public Law 94-142), which requires a two-dimensional definition; this poses a critical question for pupil appraisal practitioners and other concerned individuals and agencies. What will happen, educationally, to those individuals who are excluded from special education because of the inclusion of adaptive behavior? This is the most often asked question by pupil appraisal practitioners, who see special education as the only potentially available intervention resource for many failing students. The debate surrounding this question has only begun.

A third issue revolves around the measurement of adaptive behavior and its relationship to intelligence. Can adaptive behavior replace intelligence as the single most important measure used in psychological assessment for identification/placement? Certainly the relative infancy in the conceptual development of adaptive behavior argues against imminent change. However, three factors may have an important impact on the future answer to this question. First, there is widespread dissatisfaction with the concept of learning potential as expressed by the IQ score (e.g., Dworkin & Block, 1976; Jackson, 1975; Kamin, 1974; Williams, 1975) that appears stalled without a reasonable alternative. Adaptive behavior has been suggested by some to be the more reasonable alternative (Leland, 1973). Some would argue, and quite persuasively, that adaptive behavior and intelligence/learning potential are compatible, exclusive, and mutually useful in multidimensional assessment (Mercer, 1977b; Tucker, 1976). Second, the learning potential concept's utility in psychological assessment is receiving criticism (Kamin, 1974; Ross, 1974) and may not stand the test of empirical investigation. If learning potential passes from fashion as a useful concept, the intelligence test may no longer offer sufficient information to justify its usefulness. Third, strong aversion to labeling as a basis for providing services (which requires an almost statistical approach[2]) may eventually lead to a different service delivery method requiring precise measurement of academic achievement skills needed as the primary basis for eligibility.

The concept of adaptive behavior when used in psychological assessment for identification/placement presents specific definitional problems. What is the difference between adaptive behavior and intelligence in early years (0 to 5 years)? Considerable overlap and some congruence is apparent when examing the skills exhibited by infants and young children and the definitions of intelligence and adaptive behavior (Bower, 1974; Meier, 1976; Sattler, 1974). If there is, in fact, little or no difference

---

[2] An excellent example of the statistical requirement is recent federal legislation (Public Law 94-142) which places a ceiling of 12 percent of the regular school population as eligible for federal funds for special education.

between the two concepts (intelligence and adaptive behavior) at these early ages, then what can be said about the measurement of both as well as the justification for a two-dimensional definition of mental retardation? Early identification of handicaps is repeatedly stressed (Meier, 1976), but if the critical variables are vague, how can the appraisal practitioner identify children early? Indeed, many would consider autism an extreme case of maladaptive behavior which should be detectable early (Hamblin, Buckholt, Ferritor, Kozloff, & Blackwell, 1971; Rimland, 1974; Ross, 1974). Also, given little or no difference, what can be said about the two concepts (intelligence and adaptive behavior) at later ages? With the present development of the concept of adaptive behavior, it appears as though adaptive behavior emerges as a separate psychological entity at approximately 5 years and disappears in adolescence. However, this may not be an accurate representation of the concept. More examination is needed to explicate what adaptive behavior means at different ages (Nihira, 1976).

Another definitional question can be posed regarding the severity of a handicap. Clausen (1972) points out that some authors are discussing adaptive behavior only for those individuals who exhibit mild to moderate intellectual deficits. To be sure, in the assessment for identification/placement the primary use of adaptive behavior is to ensure least-biased placement of minority groups who were being labeled as educable mentally retarded (Mercer, 1973). However, adaptive behavior for the severely handicapped may in fact imply radically different components. Of course, some of the confusion can be readily understood when the reader realizes that few authors explain the specific purpose or function of the concept in psychological assessment. Indeed, one major point of Chapter 1 that has been repeatedly emphasized is that the present confusion regarding adaptive behavior could, in part, be explained by a functional conception of psychological assessment (i.e., identification/placement versus intervention/programming). Most of the concern in the concept and measurement of adaptive behavior relevant to the severely handicapped individual is oriented to the intervention/programming dimension of psychological assessment. The danger of mislabeling is not a serious issue because evidence of organicity, etc., usually exists to corroborate the identification of the handicap.

Given the importance of adaptive behavior in the identification of mental retardation, is the concept and its measurement also important in the identification of other handicaps? Initially it would appear useful to include adaptive behavior in the identification of emotional disturbance, especially including out-of-school behaviors. Hence, an individual should be emotionally disturbed at home as well as at school to satisfy eligibility requirements (thus reducing the risk of unfair stigmatization). Adaptive behavior could assist in this type of multidimensional assessment. What about other handicaps such as learning disability? Probably it could not be used for the identification of learning disability but possibly in intervention/programming to provide out-of-school survival skills where needed.

Several specific issues regarding the *measurement* of adaptive behavior for identification/placement need to be considered. First, because this measurement is usually dependent upon norms specific to particular groups, not all the relevant groups have been included in norms of available measures. Do other minority groups present a case for specific norms? To date no significant difference has been found between Anglo, Hispanic, and black groups on measures of adaptive behavior (Chapters 9, and 10). There is an indication that low socioeconomic Hispanics in southern Texas are significantly different from other groups on a measure of adaptive behavior (Mastenbrook, 1977). The answer to the above issue will require further research, including a large number of studies dealing with various ethnic groups across the United States.

Second, how is adaptive behavior measured from ages 13 to 21? The requirement of an adaptive behavior measure in the identification of mental retardation (Public Law 94–142) has produced a problem for appraisal practitioners. Measures with adequate norms are only available for ages 5 through 12 (see Chapter 8). What is the appraisal practitioner to do until measures for this age range are developed? Is there any reasonably objective method beyond the perfunctory recommendation of using professional judgment?

Third, some disagreement presently exists as to who is the most appropriate source of information for the measurement of adaptive behavior, parents or parent surrogates versus teachers (Chapters 9 and 10). This question is critical to appraisal practitioners who are concerned with obtaining the most valid and reliable measurement. More discussion and research is necessary before a full explication of this issue can be presented. Also, can adolescents be interviewed directly?

Fourth, and related to the previous questions, is who is capable and competent to collect adaptive behavior data. Paraprofessionals have been used in some instances (Chapter 10), while school psychologists were required in others (Mastenbrook, 1977). Not only does this question arouse territorial emotions among professionals, but relatively little examination has been conducted regarding who can collect data and, probably more important, how much specific training is required.

How is validity of adaptive behavior measures to be determined? The traditional approach of establishing construct validity is to correlate a measure with other measures of similar content. However, this approach is inappropriate given the limited number of relevant measures (ABIC and

ABS—PS) and their different focus. Mercer (1977) reports that validity of the ABIC will best be established by correlation scores with independent measures from parents and peers. Presently, little construct validity evidence for either measure has been reported. Studies of other types of validity (predictive, concurrent, etc.) are also rare, though the ABS—PS manual (Lambert, Windmiller, Cole, & Figueroa, 1974) does present one study of predictive ability.

If adaptive behavior measurement is multidimensional, then is a single score or average score feasible to measure and interpret scores for identification purposes? The ABS—PS does not have a total score, while the ABIC does provide for an average scaled score. The accuracy and consequent usefulness of a single score is yet to be established. Furthermore, if adaptive behavior is a generic concept encompassing a broad spectrum of skills and abilities, how many scores need to be considered in its measurement in order to determine eligibility or identification? Future tests or procedures will have to define more explicitly what domains or types of adaptive behavior they are measuring. Also, the appraisal practitioner will have to judge professionally how much information is enough to make an eligibility decision.

In summary, the concept and measurement of adaptive behavior when applied to the function of identification/placement involves a number of critical issues surrounding the differential identification of mental retardation. The issue of least-biased assessment requires separate study from that usually associated with traditional investigations of reliability and validity.

ADAPTIVE BEHAVIOR AND
INTERVENTION/PROGRAMMING:
WHAT AND HOW MUCH MEASUREMENT IS ENOUGH?

When the concept and measurement of adaptive behavior is applied to psychological assessment for intervention/programming, many of the issues and questions that emerge are quite different from those of the previous section. The single most critical question regarding the concept of adaptive behavior within the intervention/programming context is how encompassing is adaptive behavior? As mentioned previously, the general definition (Grossman, 1973) is both flexible and vague. Adaptive behavior can be almost anything an appraisal practitioner chooses. Indeed, lists of behaviors which are theorized to be subsumed under the concept are so vast as to almost encompass human behavior in general. What is adaptive behavior to be? If it is a generic concept with multiple domains, how many domains are there?

Additionally, adaptive behavior is conceived by some as a psychological entity that can be reliably and validly measured. Clausen (1972) argues that adaptive behavior is too vague and elusive a concept to be considered a discrete entity. He further argues that because the concept is vague, measurement is unrealistic. Baumeister and Muma (1975) support Clausen's criticism on this issue:

> Upon closer analysis adaptive behavior turns out to be a rather vague and ill-defined concept, despite recent efforts to develop measurement scales for it. And it is doubtful whether any instrument can suffice in this regard. For one thing, there is no way of knowing all the contexts in which an individual will be required to function. Secondly, all relevant domains of adaptive behavior could not possibly be tapped by a single instrument (p. 302).

This type of criticism must be addressed and countered with sufficient modifications in the concept (especially definition) to assist in the development of effective measures.

Other related definitional issues must be considered. Does adaptive behavior exist in adulthood? If so, what behaviors encompass the concept? Whereas the concern regarding the age variables of the definition within assessment for identification center on early childhood, the focus of concern changes in intervention/programming. If the optimum goal in intervention/programming is the training of skills so that individuals deficient in the necessary adaptive skills can become independent or normalized. (President's Committee on Mental Retardation, 1976), then an estimate must be made of what minimum (and possibly maximum) skills are necessary for an adult to function. This estimate forms the long-term goals for training and the parameters for adaptive behavior measurement.

Fundamental to the entire conception of adaptive behavior as relevant to intervention/programming is the assumption that the behaviors being measured can, in fact, be trained or programmed. What do we know of the effectiveness of programs to train adaptive behavior skills? What large-scale efforts have been reported or are underway to document the program efficacy and value of adaptive behavior measurement in those efforts? Is it possible that too much has been assumed regarding the capability of the training technology to inculcate skills? Or perhaps the more appropriate question is, Who among the handicapped can be trained? With the long-term goal of abolishing large residential, custodial institutions (President's Committee on Mental Retardation, 1976), which individuals require the greatest efforts in technological development and implementation to attain the goal?

The issues or questions regarding application of the concept of adaptive behavior in assessment for intervention/programming arise from a need to plan precisely and implement training programs. The *measurement* of adaptive behavior within the same functional context of assessment also presents a number of critical questions. First, how much measurement is enough? This question is easier to answer when considering identification/placement because only data necessary to make the differential discrimination of the handicap would be required. The decision regarding whether the handicap exists is a one-time or yearly event. In assessing adaptive behavior for intervention/programming, however, a greater degree of detail is usually needed to plan for training. How much more detail is required? Additionally, how often is measurement necessary in order to maintain surveillance of program progress and to implement new programs when needed? Very few studies exist that begin to address this problem.

A highly practical problem already mentioned (Chapter 8) is the paucity of information regarding what specific social and prevocational skills are important at adolescent or upper functioning levels. Very few measures have been developed to assist in this regard. The issue is not the development of a technology to analyze appropriately and assess behaviors. That technology already exists to a large extent (Gold, 1972; Mercer & Ysseldyke, 1976). The key question is, What behaviors are important, vital to independence and to normalized functioning?

As in the focus on identification/placement, how much training is required to administer available measures? Who should/can collect this type of information and from whom should it be obtained? Where tests or scales (as opposed to observational methods) are used, is it possible to directly interview adolescents and adults who are to be trained? These issues regarding the process of assessment for intervention/programming become more critical when roles and staff requirements of community centers and other intervention units are considered.

In summary, the concept of adaptive behavior and its measurement, when focused on the function of intervention/programming, provokes an additional set of questions from those already presented. The focal issues related to specific programs required to train skills and achieve the goal of normalization for as many handicapped individuals as possible.

To say that the future of adaptive behavior is best summed as research is to oversimplify the highly complex environment in which these issues have been raised. The present and near future is dictated more by political-legal directions taken by society and various groups that encompass the diverse environment in which we live than by any gains made in scientific knowledge. Science and society are inextricably intertwined in the decisions that are made. The values associated with the concept of adaptive behavior and its measurement (as yet not fully explicated or understood) perhaps carry the greatest weight in the future of the concept and measurement of adaptive behavior.

REFERENCES

Baumeister, A., & Muma, J. On defining mental retardation. *Journal of Special Education,* 1975, *9,* 293–306.
Bower, T. G. R. *Development in infancy.* San Francisco: Freeman, 1974.
Clausen, J. The continuing problem of defining mental deficiency. *Journal of Special Education,* 1972, *6,* 97–106.
Dworkin, G., & Block, N. J. (Eds.) *The I.Q. controversy.* New York: Pantheon Books, 1976.
Gold, M. W. Stimulus factors in skill training of the retarded on a complex assembly task: Acquisition, transfer and retention. *American Journal of Mental Deficiency,* 1972, *76,* 517–526.
Grossman, H. J. (Ed.). *Manual on terminology and classification in mental retardation* (Special Publication No. 2). Washington, D. C.: American Association on Mental Deficiency, 1973.
Hamblin, R. L., Buckholdt, D., Ferritor, D., Kozloff, M., & Blackwell, L. *The humanization process: A social, behavioral analysis of children's problems.* New York: Wiley, 1971.
Jackson, G. Another psychological view from the Association of Black Psychologists. *American Psychologist,* 1975, *30,* 88–93.
Kamin, L. *The science and politics of IQ.* New York: Wiley, 1974.
Lambert, N. M., Windmiller, M., Cole, L., & Figueroa, R. *AAMD Adaptive Behavior Scale: Public School Version* (1974 Rev.). Washington, D. C.: American Association on Mental Deficiency, 1974.
Leland, H. Adaptive behavior and mentally retarded behavior. In C. E. Meyers, R. K. Eyman, & G. Tarjan (Eds.), *Sociobehavioral studies in mental retardation: Papers in honor of Harvey F. Dingman.* Washington, D. C.: American Association on Mental Deficiency, 1973.
Mannheim, K. *Ideology and utopia.* London: Kegan Paul, 1936.
Mastenbrook, J. Personal communication, May 1977.
Meier, J. M. *Developmental and learning disabilities.* Baltimore: University Park Press, 1976.
Mercer, J. R. IQ: The lethal label. *Psychology Today,* 1972, *6* (4), 44.
Mercer, J. R. *Labeling the mentally retarded: Clinical and social system perspectives on mental retardation.* Berkeley and Los Angeles: University of California Press, 1973.
Mercer, J. R. *System of Multicultural Pluralistic Assessment: Technical manual.* New York: The Psychological Corporation, 1977. (a)
Mercer, J. Personal communication, July 1977. (b)
Mercer, J. R., & Ysseldyke, J. Designing diagnostic intervention programs. In T. Oakland (Ed.), *With bias toward none: Non-biased assessment of minority*

group children. Lexington, Ky.: Coordinating Office for Regional Resource Centers, 1976.

Nihira, K. Dimensions of adaptive behavior in institutionalized mentally retarded children and adults: Developmental perspective. *American Journal of Mental Deficiency*, 1976, *81*, 215–226.

President's Committee on Mental Retardation. *Mental retardation: Century of decision*. Washington, D. C.: Government Printing Office, 1976.

Rimland, B. Infantile autism: Status and research. In A. Davids (Ed.), *Child personality and psychopathology: Current topics*. New York: Wiley, 1974.

Ross, A. O. *Psychological disorders of children: A behavioral approach to theory, research and therapy*. New York: McGraw-Hill, 1974.

Ross, A. O. *Psychological aspects of learning disabilities and reading disorders*. New York: McGraw-Hill, 1976.

Sattler, J. *Assessment of children's intelligence* (Rev. ed.). Philadelphia: Saunders, 1974.

Texas Education Agency. *Texas state planning design for the education of exceptional children*. Austin: Author, Department of Special Education, 1977.

Tucker, J. A. Operationalizing a nonbiased appraisal process. In T. Oakland (Ed.), *With bias toward none: Non-biased assessment of minority group children*. Lexington, Ky.: Coordinating Office for Regional Resource Centers, 1976.

Williams, R. L. The bitch-100: A culture-specific test. *Journal of Afro-American issues*, 1975, *3*, 103–116.

W. Alan Coulter,
Henry W. Morrow,
Judi L. Coulter

12

An Annotated Bibliography of Research in Adaptive Behavior

Aanes, D., & Moen, M. Adaptive behavior changes of group home residents. *Mental Retardation*, 1976, *14*, 36–40.

Aanes and Moen cite the current trend from institutional placement for the mentally retarded toward community based residential care. The authors view the Adaptive Behavior Scale as an objective measure to evaluate improved functioning of mentally retarded individuals placed in residential homes versus lower functional levels for these same types of individuals who are in institutional settings. To support their hypothesis, the authors evaluated 46 adult MR residents at a one-year interval on the ABS covering more than 27 different areas of adaptive functioning.

Comparison of the 1974 ABS ratings to the 1975 ratings supported significant increases in four major adaptive behavior areas: (1) eating skills, (2) cleanliness, (3) appearance, and (4) care of clothing. The subdomain area of comprehension revealed a significantly lower level of functioning from the first to second ABS evaluation. The implication of the lowered comprehension score, suggest Aanes and Moen, is the use of ABS ratings for locating potential programming needs. Based on study results, the authors support two broader applications of the ABS: (1) the use of pre- and post-ABS ratings for determining the effectiveness of residential care for the mentally retarded and (2) its use for quantitative assessment to compare the overall effectiveness and specific strengths and weakness of differing group home programs.

Some of the references in Chapter 12 were compiled from a document on adaptive behavior: N. Carlson. *The contexts of life: A socio-ecological model of adaptive behavior and functioning*. East Lansing: Michigan State University, College of Human Ecology, 1976.

Adams, J. Adaptive behavior and measured intelligence in the classification of mental retardation. *American Journal of Mental Deficiency*, **1973,** *78,* **77–81.**

The American Association on Mental Deficiency has defined mental retardation in terms of both adaptive behavior and measured intelligence. Adaptive behavior, when determined by the Vineland Social Maturity Scale, is seen by many clinicians as very limited in practical value. Adams's study investigates types of information used to define mental retardation. The results indicate that psychologists and physicians relied almost entirely on the IQ score when the psychological reports were available.

The author contends that in the classification of mental retardation adaptive behavior should be cast in a more central role. He feels that many other factors besides IQ and current interpretations of adaptive behavior are operative, and should be identified and systematically included in the MR classification. In his opinion many of these factors are societal-environmental in nature (family, educational, community). These variables, like adaptive behavior, are very difficult to weigh and measure accurately. Thus, arriving at appropriate decision in the classification of the retarded is difficult.

Meanwhile, since clinicians continue to use IQ tests as primary determinants of major decisions in children's lives, the author stresses the importance of correcting this gross injustice by immediate, intensive, and systematic study and/or action.

Allen, R., Loeffler, F., Levine, M., & Aiker, L. Social adaptation assessment as a tool for prescriptive remediation. *Mental Retardation,* **1976,** *14,* **36–37.**

The Adaptive Behavior Checklist (ABC) is the tool used to illustrate the efficacy of formally evaluating adaptive behavior for a continuum of residentially placed mentally retarded individuals (e.g., children to adults, all levels of measured intellectual functioning, physically handicapped, etc.). The authors propose that the ABC not only yields information necessary for placement and administrative criteria, but also that the adaptive behavior (AB) profile results are most effectively applied to programming for remediation. To illustrate the prescriptive value of the ABC, a computer printout of basic AB functions for an adolescent male MR is reviewed and interpreted via specific AB strengths and weaknesses with accompanying program suggestions. The authors also emphasize that effective remedial AB evaluation depends on selecting the appropriate evaluative tool. Therefore, the relevant use of the ABC includes noting the appropriateness of the standardization population to the client being evaluated.

Baroff, G. *Mental retardation: Nature, cause, and management.* *Washington, D. C.:* **Hemisphere Publishing, 1974.**

According to Baroff, adaptive behavior, which is included in the American Association on Mental Deficiency's definition of mental retardation, is defined as "the degree to which an individual meets the standards of personal independence and social responsibility expected of his age and cultural group." Therefore, measurement of adaptive behavior will vary at different ages in different environmental settings.

For the preschool child, adaptive behavior is reflected in acquisition of motor skills, language, cognitive skills, self-help skills, and socialization. The author feels that cognitive deficiences, reflected by learning difficulties, are the most direct consequences of an impairment of general intelligence. He sees a strong need for social skills, often overlooked in retarded children, to be encouraged. Preschool experience would provide these social experiences.

Baroff contends that parental reaction to a retarded child strongly influences the child's self-esteem. Some of the reactions that detract from a child's sense of worth are parental shock, grief, shame, and tendency to isolate. The nature of mental retardation is such that it may cause many coping problems for the family. The author views the ideal role of the parent as being warm and loving while conveying a sense of worth to the child, who, in turn, learns to trust and approach new people and experiences. The author points out that impaired intelligence can lead to behavior patterns which differ from what is expected of the "average" individual of that age.

Baumeister, A., & Muma, J. On defining mental retardation. *Journal of Special Education*, 1975, *9*, 293–306.

Baumeister and Muma discuss the sparsity of empirical studies which are necessary to develop a more comprehensive criteria for assessing mental retardation. They particularly criticize the almost total reliance of psychologists/educators on the AAMD definition of mental retardation for delineating diagnostic assessment criteria. The article systematically presents the strong need to reassess use of the IQ measure as a major component of mental retardation diagnosis. The authors propose that research and development efforts be directed toward an adaptive behavior continuum which accounts not only for individual behavior but also for the interaction of that person with the contingencies of the person's significant living environments (i.e., home, school, job).

Bernal, E. A response to educational uses of tests with disadvantaged subjects. *American Psychologist*, 1975, *30*, 93–95.

Bernal states that the current draft of "Educational Uses of Tests with Disadvantaged Students" is an improved and more complete review of the literature than previous drafts. He urges, however, a constructive, rather than defensive, evaluation of the state of the art regarding pertinent minority testing issues:

1. Focusing misuse and abuse of minority evaluations onto the field practitioner avoids the issue of the test developers' responsibilities to label tests appropriately, to delineate application to oversee dissemination, and to direct use and interpretation.
2. Alternatives to formalized tests for evaluation and prescription need more extensive review.
3. The predictive validity of a test (i.e., initial success in school) needs to be

weighed against the construct and factorial validity of the test for both dominant ethnic and nondominant ethnic groups. The "psychometrically naive"
require special attention.
4. A major issue not adequately addressed involves researching why so many
    norm-referenced tests appear inappropriate for assessing disadvantaged stu-
    dents.

Blackman, L. An active-passive dimension in the definition of mental retardation.
***Journal of Special Education*, 1972, *6*, 67–70.**

Blackman reviews Clausen's critique of the AAMD definition of mental retardation. He then distinguishes between an active and passive diagnostic appraisal and
explains that the passive evaluation aims for identification only and psychometrics
alone suffice. Next there is a detailed discussion on the active diagnostic dimensions, including treatment and prevention goals.

**Brantley, J. *Adaptive behavior: Uses and misuses*. Unpublished manuscript, Univer-
sity of North Carolina, 1977.**

Brantley states that federal legislation has created a critical need to clarify specific
definitions and measures of adaptive behavior appropriate to the client served and
the intent of the evaluation. He presents three perspectives in delineating valid
application and measurement of the adaptive behavior concept: (1) the developmental, (2) the psychosocial, and (3) the social-system models.

Competent behavioral functioning tied to specific age appropriate expectancies comprises a developmental model for measuring adaptive behavior. Brantley
cites specific rating scales and tests currently in use as representative of developmental measures of adaptive behavior.

The psychosocial approach centers on the environmental impact on a person's behavior and is best illustrated by the American Association on Mental
Deficiency's definition of adaptive behavior (1961). He again cites specific tests,
rating scales, and behavioral observation procedures as representative of a psychosocial measure of adaptive behavior.

The third perspective focuses on legislation designed to measure adaptive
behavior of the ethnic/racial minority child in noneducational settings. The
social-system model is exemplified by Jane Mercer's definition of adaptive behavior: The performance of social roles appropriate to age/sex criteria and behavioral expectancies of a child's "social systems." Her method incorporates a
multidimensional assessment of the child's functioning in the school and community and with family and peers. The assumptions underlying Mercer's System of
Multipluralistic Assessment (SOMPA) include (1) multidimensionality of behavior
and (2) contextual appropriateness of behavior among differing cultures/social
systems.

Brantley differentiates the assessment of adaptive behavior for descriptive
purposes versus assessment for evaluative purposes. He strongly urges professionals to determine the most appropriate framework for adaptive behavior assessment prior to selection of measuring devices.

Bryant, J. L. *Comparison of two methods of evaluating educable retarded children.* **Unpublished doctoral dissertation, University of Iowa, 1976.**

The System of Multicultural Pluralistic Assessment is compared to a traditional evaluation program for providing relevant placement information to professional staffings (the evaluator, appropriate school personel, and parents). The SOMPA evaluation included comprehensive assessment of the child's adaptive behavior skills, intellectual potential, environment, family structure, health information, and cultural data. The traditional assessment was left to the discretion of school personnel and the evaluator and varied from a comprehensive evaluation to no evaluation.

Significant finds indicate:

1. More children would be removed from mental disabilities educable programs if Estimated Learning Potential (SOMPA) scores were used in place of WISC—R scores.
2. Students from lower socioeconomic families scored higher on SOMPA than on the WISC—R.
3. Parents whose children were evaluated according to SOMPA attended more staffings than parents of children in the traditional evaluation group.

Buck, M. The multi-dimensional model for the assessment of children referred for classes for mental retardation. *Journal of Afro-American Issues*, **1975,** *3,* **91–102.**

Buck urges that educational retardation be excluded from the definition of mental retardation. She cites Dunn's definition of mental retardation for assessing minority group children: Children labeled mentally retarded should (1) include no more than 1 percent of the ethnic/racial group who are so deficient in self-care that they are unable to function adaptively when compared to their age/ethnic group and (2) score no higher than the second percentile for their ethnic/racial group on verbal/nonverbal individual intellectual assessments.

Buck recommends minimizing and/or excluding labeling as criteria for individualized educational services. Her multidimensional model for assessing minority group children includes:

1. Complete physical examination.
2. Measure of academic achievement via criterion-referenced tests.
3. Verbal and nonverbal assessment of cognitive style and intellectual potential.
4. Visual/motor perceptual functioning.
5. Evaluation of adaptive behavior, including coping skills *outside* the school environment.

Clausen, J. The continuing problem of defining mental deficiency. *Journal of Special Education,* **1972,** *6,* **97–106.**

Clausen presents the views of seven professionals in an attempt to formulate a standard definition of mental deficiency. Some issues addressed in the article include:

1. Critique of American Association on Mental Deficiency 1961 definition of mental retardation.
2. Limitations of intelligence testing.
3. Inclusion of adaptive behavior in the definition of MR.
4. Needs of the classroom teacher.
5. Clarification of the appropriateness and operational application of adaptive behavior in defining MR.

Clausen, J. Quo vadis, AAMD? *Journal of Special Education*, **1972,** *6,* **51–60.**

Clausen addresses the state of the art in defining mental retardation. He delineates three different directions in conceptualizing mental deficiency for practitioners: (1) inclusion of adaptive behavior as the central variable, (2) focus on etiology and pathology, and (3) retention of a measure of intellectual functioning as the main criterion for diagnosis. The author then argues in favor of intelligence testing and improvement of existing intelligence measure as the most viable method of diagnosing mental retardation.

Cleary, T. A., Humphreys, L. G., Kendrick, S. A., & Wesman, A. Educational uses of tests with disadvantaged students. *American Psychologist*, **1975,** *30,* **15–41.**

This report details in five comprehensive sections current guidelines for assessing ethnic/racial/disadvantaged students. The five sections of the report deal with:

1. The 1968 Black Psychological Associations' call for a moratorium on intellectual testing with minority/disadvantaged students.
2. Specific definitions of learning/developmental coping abilities with special emphasis on general intelligence.
3. Guidelines for avoiding inappropriate testing procedures and misinterpretation of test results.
4. Statistical knowledge necessary to develop effective testing programs.
5. Current assessment alternatives to standardized ability testing.

Corpus Christi Independent School District. *Adaptive Behavior Newsletter*, **1977,** *1.*

The rationale for the publication of an adaptive behavior newsletter to facilitate the dissemination of current information to interested professionals is presented. The American Association on Mental Deficiency's definition of adaptive behavior is presented, along with an explanation of the relevancy of adaptive behavior measurement to education. Other articles present research projects on adaptive behavior implemented by the Corpus Christi ISD and list upcoming workships.

Cromwell, R., Blashfield, R., & Strauss, J. Criteria for classification systems. In N. Hobbs (Ed.), *Issues in the classification of children: I.* **San Francisco: Jossey-Bass, 1975, 4–5.**

Development of a multidimensional classification system for evaluating exceptional children is given in a proposed step-by-step procedure by the authors.

According to their hypothesis, a child referred for evaluation would be assessed on three levels: (1) syndromes or types of problems; (2) methods of treatment/prevention/prognosis; and (3) context of functioning, i.e., environmental/age norms, etc. The article includes detailed recommendations for developing "multi-axial" assessment programs. For example, diagnostic programs should allow for preventive measures and methods of evaluating direct benefits and liabilities to the student evaluated.

Cronbach, L. J. **Five decades of public controversy over mental testing.** *American Psychologist,* **1975,** *30,* **1–14.**

Cronbach follows the initial testing movement in the United States through to current testing policies and controversies. He parallels professional test development and research with social response to testing for specific historical periods. For example, he details media and lay response to Arthur Jensen's postulations on the etiology of intellectual potential. He cites the *Pygmalion in the Classroom* controversy as well as the opposition in the 1940s and 1950s to standardized testing. His concluding summation emphasizes professional awareness beyond scientific test development to include the possible societal effects a test might exert on students' educational potentials and opportunities.

Drew, C. J. **Criterion-referenced and norm-referenced assessment of minority group children.** *Journal of School Psychology,* **1973,** *11,* **323–329.**

Drew articulates the state of the art in assessing minority/ethnic children. There are a compendium of problems. One recognized problem is the inadequacy of norm-referenced tests for assessing minority children. Efforts directed toward developing nonbiased testing instruments is one response to the minority testing situation. Drew reviews the problems of norm-referenced testing and presents alternatives, particularly criterion-referenced testing. He also addresses the potential bias of criterion-referenced testing and proposes a challenge for developing relevent criterion-referenced measurements for multicultural assessments.

Fitzpatrick, A., & Rogers, D. *A critique of the AAMD Adaptive Behavior Scale, Public School Version.* **Unpublished manuscript, 1977. (Available from Northside Independent School District, Pupil Appraisal Center, 1827 Westridge, San Antonio, Texas 78227.**

The paper cites recent court decisions dictating a reappraisal of current testing practices in public education. The Texas Education Agency's policy and guidelines on assessing adaptive behavior is reviewed, noting that only two adaptive behavior instruments have been approved for use. One is not yet available, and the second is the American Association on Mental Deficiency's Adaptive Behavior Scale, Public School Version (1974 revision). The authors then show that the AAMD ABS—PS does not adequately differentiate among its standardization populations in the standard deviations among ABS domains. They also support the inadequacy of the AAMD ABS—PS with specific case histories.

Foster, R., & Foster, C. The measurement of change in adaptive behavior. *Project News* (Parsons State Hospital and Training Center), 1967, *3*, 21–29.

Forty-one subjects were chosen from a group that had received an adaptive behavior scale (ABS) rating two years previously. Of these subjects, 26 had been part of a demonstration program based on operant procedures to change various behaviors from inappropriate sexual behavior to learning to tell time. A group of 15 controls were used. All subjects were rerated with the ABS. Results indicate that the experimental subjects made a significant gain in their total Part I scores. Of the experimental group, 50 percent changed AB levels (increase), while only 13 percent of the control group increased. Subgroup results of the experimental subjects displayed differential change. The change in adaptive behavior was highly significant for the younger group, but it was not significant for the two older groups. For the younger group increases were seen in language development, self-direction, and domestic occupation. One of the other subgroups showed a significant increase in self-direction only. The study lends support to the notion that programmatic increases in adaptive behavior as defined in this study can occur.

Garza, P. *Non-biased assessment of minority group children: Considerations.* Conference on nonbiased assessment of minority children, Austin, Texas, 1976.

Garza covers in detail four major nonbiased assessment considerations: (1) selecting testing instruments (intelligence and achievement measures), (2) gathering formal evaluation data, (3) collecting family history and appropriate medical/health information, and (4) adoption of appropriate nonbiased assessment techniques for local school districts. For example, under formal data collection Garza discusses procedures for selecting test instruments. In so doing he reviews the relevant application of the standardization of test instruments for students referred, the ethnic status of the test examiner, and the cultural bias of the test as several important considerations in achieving valid nonbiased educational evaluations.

Gold, M. An adaptive behavior philosophy: Who needs it? A paper published in the *Proceedings of the National Association of Superintendents of Public Residential Facilities,* Region V Interaction Workshop on Community Living for Institutionalized Retardates, Chicago, May 1972.

The current trend to move the moderate to severely retarded individual from institutionalized care to community environments (i.e., supervised apartment living, sheltered workshops) requires a refocusing of adaptive behavior considerations. While the adaptive behavior skills of the retarded are the focus of professionals, Gold suggests that the adaptive skills of the community—parents, workshop supervisors, educators, and others—also need evaluation and remediation. Changing community expectancies for the retarded involves clarifying the daily living skills which depend more on training than on measured intelligence. Those whom professionals *label* MR are still capable of learning many self-supporting behaviors, including earning their own income, if properly trained. To assure adaptive community living success for mentally retarded citizens, labor laws, import laws, labor unions, and other community groups must first recognize the full potential of the retarded to manage their lives and sustain a living and then offer work opportunities.

Guide to adaptive behavior assessment: A resource manual for the development and evaluation of special programs for exceptional students. Tallahassee, Fl.: Leon County Adaptive Behavior Assessment Project, 1977.

The document presents in a concise format the current status of adaptive behavior assessment. The rationale for incorporating AB information into the educational evaluation is presented, along with a suggested strategy for collecting and using AB data. A second section details programming implications derived from adaptive behavior assessments. The appendices include guidelines for an evaluation system and a historical perspective on adaptive behavior.

Harbin, G., & Haigh, J. *Position paper on the measurement of adaptive behavior.* Unpublished manuscript, Mideast Regional Resource Center, Washington, D.C., 1977.

Harbin and Haigh briefly review the current status of adaptive behavior assessment and then present a supportive framework for the development of their Haigh-Harbin Adaptive Behavior Scale (H-HABS). The etiology of the adaptive behavior concept is presented, followed with an in-depth comparison of three major operational definitions/measuring systems for adaptive behavior assessment: (1) the developmental, (2) the psychosocial, and (3) the social-system models.

The three current methods of defining/assessing adaptive behavior are critiqued for weaknesses:

1. The developmental model is viewed as potentially biased against ethnic/racial minority children primarily due to its focus on dominant culture behavioral expectancies.
2. The psychosocial measure of adaptive behavior focuses on the "pathological" model of adaptability, and thus, is too narrow to encompass normative functioning in home, school, and community environments.
3. Mercer's Adaptive Behavior Inventory for Children represents the social-system model and is viewed by the authors as too time-consuming and as inadequate in programming for remediation.

The next section presents the strengths of the H-HABS and the procedural phases of development. Briefly, the H-HABS covers birth through adolescence, consists of five scales based on the AAMD definition of mental retardation, uses pluralistic norms, attempts to measure behavior appropriate to age/sex/culture of child, and interviews the parent/parent surrogate for information. The authors emphasize that one major strength of the H-HABS is the profile presentation of the child's behavior versus the inadequate derivation of a single score. A concise table compares assumptions, content, environment(s) measured, norms, and applicability to intervention for developmental, psychosocial, and social-system models versus the H-HABS. An appendix describes an introduction to the Individualized Intervention System, which ties comprehensive assessment results, including the H-HABS profile, to specific remediation strategies.

Jackson, G. Another psychological view from the Association of Black Psychologists: *American Psychologist*, 30, 88–93.

Jackson thoroughly reviews and documents a critique of the "Report of the Ad Hoc Committee on Educational Uses of Tests with Disadvantaged Students." The report is viewed by Jackson and other members of the Black Psychological Association as supporting racist psychometric techniques and taking a political position to perpetuate the model of "intellectual deficits." The black psychologists represented in the critique also question the assertion that test invalidity comes not from the instrument but from the test user. Jackson strongly states that the test itself is invalid when not designed for specific cultural/ethnic groups, i.e., black, Chicano. Based on the outcome of the Ad Hoc Committee on Educational Uses of Tests with Disadvantaged Students (1975), Jackson suggests that the Black Psychological Association call for federal legislation to correct current psychometric techniques used with minority students.

Kohn, M., & Rosman, B. A social competence scale and symptom checklist for the preschool child: Factor dimensions, their cross-instrument generality and longitudinal persistence. *Developmental Psychology*, 1972, 6.

Reported are the results of an experiment designed to measure the longitudinal persistence of the factor dimensions extracted from two teacher rating instruments: The Social Competence Scale, intended to measure the preschool child's mastery of the environment, and the Symptoms Checklist, an observational inventory of clinical symptoms manifested in the preschool child. By focusing on overt classroom behavior, the authors presumably assessed social-emotional functioning.

Although the study is primarily considered with the factor analytic study of the two major dimensions of social-emotional functioning across two instruments and across time, it has application to the study of adaptive behavior in the preschool child. The dimensions which emerged from the factor analysis of the Social Competency Scale have been interpreted by the authors to reflect the major adaptive demands that the preschool setting makes on a child. This entails both (1) using the opportunities for learning, pleasure, and peer interaction and (2) living within the limits of the environment so that a normal group process can be maintained. In addition, the results suggest that the preschool teachers' ratings of good function were related more to the extent of the child's involvement in activities than to cooperation and compliance with routines. Both the teacher's perception of the child and the child's reaction to the adaptive demands of the preschool environment will influence the child's overall adjustment to the school setting.

Lambert, N. M. Validity of the AAMD Adaptive Behavior Scale for the public school populations. Paper presented as part of a symposium entitled *Psychoeducational assessment in the seventies—A look at measures and concepts.* American Psychological Association Convention, New Orleans, September 1974.

This paper is a report on the standardization of the public school version of the American Association of Mental Deficiency's Adaptive Behavior Scale (AAMD ABS). Determinations in the pilot phase of the study were (1) how the scale performed on a public school population, (2) what contributions parents and teachers made in assessing a child's adaptive behavior, and (3) what procedures were most successful in supplying data called for by the scale. The standardization phase required the development of the sampling plan, determined by a multiethnic advisory board.

The sampling plan called for 200 "trainable mentally retarded" pupils, 400 "educationally handicapped" children, with the remainder of the 300 subjects distributed equally between pupils from "regular" and "educably mentally retarded" classes. The final population was 2600 children. Results of the pilot showed that teachers' and parents' reports of adaptive behavior were equivalent in the standardization population. The sample was defined on the basis of class placement, sex, population, density of residence, socioeconomic status, ethnic status, and age. The evidence from the analysis of the contribution of sex, ethnic status, population density, and socioeconomic status suggests that Part I of the scale can be thought of as relatively independent of sex and ethnic status effects; thus, a single set of norms is appropriate for children of both sexes who are white or black, or of Spanish-speaking backgrounds. When interpreting the domain scores on Part II of the scale based on a single set of norms, one should proceed cautiously; one should consider the child's domain scores with respect to the norms for sex and ethnic status in order to have as much comparative information as possible. According to the authors, the results of the public school standardizations of the AAMD ABS appear to demonstrate that the scale can provide a valid, useful assessment of elementary school children's adaptive behavior and, with other data on the child, can be used to help formulate an educational plan for the individual child.

Lambert, N. M., & Nicoll, R. C. Dimensions of adaptive behavior of retarded and nonretarded public school children. *American Journal of Mental Deficiency,* 1976, *81*, 135–146.

This study evaluated 2618 students (from ages 7 to 13) on the AAMD Adaptive Behavior Scale, Public School Version. The student sample selected included white, black, and Spanish surname children from both regular and special education programs. For all groups three dimensions of adaptive behavior were significant in the factoral analysis: (1) functional autonomy, (2) interpersonal adjustment, and (3) social responsibility. Based on the outcome of their study, Lambert and Nicoll discuss the potential applications of adaptive behavior assessments.

Lambert, N. M., Windmiller, M., Cole, L., & Figueroa, R. Standardization of a
public school version of the AAMD Adaptive Behavior Scale. *Mental Retardation*, 1975, *13*, 3–7.

The study details the effort of the California State Department of Education to
standardize the AAMD Adaptive Behavior Scale, Public School Version on a
large California public school population. The authors attempt to show the appropriateness of the AAMD ABS—PSV in assessing students referred for EMR and
other special education services in the state of California. Results of the study are
compiled in an interpretative manual, including the normative data.

Leland, H. Introduction and theoretical considerations. In E. Kagin (Ed.), *Conference on measurement of adaptive behavior: III*. Parsons, Ks.: Parsons State
Hospital and Training Center, 1968.

The author defines adaptive behavior and its components: independent functioning, personal responsibility, and social responsibility. The critical demands of the
community in which the individual is residing are stressed and the concept of
visibility is discussed. Age-specific expectations modify the community's critical
demands and permit increased tolerance at lower ages. The value of the concept in
training and program planning is briefly reviewed.

Leland, H. Mental retardation and adaptive behavior. *Journal of Special Education*,
1972, 71–80.

The problem of interrater reliability in the Adaptive Behavior Scale is defended by
the author. "Environmental and cultural biases and priorities cause different
ratings to be given in different situations, according to the author." A person's
coping behavior in a particular situation depends as much upon his own abilities to
cope as it does upon the perceptions and biases of the individuals who spend time
with him. These perceptions of the person who spends time with the individual in
a particular situation are, therefore, deemed important and credible in yielding an
accurate description of the individual being rated, in light of that particular
environmental setting. Intervention and programming must be designed to help
the individual cope with his environment, for his environment and the people who
work with him inside that environment are responsible for his success or failure.
Retardation is defined as behaviors an individual exhibits that exclude him from
his social environment. The author calls for a greater concern in reversing and
modifying behaviors that exclude individuals rather than the current practice of
allowing the label of mentally retarded to be used as a stopping point for any
possible intervention.

Leland, H. Adaptive behavior and mentally retarded behavior. In C. E. Meyers, R.
K. Eyman, & G. Tarjan (Eds.), *Sociobehavioral studies in mental retardation.
Papers in honor of Harvey F. Dingman*. Washington, D. C.: American Association on Mental Deficiency, 1973.

Mentally retarded behavior is discussed in terms of adaptive behavior. In the
author's perspective, the three behavioral dimensions of adaptive behavior—

independent functioning, personal responsibility, and social responsibility—are prerequisites for coping with personal, social, and societal demands. Intelligence is presented in terms of a social and cultural definition. A person who is seen as not coping with his social adaptive environment is visible because he is different and is in need of some form of mediation. The goal for every mentally retarded and developmentally disabled person is to exhibit coping behavior, defined as invisibility in the social adaptive environment.

Leland, H., & Husseini, M. *Adaptive behavior and social adjustment.* **Paper presented at the annual meeting of the American Psychological Association, Montreal, September, 1973.**

The Adaptive Behavior Scale (ABS) is discussed in terms of treatment and training. The three factors which emerge from the ABS are personal independence, personal adaptation and responsibility, and social adaptation. These factors are considered as elements of coping strategies that a retarded person needs to learn. The issues of visibility and social tolerance are presented in detail, and studies are used to demonstrate that social adjustment is a prime requisite for a retarded person to succeed in leading an effective life—be it in a school, an institution, a half-way house, or a community environment. The authors conclude that more emphasis is needed in the treatment and training of retarded individuals so that "adaptive behavior and social adjustment" may take place.

Leland, H., Nihira, K., & Shellhaas, M. The demonstration and measurement of adaptive behavior. In B. W. Richards (Ed.), *Proceedings of the First Congress of the International Association for the Scientific Study of Mental Deficiency.* **Reigate, Eng.: Michael Jackson, 1968.**

This paper discusses historical precedents, research, and critical sociocultural factors relevant to adaptive behavior as a classification dimension in mental retardation. The shortcomings of the IQ method of classification are pointed out relative to adaptive behavior as a means of evaluation. The importance of adaptive behavior as the reversible aspect of retardation is stressed in potential evaluation, program placement, and training. The sociocultural elements, embodied in particular environmental expectations and the individual's ability to discern these critical demands, are emphasized. The "bookkeeping" aspect of adaptive behavior (designation of levels) is of far-reaching practical utility in effective individual management.

Leland, M., Shellhaas, M., Nihira, K., & Foster, R. Adaptive behavior: A new dimension in the classification of the mentally retarded. *Mental Retardation Abstracts,* **1967, *4,* 359–387.**

This overview of the development of adaptive behavior as a concept of classification acknowledges that, despite interest, there has been some difficulty defining the concept precisely. Research on the measurement and definition of adaptive behavior is needed to provide an improved instrument for evaluation, treatment, and placement. The article reviews current definitions, research on adaptation, mental retardation in general and sociocultural considerations, and work in the development of some form of assessment device to measure adaptive behavior. A bibliography including all material pertinent to adaptive behavior up to 1967 is included.

Littell, W. The Wechsler Intelligence Scale for Children: A review of a decade of research. *Psychological Bulletin*, **1960,** *57,* **132–156.**

Littell reviews the research literature on the WISC from its publication in 1949. His review attempts to assess the WISC as a measure of psychological variables and concurrently to present to interested professionals a complete overview of WISC research. Three areas of concern about the WISC arise from the research cited: (1) its inadequate theortical framework, (2) its predictive validity, and (3) its use as a measuring device. Systematic investigation of the last seems warranted based on evidence that the WISC is reflecting variables *in addition* to intelligence (i.e., the examiner–examinee relationship).

MacMillian, D. L., & Jones, R. Lions in search of more Christians. *Journal of Special Education*, **1972,** *6,* **81–91.**

MacMillian and Jones address their article on mental retardation to Clausen's (1971) premises presented in "Mental Deficiency: Development of a Concept." They argue in support of the AAMD inclusion of adaptive behavior in the definition of mental deficiency. The lack of appropriate adaptive behavior assessment devices does not in their opinion preclude omitting adaptive behavior in the conceptualization of mental deficiency. They especially emphasize that the use of IQ alone to determine mental deficiency is greatly inadequate.

McCarthy, J. Region IV Education Service Center Conference regarding appraisal and programming for preschool children. *Today's Educational Consultant*, **1977,** *4,* **4–5.**

McCarthy outlines a procedure for selecting appropriate adaptive behavior tests. She also states her belief that the AAMD Adaptive Behavior Scale is *not* an appropriate adaptive behavior measurement for regular education programs.

McClelland, D. C. Testing for competence rather than for "intelligence." *American Psychologist*, **1973,** *28,* **1–13.**

McClelland addresses the politics and social power issues of tests as they are now used in the United States. He supports his view of challenging the purposes and outcomes of currently accepted test procedures by citing landmark correlational studies. The research cited indicates low, really nonexistent, positive correlations between achievement/aptitude test scores and later job success or proficiency. The author also notes that socioeconomic status has been shown to be positively and significantly related to intelligence test scores, pointing to possible bias in the test use. He concludes with five suggestions for correcting current biased testing procedures (e.g., the development and use of criterion-referenced tests and the investigation and specification of competencies required for success in order to maximize successful job/educational training). Last, McClelland calls for correcting the fallacious concept that lack of success in school precludes success and competent coping skills in other environments.

McIntosh, E., & Warren, S. Adaptive behavior in the retarded: A semi-longitudinal study. *The Training School Bulletin,* **1969,** *66,* **12–22.**

This five-year study compared annual Vineland Social Maturity Scale scores for 119 institutionalized mentally retarded children. Staff psychologists served as data collectors via direct observation, and study results indicated VSMS scores were highly consistent across the five administrations. The authors discuss the possible remedial/programming value of the VSMS based on study findings.

Mercer, J. R. *An analysis of factors in the family's withdrawal of a patient from a hospital for the mentally retarded.* **Unpublished doctoral dissertation, University of California, 1963.**

The dissertation is a sociological study of families having a mentally retarded member hospitalized in an institution for the mentally retarded. The objective of the study was to determine what factors are related to the family's withdrawal of the patient from the hospital. A comparison of the families of retardates who had been discharged from the hospital with the families of retardates who were still residents at the hospital at the time of the study was the method used to determine the factors. The information about the families was obtained by interviewing one member of the family, usually the mother.

The following findings seem relevant: (1) Resident patients were found to have more physical handicaps than discharged patients. (2) Resident patients were more frequently diagnosed into categories having specific clinical symptoms, while discharged patients were more frequently diagnosed as familial or undifferentiated. (3) The socioeconomic status of the families of discharged patients was lower than that of resident patients. (4) There was a closer consanguinity between the discharged patient and his current family than between the resident patient and his current family. (5) The mothers of discharged patients were younger than the mothers of resident patients. (6) Resident patients of low socioeconomic status came from families with low marital stability more frequently than did discharged patients of low socioeconomic status. (7) Resident patients were reported as having caused their families more problems than discharged patients. (8) Mothers of discharged patients were more likely to blame themselves for the retardation than mothers of resident patients. (9) The families of resident patients were more favorable toward the original placement of the retarded member. (10) The discharged patient was more likely to have been placed in the hospital because of community pressures, while the resident patients were more likely to have been placed because of family problems.

The differences found in this sociological analysis suggest multiple, complex, interactive processes within family systems. The discharged patients seemed more likely to be able to adapt to a changed environment—less a function of the individual than a function of the different environment.

Mercer, J. R. Sociological perspectives on mild mental retardation. In. H. C. Haywood (Ed.), *Social-cultural aspects of mental retardation.* **New York: Appleton-Century-Crofts, 1970, 378–391.**

The perspective taken toward mental retardation is a fundamental issue in the handling of retardates. Children with comparable disabilities receive different treatment in a medical environment than they would in a home. In the medical environment children are usually restricted and grouped by age and handicap. In homes children are more likely to be free and unregimented, of widely differing ages, with outside contacts. From a clinical perspective, a pathological model borrowed from medicine, mental retardation is regarded as a disease process involving biological damage, and the retardate (when placed in a hospital) is a "patient" or "inmate." This "disease model" involves many communities, influences the vocabulary of professionals, and promotes the use of more precise diagnostic instruments: perhaps only for the severely and profoundly retarded does it furnish an adequate frame of reference.

A social-system mental retarded analysis (more frequently applied to mild retardation) has the ability to create deviant, unesteemed status for those who do not fulfill expected roles in society. Mental retardation from this perspective is viewed not as individual pathology but as a description of one's social position. Effects may been seen in the school systems, where mere enrollment for the retarded child gives him the status of EMR—thus predicting at least a reading problem, a speech problem, and underachievement. Clearly, the perspective has an influence on life's alternative pathways for the labeled child.

Mercer, J. R. Institutionalized Anglocentrism: Labeling mental retardates in the public schools. In P. Orleans & R. Ellis (Eds.), *Race, change, and urban society: Urban affairs annual reviews.* **Los Angeles: Sage Publications, 1971.**

Mercer cites illustrative case histories to question the current practice by many school systems of placing a disproportionate number of Mexican-American and black students in classes for the educable mentally retarded based on dominant culture/ethnic criteria. She then presents an intensive look at alternatives for nondominant ethnic/cultural evaluations. The concluding section of the paper deals with the presentation of her own system called "pluralistic evaluation of intelligence." The pluralistic assessment procedure is then outlined for both Mexican-American and black student populations.

Mercer, J. R. *Anticipated achievement: Computerizing the self-fulfilling prophesy.* **Paper presented at the Annual Convention of the American Psychological Association, Honolulu, 1972.**

The paper presents the proceedings of the APA symposium dealing with the appropriate use of standarized tests in education. Mercer reviews the literature supporting the premise that intelligence tests measure abilities distinct and different from abilities measured by achievement/aptitude tests. She then asserts that artificial distinctions separate intelligence test outcomes from achievement test outcomes. The remainder of her paper presents specific evidence supporting the possible educational liabilities of assuming that intelligence tests measure more global concepts than situation/skill specific achievement tests.

Mercer, J. R. Who is normal? Two perspectives on mild mental retardation. In E. Gartley Jaco (Ed.), *Patients, physicians, and illness* **(Rev. ed.). New York: Free Press, 1972.**

Mercer evaluates three models of conceptualizing normality: (1) the medical, (2) the statistical, and (3) the social-system models. She presents the strengths and weaknesses of each, noting that in cases of extreme deviance (i.e., severe retardation) all three systems concur on the abnormality. The thesis of her articles centers, however, on borderline cases on normality. For these she supports the use of the social-system model for identification of treatment needs. She particularly supports this model of assessment for nondominant ethnic/cultural groups. In addition, the social-system model works toward normalizing environments as well as people.

Mercer, J. R. *Labeling the mentally retarded: Clinical and social system perspectives on mental retardation.* **Berkeley: University of California Press, 1973.**

This book is the product of an eight-year study of the labeling process of mentally retarded persons in the city of Riverside, California. The author comprehensively investigates and describes the process. She discusses the implications of the existing systems and makes recommendations for the future.

Mercer describes two contrasting points of view from which mental retardation can be considered: the clinical perspective and social-system perspective. The clinical perspective, which is by far the more common position, classifies mental retardation as a handicapping condition existing within the individual. From the social-system perspective, mental retardation is not an individual attribute. Rather, it is an achieved social status; being mentally retarded consists of playing the role of a retardate in one or more social systems. Within this framework a low test score or an organic defect is not a symptom of retardation; it is rather a characteristic that will increase the probability of an individual's being labeled retarded. Thus, it is possible for a person to be mentally retarded in some social systems and not in others.

After an in-depth study of the population and social systems in Riverside, the author concludes that there are some modifications that could be made in the clinical perspectives that would maximize convergence between the clinical and social-system definitions of mental retardation. She suggests that a two-dimensional model of retardation be adopted. According to this model, a person would have to fail both the intellectual dimension and the adaptive behavior dimension to be labeled retarded. From the results of the Riverside study, she demonstrates that adaptive behavior and intellectual functioning are, in fact, two independent dimensions and should be measured accordingly. She also finds that the percentages of retardation in Anglos are not affected by the addition of the adaptive behavior dimension, but that the percentages for Mexican-Americans and blacks are greatly reduced by this addition. She hypothesizes that many members of these latter populations do not have as great an opportunity to learn cognitive skills and, therefore, do not acquire the knowledge needed to pass an intelligence test. They can, however, demonstrate their ability to cope intelligently with problems outside the academic setting, and by achieving within the adaptive behavior dimension they, therefore, should, not be labeled retarded.

Mercer, J. R. A policy statement on assessment procedures and the rights of children. *Harvard Educational Review*, **1974**, *44*, **125–141.**

The article presents the results of an eight-year study of a large public school system's educational assessment and placement procedures. Results indicate a disproportionate number of minority group children assessed were placed in classes for the mentally retarded. Mercer asserts that present classification procedures violate five basic rights of children: (1) to be assessed in an appropriate cultural context, (2) to be evaluated as a multifaceted person, (3) to have access to all possible educational options, (4) to avoid stigma via negative diagnostic labels, and (5) to have one's own cultural identity and consequent self-respect. She concludes that placement in classes for the mentally retarded should require IQ *and* adaptive behavior scores at or below the third percentile on standardized tests.

Mercer, J. R. Sociocultural factors in educational labeling. In M. G. Begab & S. A. Richardson (Eds.), *The mentally retarded and society: A social science perspective*. **Baltimore: University Park Press, 1975.**

The author cites previous research to support this study on multicultural pluralistic assessment. She lists five premises relevant to the findings of her study: (1) tests measure only what has been learned, so all are basically achievement tests; (2) there are *no* "culture-free" tests; (3) only arbitrary differences exist between tests labeled "intelligence" and those labeled "achievement" or "aptitude"; (4) norms for these tests are not relevant to all of the school population; and (5) ethnic/racial factors need better specification to include the sociocultural factors relevant to the child's family/community environment.

Study design involved selecting a representative California school population consisting of Anglo, Mexican-American, and black children who were pluralistically assessed via WISC—R and a comprehensive collection of sociocultural data from the family and other significant adults. In addition to findings based on data collected with 1924 children and their parents, Mercer applies the outcome of these findings to several case histories of Chicano children. She concludes by emphasizing that the estimated learning potential derived from WISC—R and sociocultural assessment requires expansion to include other important variables (i.e., child's physical health, social competence in nonacademic situations).

Mercer, J. R. *Cultural diversity, mental retardation, and assessment: The case for nonlabeling*. **Paper presented at the Fourth International Congress of the International Association for the Scientific Study of Mental Deficiency, Washington, D. C., 1976.**

Mercer states that assessment techniques used to identify the mentally retarded are particularly weak in differentiating the organically intact person from a nondominant cultural/ethnic group and a bona fide mentally retarded person. She presents two conceptualizations basic to educational assessment: (1) the conformity model of society, which focuses on one main cultural group in identifying normative behavior for the population at large, and (2) the pluralistic model of society, which is based on a multicultural system and avoids misidentifying nondominant ethnic persons as MR.

The paper includes a detailed description of the components and effective use of the System of Multicultural Pluralistic Assessment (SOMPA). The three conceptual models (medical, social system, and pluralistic) are presented, along with pertinent similarities and differences and the role of each in the pluralistic assessment process.

Mercer, J. R. *Identifying the gifted Chicano child*. **Paper presented at the First Symposium on Chicano Psychology, University of California, Irvine, May 1976.**

The author thoroughly assesses the impact of monocultural educational testing techniques on the educational opportunities of the Chicano student in the United States. While noting the disproportionate number of Chicano students placed in classes for the mentally retarded, the primary topic of her paper deals with the difficulty of identifying educationally gifted Chicano children.

She begins with the historical context of Anglo-centered test development and details the negative impact of anglicizing Chicano children in the public school system. Mercer follows her critique of the monoculturally centered testing program with a description of a constructive alternative, the System of Multicultural Pluralistic Assessment (SOMPA).

Mercer, J. R. *Test "validity," "bias," and "fairness." An analysis from the perspective of the sociology of knowledge*. **Submitted to *Interchange*, The Ontario Institute for Studies in Education, Toronto, Canada, 1976.**

Mercer uses the concept sociology of knowledge to contrast and analyze the views of APA psychologists who support the status quo in testing as opposed to minority group professionals who are calling for a moratorium on traditional testing and consequent legislative action to ensure equal educational and employment opportunities for minority groups. The sociology of knowledge construct places the acceptance of beliefs as knowledge in a societal/environmental/cultural framework. Therefore, Mercer presents the Anglo conformity model as representative of psychometric psychologists who deal with the issues of test "validity," "fairness," and "bias." The minority psychologists, in contrast, use a pluralistic model as the basis for developing test "validity," and "fairness" and for dealing with test "bias." Mercer concludes that the differences in testing constructs among the two groups center on a political context and require political resolution, not academic or scientific resolution.

Mercer, J. R. *When you're up to your waist in alligators . . . SOMPA . . . or find a system for multicultural pluralistic assessment.* **Keynote address to Michigan Council for Exceptional children, Grand Rapids, March 1976.**

The address centered on the System of Multicultural Pluralistic Assessment (SOMPA) of elementary school-aged children and how the system fits into three different but mutually compatible models. There are two parts to SOMPA: (1) interview with mother and (2) test session. In an interview with the mother sociocultural modalities (family background) are discussed as well as questions relating to the child's "nonscholar" roles (i.e., family, peer group, community, nonacademic school). A health history inventory is also taken during the interview. In the test session additional information is gathered: WISC—R, physical dexterity, Bender-Gestalt, height/weight, and vision.

All information is categorized according to degree of fit to one of the three models which are simultaneously used to view each child. Each of the three models—medical, sociological, and pluralistic—is described in terms of particular dimensions: definition of normal/abnormal, assumptions of model, characteristics of model, properties of statistical distributions of scores on measures, characteristics of appropriate measures, interpretation of scores, and appropriate SOMPA measures.

The information gathered can thus be evaluated against the particular model. Current (and previously unpublished) research evidence indicates that when used in multiple-regression analysis, it is possible to assess more accurately the degree to which any individual can be judged as adaptive or maladaptive, allowing for differences in socioecological contexts. One of the important suggestions is that this process does not involve new "culture-free" instruments, but rather that existing instruments can be used and analyzed against an appropriate individualized context.

Mercer, J. R. **The struggle for children's rights: Critical juncture for school psychology.** *School Psychology Digest* **(in press).**

The paper centers on a historical development of educational testing and the role of the school psychologist. The Anglo conformity model of test development and the school psychologist's assessment for placement is well detailed, along with consequent legislative action to redirect educational assessment and placement procedures to include ethnic/culture-fair assessment and placement procedures, due process, and appropriate services to handicapped children and their parents. Mercer concludes with a five-point challenge to school psychologists: (1) realize the inadequacy of the Anglo conformity model of educational testing, (2) recognize a pluralistic model of society as a more valid representation of American society, (3) include pluralistic conceptualizations in testing procedures, (4) use a team appraisal approach for diagnosis, and (5) develop more complete educationally relevant diagnostic constructs.

Mercer, J. R. *System of Multicultural Pluralistic Assessment: Technical manual.* **New York: The Psychological Corporation, 1977.**

Mercer explains in detail her theoretical models for assessment and the statistical background of the SOMPA measurement process. The research background of the system, the statistical rationale, and related findings of other studies are discussed in detail. One chapter focuses on a theory of adaptive behavior which explains a sociological view of how a child adapts to the increasing complexities of the environment. Another chapter focuses on how the ABIC (Adaptive Behavior Inventory for Children) was developed in contrast to other adaptive behavior scales.

Nagler, B. A change in terms or in concepts? A small step forward or a giant step backward? *Journal of Special Education*, 1972, *6*, 61–64.

Nagler critiques the American Association on Mental Deficiency's definition of mental retardation. He cites a list of other historical terms previously used to describe intellectual subnormality and states that each was replaced by a more current term due to the original acquiring a highly negative meaning with the public (i.e., idiot replaced by imbecile). He asserts, however, that each change in terminology did not change the basic construct of what comprised mental retardation. Now with the addition of adaptive behavior as a criteria for assessing retardation, Nagler contends that the construct of mental retardation has changed, and may have harmful consequences for the handicapped and persons working with the handicapped.

Neer, W., Foster, D., Jones, J., & Reynolds, D. Socioeconomic bias in the diagnosis of mental retardation. *Exceptional children*, 1973, *40*, 38–39.

An analysis of variance study explored the relationship between diagnosis of mental retardation and socioeconomic status of the child. Thirty-one staff psychologists reviewed identical assessment data for three cases with the variable of socioeconomic status manipulated to include low, middle, and high socioeconomic differentiations. Results of the ANOVA indicated a significant difference supporting low socioeconomic status and a resultant diagnosis of mental retardation versus a recommendation against such a diagnosis for the middle/high socioeconomic cases.

Nihira, K. A study of environmental demands as an aid to construct a behavior rating scale. *Project News of Parsons State Hospital and Training Center*, 1967, *3*, 2–21.

A critical-incident technique was utilized to determine what behaviors would be problematic in several environments (i.e., in 2 state institutions, special education classes of a public school system, and 23 state day-care centers). Differential importance was attributed to self-help skills and the domains of emotional and conduct disorders. It was found that self-help skills are more problematic in the institution, while emotional and conduct disorders are more so in the community. Two possible reasons are given: (1) institutional residents are generally thought to be lower functioning, and (2) community individuals have acquired adequate self-help skills. Implications for treatment and training program placement are mentioned.

Nihira, K. Factorial dimensions of adaptive behavior in mentally retarded children
and adolescents. *American Journal of Mental Deficiency*, 1969, *74*, 130–141.

This factor analysis study includes adaptive behavior data on 313 institutionalized
children and adolescents. Three main adaptive behavior domains appear significant for this population: (1) personal independence, (2) social maladaptation,
and (3) personal maladaptation. Results across age groups support the adaptive
behavior factors as constructed. The author discusses application of the results to
commonly used coping skills of institutionalized retardates.

Nihira, K. Factorial dimensions of adaptive behavior in adult retardates. *American
Journal of Mental Deficiency*, 1969, *73*, 868–878.

Nihira explores the relationship between the differences of coping skills among
retardates and the then measurable dimensions of adaptive behavior. A newly
developed adaptive behavior scale was used to measure objectively 919 institutionalized adult retardates for functional living skills in their institutional
environments. Factorial analysis of the data indicated two significant adaptive
behavior dimensions (personal independence and social maladaptation) among 10
domains in personal independence and 12 domains in personal and social responsibility.

Nihira, K. Environmental expectations and adaptive behavior. *Proceedings of the
79th Annual convention of the American Psychological Association*, 1971, *6*,
619–620.

A critical-incident survey was conducted to determine the types of behavioral
expectations imposed upon retardates. Three environments were tapped: 2 state
institutions, public school special education classes, and 23 day care centers. The
IQs of all groups were roughly comparable, ranging from 0 to 95. The behaviors
fell into two broad categories: those due to lack of skills and abilities and those
due to emotional or behavioral disturbances. When the investigations moved
from the institutional environments to day-care centers or to special educational class groups, the incidents due to lack of skills or abilities gradually de-
creased while the emotional or behavioral disturbances increased. Possible interpretations for the results included (1) a difference in actual behavior between
the groups and (2) a difference in demands and expectations present in the
environments.

Nihira, K. Importance of environmental demands in the measurement of adaptive
behavior. In C. E. Meyers, R. K. Eyman, & G. Tarjan (Eds.), *Sociobehavioral
studies in mental retardation: Papers in honor of Harvey F. Dingman*. Washington, D. C.: American Association on Mental Deficiency, 1973.

The premise for this study stems from the American Association on Mental
Deficiency's definition of mental retardation, which includes sociocultural factors
in addition to a measure of intellectual functioning. Nihira's project sought to
develop an objective adaptive behavior measure to be used with residentially and
institutionally placed retardates. The study describes the technique used in the

first phase in developing the adaptive behavior instrument. The critical-incident technique generated the objective items needed for establishing the continuum of adaptive to maladaptive behaviors. Nihira also reports significant differences between appropriate adaptive behavior for community-based retardates versus institutional retardates. In the discussion section he elaborates on an operational definition of adaptive behavior to include the relationship between a person's skills and resources and the behavioral/social requirements of his/her environment.

Nihira, K. Dimensions of adaptive behavior in institutionalized mentally retarded children and adults: Developmental perspective. *American Journal of Mental Deficiency*, 1976, *81*, 215–226.

The AAMD Adaptive Behavior Scale, Part I, was administered to 3354 institutionally placed children and adults, and the subscale scores were then factor analyzed for eight age groupings. The hypotheses under study included:

1. Determining the applicability of specific adaptive behaviors of the scale in the assessment of different age groups.
2. Pinpointing consistency of adaptive behavior factors across age groups.
3. Noting developmental differences among adaptive behavior subscales.
4. Finding any significant relationships between the above three factors and level of retardation. Results were presented according to the level of retardation and minimum and maximum growth rates and critical developmental periods.

Nihira, K., Foster, R., Shellhass, M., & Leland, H. *American Association on Mental Deficiency Adaptive Behavior Scale, 1975 revision*. Washington, D. C.: American Association on Mental Deficiency, 1975.

The Adaptive Behavior Scale (ABS) is an assessment tool employed to measure a varied range of behaviors of the mentally retarded, emotionally impaired, and developmentally disabled. Its primary purpose is to provide objective profiles of an individual's effectiveness in coping with the demands of the environment (i.e., adaptive behavior as defined by the American Association on Mental Deficiency). Developed to provide useful behavioral information and designed to be used in conjunction with other objective measures (IQ tests, for example), the ABS provides a description of the way in which the individual maintains independence in daily living situations and how these behaviors approach the social expectations of a particular environment.

This test is composed of two parts. Part I assesses adaptive behaviors using a normal development paradigm as a measuring standard. This section comprises 10 behavioral domains and 21 subdomains. The 10 domains are Independent Functioning, Physical Development, Economic Activity, Language Development, Number and Time Concepts, Domestic Activities, Self-directiveness, Responsibility, and Socialization.

Part II assesses maladaptive behaviors related to personality and behavioral disorders and is comprised of 14 domains: Violent and Destructive Behavior, Antisocial Behavior, Rebellious Behavior, Untrustworthy Behavior, Withdrawal

Stereotyped Behavior and Odd Mannerisms, Inappropriate Interpersonal Behavior, Unacceptable Vocal Habits, Unacceptable or Eccentric Habits, Self-destructive Behavior, Hyperactive Tendencies, Sexually Aberrant Behavior, Psychological Disturbances, and The Use of Medication.

This test is administered using an interview-informant method. Easy-to-follow directions and score response sheets make the administration of the ABS relatively easy and highly reliable. Response scores are normalized to institutionalized mentally retarded persons ages 3 to 69. Response profiles are determined by using a simple scoring procedure and then matching the subject's scores with normalized data, thus adequately identifying both strengths and weaknesses of the subject in relation to chronological age peers as well as peers in similar environmental situations.

The authors suggest that ABS profiles can be used to facilitate proper placement in habilitative programs, to assess behavioral changes resulting from these programs, to compare the subject's behavior in a variety of situations as well as with different people, to provide a common information exchange system, and to assess the effectiveness of existing programs, as well as to determine the need for developing new programs.

Nihira, K., Foster, R., & Spencer, L. Measurement of adaptive behavior: A descriptive system for mental retardates. *American Journal of Orthopsychiatry*, 1968, *38*, 622–634.

Adaptive behavior is defined as "the effectiveness with which (1) the individual is able to maintain himself independently and (2) the degree to which he satisfactorily meets the culturally imposed demands of personal and social responsibility." The authors note that the traditional practice of using a unidimensional score to serve as a summary of adaptive behavior is fruitless, and they suggest a multivariate approach. They sampled existing measures of adaptive behavior, along with an informally developed list of ward behaviors, and from this information produced a preliminary behavior checklist with 325 specific behaviors in 10 domains. This preliminary scale was used by 27 ward attendants to rate 307 retardates. The 10 behavioral domains were compared to determine how well they discriminated between and correlated with adaptive behavior levels. Intercorrelations were also done between the 10 hypothesized behavioral domains. The authors note that the applications of specific weighting systems will yield measures for predicting specified criteria.

Nihira, K., & Shellhaas, M. Study of adaptive behavior: Its rationale, method, and implication in rehabilitation programs. *Mental Retardation*, 1970, *8*, 11–16.

After briefly reviewing the development of the Adaptive Behavior Scale, the authors address the concept of adaptation as "a matching between the resources of an individual and the requirements of his environment." Several studies are reviewed: Nihira's studies on reasons for referral, three major dimensions of adaptive behavior, and Shellhaas's study of general tolerance. These studies are also related to rehabilitation. The authors state that knowledge of the retardate's resources and limitations plus the demands of specific environments are necessary for the development of effective rehabilitation programs. Knowledge of the environment in which the retardate may be placed has several advantages: (1) if specific environmental requirements are delineated, one may be able to predict the retardate's possible success in adapting to it; (2) more effective placement may be made (i.e., locating an environment tolerant of the retardate's limitations); (3) an individual may be specifically trained to the environmental demands; (4) prejudices and misconceptions about the mentally retarded can be isolated in particular environments and then studied.

Nihira, L., & Nihira, K. Normalized behavior in community placement. *Mental Retardation*, **1975,** *13,* **9–13.**

Nihira and Nihira conducted a survey with 109 caretakers for 425 mentally retarded persons in community-based facilities. They present a spectrum of normative, positive behaviors cited by the interviewees. Their results indicate the development of self-care skills among retarded residents to be a major priority for the caretakers.

Oakland, T. *The concept of adaptive behavior.* **Paper presented at the Annual Meeting of the Texas Psychological Association, Houston, 1976.**

The address introduced a symposium on adaptive behavior and served as a backdrop for other presentations on adaptive behavior measures and research. Oakland briefly traced the historical development of adaptive behavior as a concept and then illustrated and contrasted two differing perspectives and measures of adaptive behavior (the Vineland Social Maturity Scale and Mercer's System of Multicultural Pluralistic Assessment). He concluded his address with some cautions concerning the limits, efficacy, and multiconceptual attributes of adaptive behavior as applied to public education.

Penrose, L. Mental deficiency. *Journal of Special Education,* **1972,** *6,* **65–66.**

Penrose considers that the two major directions in defining mental retardation are the medical approach and the social context. He asserts that the medical definition of mental retardation is the most appropriate, and most valid approach. He continues to explain the rationale for a "disease" model of retardation.

Schwartz, B., Allen, R., & Cortazzo, A. Factors in the behavior checklist revisited and revised. *Training School Bulletin,* **1974,** *70,* **248–254.**

Data from 3,000 Adaptive Behavior Check List ratings on institutionally placed retardates was factor analyzed for revision purposes. The study analyzed items for inclusion or omission in the revision, appropriate placement in the three major behavioral categories, and need for rephrasing ambiguous items. Results yielded a 60-item revision on the ABCL.

Tucker, J. A. Operationalizing a non-biased appraisal process. In T. Oakland (Ed.), *With bias toward none: Non-biased assessment of minority children.* Lexington, Ky.: Coordinating Office for Regional Resource Centers, 1976.

This seminal article details a nonbiased process for educational assessment and intervention in public education. Tucker states that the aim of comprehensive nonbiased assessment programs is to prevent errors in placement and to maximize intervention techniques. Tucker emphasizes assessment as opposed to testing, and thoroughly presents nine components of an individual comprehensive assessment (i.e., observational data, language dominance, educational assessment, etc.). With each component he presents the objective and evaluation of the component, procedures and interpretation appropriate to that section, and options and rationale for the data collected.

Walls, R., & Werner, T. *History and future of behavior checklists.* Paper presented at the Annual Convention of the Midwestern Association of Behavior Analysis, 1976.

The authors offer a wealth of information on behavior checklists. They review 157 lists in an annotated bibliography. Walls and Werner trace the possible inception of the behavior checklist to the development and use of achievement instruments, adjustment-personality inventories, and developmental evaluations. They then discuss categories of checklists from basic adjective checklists to prescriptive ones detailing remediation/treatment programs. The authors foresee two major future trends in the use of these instruments: (1) as supplemental data in comprehensive individual assessments and (2) as another resource in individualized educational/vocational programming.

Walls, R., Werner, T., & Bacon, A. Behavior checklists. In J. Cone & R. Hawkins (Eds.), *Behavioral assessment: New directions in clinical psychology.* New York: Brunner/Mazel, in press.

The authors have compiled and categorized 136 behavior checklists. The intent of their review is to facilitate the appropriate selection of checklists by assessment professionals. The checklists are grouped according to the descriptive and/or prescriptive value of each one. Prescriptive behavior checklists specifically include remediation/training suggestions or techniques.

Wilson, J. Is the term "adaptive behavior" educationally relevant? *Journal of Special Education*, 1972, *6*, 93–95.

The article responds to Clausen's argument against including adaptive behavior as a criteria for diagnosing mental retardation. Wilson asserts that as a school psychologist/educator he finds adaptive behavior is educationally relevant and a necessary component in a thorough diagnostic/intervention program. He disputes Clausen's contention that adaptive behavior assessments will lead to more false positive mental retardation diagnoses.

Index

Boldface page numbers indicate material in tables or figures. An *n*. after a page number refers to a footnote or reference.

"AAMD Manual on Terminology" (Heber), 158

Aanes, D., 227

Achievement tests, 41, 128, 192, 194

"Active-passive dimension, An" (Blackman), 230

Adams, J., 228

Adaptive behavior. *See also* Adaptive behavior scales

  definition of, 67, 89, **89**, 90, 97, **97**, 115, 129, 216, 221

  and diagnosis, general, **97**, 97–98

  measurement of, 98, **98**

  and social competence, 61

"Adaptive behavior" (Brantley), 230

"Adaptive behavior" (Leland et al.), 239

"Adaptive behavior and measured intelligence . . ." (Adams), 228

"Adaptive behavior and mentally retarded behavior" (Leland), 238

"Adaptive behavior and social adjustment" (Leland & Husseini), 239

"Adaptive behavior changes . . ." (Aanes & Moen), 227

Adaptive Behavior Check List (ABCL), 228, 251

"Adaptive behavior in the retarded" (McIntosh & Warren), 241

Adaptive Behavior Inventory for Children (ABIC), 14, 16, 68, 75–76, 79, 80, 85, 86, 91, 93–94, 98, 100, 113, 116, 145, **146, 155,** 185, 191, 193, 202–207, 209, 211, 220, 221, 235, 247

Adaptive Behavior Newsletter, 232

"Adaptive behavior philosophy, An" (Gold), 234

Adaptive Behavior Project, 23

Adaptive behavior scales (ABSs), 1, 2, 8, 13, 15, 16, 21ff., 47, 48, 67, 86, 88, **88,** 90, 91, **155,** 227, 234, 237, 239, 240, 249, 250

  administrative aspects, 131–32, **135–36**

  age-related behaviors, 31–33

  categorization of, 144ff.

  and competence, 34–39

  definition, of adaptive behavior, 39–41, 89–90, 97, 115, 129, 216, 221

  elements of, 23–25

  evaluated, 159

  factor analysis of, 45ff., **46, 47**

group decision form, 137
group rating, **120–123**
and intelligence, 25–26
rating form, 116–117, 119, 127ff.,
    133–136, 138–139
reliability/validity of, 33–34
results of, 118ff., **118, 120, 121,** 129–
    131, **133–135**
stimulation exercise, 117–118
Adaptive Behavior Scale—Public
    School Version (ABS—PSV),
    15, 48, 88, 91, 93, 95, 98, **99,** 100,
    106, 113, 117, 147, 157ff., **155,**
    237, 238
adaptive behavior dimensions,
    170ff., **170**
cost/administration, 131–132
development of, 159–160
and educational programming, 169ff.
and IQ, 168
questionnaire on, 101–104, **101–104**
reliability of, 167–169
and teachers/parents, 160
validity of, 161–167, 169, 221
Adaptive fitting, 70–71, 73, 77
Adaptive measures, classification of,
    155
Adaptive trajectories, 74–75, 79–80
Adaptive typography, 75–76
Age-related behaviors, 31–34, 37
Aiker, L., 228
Allen, R., 228, 251
Amatruda, C. S., 61, 63–66, 81n.
American Association of Mental Defi-
    ciency (AAMD), **6–7,** 11, 12, 15,
    16, 22, 23, 45, 45n., 60, 61, 65,
    67, 91, 157, 158, 204, 228–30,
    232, 233, 235, 240, 247–249
American Guidance Services, **150**
*American Journal of Mental De-
    ficiency,* 228, 237, 248, 249
American Journal of Orthopsychiatry,
    250
American Psychologist, 229, 232, 233,
    236, 240
"Analysis of factors in the family's
    withdrawal, An . . ."
    (Mercer), 241

Anastasi, A., 4, 17n.
Anglicization, measured, 196
"Another psychological view . . ."
    (Jackson), 236
ANOVA, 247
"Anticipated achievement" (Mercer),
    242–243
Anticipatory socialization, 73–74,
    203–204
Antisocial Behavior, in behavior scale,
    47, 48, 164, 165, 171, 249
Aptitude tests, 192
Aristotle, 215
Assessment, psychological. *See* Psy-
    chological assessment
Auditory Acuity, 201
Ayers, F. W., **148**

Bacon, A., 252
Balthazar, E. E., **6,** 7, 17n.
Balthazar Scales of Adaptive Behavior,
    147, 155
Baroff, G., 228, 229
Bartlett, D. P., 105, 107n.
Baumeister, A., 83, 83n., 215, 216, 222,
    224n., 229
Begab, M. G., 244
Behavioral assessment (Cone & Haw-
    kins, eds.), 252
Behavioral Checklist Manual, 117
Behavioral checklists, 129, 141, 251,
    252
Behavioral Specificity of Items, in be-
    havior scale, 119
Behavior Characteristics Progression
    Chart (BCPC), 88, 132, **147, 155**
"Behavior checklists" (Walls et al.),
    252
Bell, R. Q., 71, 81n.
Bender, L., 185, 211n.
Bender Visual Motor Gestalt Test, 185,
    197, 199, 200, 202, 246
Bennett, F. A., 41, 42n.
Berdine, **150**
Bernal, E., 10, 17n., 229
Bernardoni, L. C., 4, 20n.
Bias, in assessment, 105, 221, 245, 247,
    252

Binet, A., 11, 12, 60, 81*n.*, 157
Blackman, L., 230
Black Psychological Association, 232, 236
Blackwell, L., 219, 224*n.*
Blashfield, R., 232
Block, N. J., 218, 224*n.*
Bower, T. G. R., 218, 224*n.*
Brantley, J., 230
Bryant, J. L., 231
Buck, M., 231
Buckholt, D., 219, 224*n.*
Buros, O. K., 144, 151*n.*

Cain, L. F., 61, 81*n.*, **88**, 92*n.*, **148**
Cain-Levine Social Competency Scale, **88, 148, 155**
California Political Code, on mental competency, 59, 60
California State Department of Education, 15, 157*n.*, 158, 210, 212*n.*
California State Education Code, 15, 60, 162, 169
Callier-Azusa Scale, 88, **148**
Cambridge Area Developmental Rehabilitation and Education Center, **148**
Cambridge Assessment, Developmental Rating & Evaluation, **148**
Camelot Behavioral Checklist, 88, **99,** 117–119, **122–123,** 132, **149, 155**
Carlson, N. A., 61, 68, 68*n.*, 72, 76, 81*n.*, 227*n.*
Carver, R. P., 130, 132*n.*, 143, 151*n.*, 154, 154*n.*, 156*n.*
Cassel, T. Z., 68*n.*, 70, 72–74, 76, 81*n.*, 203, 212*n.*
Castaneda, A., 73, 82*n.*
Cattel Infant Intelligence Scale, 27
Cerebral palsy, 201
"Change in terms or in concepts" (Nagler), 247
Characteristics of Visually Impaired Persons in the United States (U.S. Public Health Series), 201*n.*
Charles S., v. Board of Education, San Francisco, 158

Checklists. *See* Behavioral checklists
Chromosomal abnormalities, 169
Classification, 1
   and adaptive behavior scales, 40–42
   bookkeeping aspects, 22
   function of, 10
   habilitative, 22
   and IQ, 177, 244
   of retardation, 12, 15, 16, 25–26, 35, 40–41, 244
Clausen, J., 11, 12, 17*n.*, 219, 222, 224*n.*, 231, 232, 240, 252
Cleary, T. A., 232
Clothing care, in behavior scale, 52, **53**
Cognitive Development, and behavior scale, 53, **53,** 54
Cole, L. J., 11, 15, 18*n.*, 48, 86, **88,** 92*n.*, 95, 107*n.*, 145, **146, 147,** 152*n.*, 160, 161, 165, 166, 182*n.*, 183*n.*, 221, 224*n.*, 238
Committee on Educational Uses of Tests with Disadvantaged Students, 236
Communication Skills, in behavior scale, 50, 54, **54, 150, 151**
Community Living Skills, in behavior scale, 53, **53,** 54
Community Self-sufficiency, in behavior scale, 49, 50, 53, 54
Comparison of two methods . . . (Bryant), 231
Competent behavior, 34–39
   legal definition, 59
   and visibility, 34
"Concept of adaptive behavior, The" (Oakland), 251
Concurrent validity, 130, **134.** *See also* Validity
Cone, J., 252
Conference on measurement of adaptive behavior (Kagin, ed.), 238
Conformity, and adaptation, 30–31, 35
Construct validity, 33, 130, **134.** *See also* Validity
Consulting Psychologists Press, **147, 148**
Content validity, 130, **134.** *See also* Validity

Contexts of life, The (Carlson), 227*n*.
"Continuing problem of defining men-
    tal retardation, The" (Clausen),
    231
Coordinating Office of Regional Re-
    source Centers (COORC), 85, 93
Coping, and adaptation, 28–30, 40
Corpus Christi Independent School
    District, 232
Cortazzo, A., 251
Coulter, J. L., 227ff.
Coulter, W. A., 3ff, 4, 17*n*., 85ff, 93ff.,
    115ff., 141ff., 215ff., 227ff.
Creativity, in behavior scale, **150**
"Criteria for classification systems"
    (Cromwell et al.), 232
Criterion-reference, 10, 33, 130, 145,
    153, 154, **155**
"Criterion-referenced and norm-
    referenced assessment . . ."
    (Drew), 233
"Critique of the AAMD ABS-PS"
    (Fitzpatrick & Rogers), 233
Cromwell, R., 232
Cronbach, L. J., 233
CTB/McGraw-Hill, **150**
"Cultural diversity, mental retardation,
    and assessment" (Mercer), 244

Dallas County MHMR Center, **149**
Daly, F. M., 158, 182*n*.
Dayan, M., 12, 17*n*.
"Declaration of General and Special
    Rights . . ." 24, 42*n*.
Deficit model. *See* Medical model
Deinstitutionalization, 41
"Demonstration and measurement of
    adaptive behavior, The" (Le-
    land et al.), 239
Denver Developmental Scale, 88
Department of Health, Education, and
    Welfare, 7
Department of Mental Hygiene, 70
Destructive behavior, in behavior
    scale, 168, 171
Developmental checklists, 129
Developmental diagnosis, 63

Developmental Evaluation Scale, **149,
    155**
Developmental Psychology, 136
Diabetes, 201
Diana v. *California State Board of
    Education*, 158, 162
"Dimensions of adaptive behavior"
    (Nihira), 249
"Dimenstions of adaptive be-
    havior . . ." (Lambert &
    Nicoll), 237
Dingman, H. F., 13, 17*n*.
DiNola, **150, 151**
Diphtheria, 201
Disabeling trajectory, and socializa-
    tion, 80
Disease model. *See* Medical model
Dixon, W., 51, 56*n*.
Dobbs, J., 88, 92*n*.
Doll, E. A., 60, 61, 64, 66, 81*n*., **88**,
    92*n*., **151**
Domain validity, 163–167. *See also* Va-
    lidity
Domestic Activity, in behavior scale,
    24, **46**, 50, 179, 249
Draguns, J. G., 105, 107*n*.
Dressing/undressing, in behavior
    scale, 49, **52**
Drew, C. J., 10, 17*n*., 145, 151*n*., 233
Drinking, in behavior scale, **52**
Dunn, L., 231
Dworkin, G., 218, 224*n*.

Earner/consumer, roles, 206
Eating, public, in behavior scale, 52, **53**
Eccentric Habits, in behavior scale, **47,**
    48, 165
Economic Activity, in behavior scale,
    24, **46**, 50, **149, 150,** 164, 166,
    168, 170, 179, 180, 249
Economy, roles in, 36–37, 79
Edmark Associates, **146, 147, 149**
Educable mentally retarded (EMR), 9,
    48, **103**, 105, 161–167, 169, 171,
    173, 216, 219, 242. *See also*
    Mental retardation
"Educational uses of tests . . ."
    (Cleary et al.), 232

Education of the Handicapped Act,
Part B, 85
Edumetric function, 211
EFG, 173–177
and class norms, **175,** 176
and EMR, **174, 176**
interpersonal problems, 177
Ellis, R., 242
Elzey, F., 61, 81*n.,* **88,** 92*n.,* **148**
Emotionally handicapped (EH), 9, 10,
161, 162*n.,* 171, 181
Engel, M., 105, 107*n.*
England, retarded in, 48
"Environmental expectations and
adaptive behavior" (Nihira), 248
Estimated Learning Potential (ELP),
185, 195, 196, 208, 209, 231
Ethclass, described, 187*n.,* 187–188
Ethics, and measurement, 22–23
Ethnicity
and adaptive behavior, 220
Anglo culture, 14, 187–188, 196
and assessment, 234
and behavior scale, **134,** 162, 166,
168, 171
Blacks, 14, 116
Caucasians, 116
Chicanos, 14, 73, 116, 245
and norms, 130
and retardation, 14, 205, 242–245
and SOMPA, 116, 186, 197, 210
and special education, 142–143
of test examiner, 234
Etiology, and medical model, 189–190
Exceptional Children, 247
Eyman, R. K., 238, 248

Face validity, 33. *See also* Validity
Factor analysis, 31, 45ff., **46, 47,** 48, 49,
61, 115
"Factorial dimensions of adaptive behavior . . ." (Nihira), 248
Factorial validity, 230. *See also* Validity
"Factors in the behavior
checklist . . ." (Schwartz et
al.), 251

Fairview Behavior Evaluation Battery,
149
Fairview State Hospital, **149**
Family, and social roles, 76–77, 193,
197, 206
Faur, P., 11, 17*n.,* 154, 156*n.*
Ferritor, D., 219, 224*n.*
Figueroa, R., 11, 15, 18*n.,* 48, 86, **88,**
92*n.,* 95, 107*n.,* 145, **146, 147,**
152*n.,* 161, 183*n.,* 221, 224*n.,*
238
Fine motor skills, **149**
Fitzpatrick, A., 15, 17*n.,* 233
"Five decades of public controversy
over mental testing" (Cron-
bach), 233
Florida, ABS-PS in, 145
Florida State Department of Educa-
tion, 171, 182*n.*
Food preparation/eating, in behavior
scale, **53**
Foreness, S., 181, 182*n.*
Foster, C., 234
Foster, D., 247
Foster, R., 5, 12, 13, 18*n.,* 19*n.,* 45,
57*n.,* 61, 67, 82*n.,* 86, 88, **88,** 90,
92*n.,* **99, 147, 149,** 159, 167,
183*n.,* 234, 239, 249, 250
Frankenberg, W., 88, 92*n.*
Fullan, M., 81*n.*
Functional Autonomy, in behavior
scale, 48–50, 170–173. *See also*
Independence, in behavior scale

Garza, P., 234
General intellectual factor. *See* "g"
factor
Gesell, A., 61, 63, 64, 66, 81*n.*
Gesell Development Schedules, 27
Gestational disorders, 169
"g" factor, 61, 64
Gleason, W. P., 15, 18*n.,* 115, 125*n.,*
159, 182*n.*
Goddard, H., 11, 60, 157
Gold, M. W., 223, 224*n.,* 234
Grooming, 49
Grossman, H. J., 6, 17*n.,* 22, 42*n.,* 45,
56*n.,* 57*n.,* 61, 67, 81*n.* 141, 142,

Grassman, H. J. (continued)
    152*n.*, 157, 169, 182*n.*, 204,
    212*n.*, 215, 216, 221, 224*n.*
Gross-motor development, **148**
Group decision form, 137
Guarnaccia, V., 47, 49, 50, 57*n.*
Guide to behavior assessment, 235
Guilford, J. P., 61, 81*n.*, 130, 133*n.*

Haigh, J., 235
Haigh-Harbin Adaptive Behavior Scale
    (H-HABS), 235, 236
Halpern, A., **150**
Halverson, C., 50, 57*n.*
Hamblin, R. L., 219, 224*n.*
Handicap, and norms, 129
Hansberry, L., 113
Harbin, G., 235
Harlow, H. F., 72, 81*n.*
Harvard Educational Review, 244
Haslan, J., 11
Hawkins, R., 252
Haywood, H. C., 242
Head Start programs, 73
Health Examination Survey (U.S. Pub-
    lic Health Series), 201, 201*n.*
Health History Inventories, in
    SOMPA, 185, 197, 200–202, 209
Heber, R. A., **5, 6,** 12–14, 16, 18*n.*,
    17*n.*, 27, 30, 42*n.*, 61, 65, 66,
    81*n.*, 86, 92*n.*, 158
Henderson, R. A., 158, 182*n.*
Hewett, F., 181, 182*n.*
H. & H. Enterprises, **150**
Hinde, R. A., 72, 81*n.*, 82*n.*
"History and future of behavior
    checklists" (Walls & Werner),
    252
Hobbs, N., 232
Horrocks, J. E., 4, 18*n.*, 143, 152*n.*,
    153, 156*n.*
Horton, L., 157, 182*n.*
Howe, J., 11
Humphreys, L. G., 232
Husseini, M., 239
Hyperactivity, in behavior scale, **47,**
    165, 165, 177, 250

Identification/placement, and adaptive

behavior, 10, 11, 14, 15, 142,
    144–146, **146,** 153, 154, **155,**
    215–221
"Identifying the gifted Chicano child"
    (Mercer), 245
"Importance of environmental de-
    mands . . ." (Nihira), 248
Inappropriate Interpersonal Behavior,
    250
Inappropriate Manners, in behavior
    scale, 165, 171
Independence, in behavior scale, 23,
    31, 34, 35, **46,** 48–50, 52, 115,
    149, 150, 164, 166, 170, 178, 179,
    248, 249
Independence, and dependence, 41
Infants, adaptive behavior in, 8
In-school behavior, 130–131
"Institutionalized Anglocentrism"
    (Mercer), 242
Intelligence. *See also,* IQ
    and adaptive behavior, 25–28, 158–
        159, 218
    intellect, structure of, 61
    and motivation, 36
    potential for, 218
    and retardation, 157–158
    tests, 51, 60, 61, 192
Interchange, 245
Intervention/programming, and adap-
    tive behavior, 145ff., **147–151,**
    153, **155,** 215, 219, 221–224
Intrapersonal Adjustment, in behavior
    scale, 171
"Introduction and theoretical consid-
    erations" (Leland), 238
IQ. *See also* Intelligence
    and ABS—PS, 95, 106
    and classification, 177, 244
    criticized, 9, 45, 239, 240
    and diagnosis, 22, 27
    and domain scores, 168
    of EMR pupils, 162
    and expectations, 248
    and identification, 10
    and intellect, functioning, 170
    and potential, 218
    reliance on, 228

and retardation, 26, 70, 229
test, 12, 15, 33, 106, 128
Irvin, L. K., **150**
Issues in the classification of children
(Hobbs, ed.), 232
"Is the term 'adaptive behavior' educationally relevant?" (Wilson), 252
Itard, J., 11, 157
Item validity, 162–163. *See also* Validity

Jackson, G., 218, 224*n*., 236
Jaco, E. G., 243
Japan, adaptive studies in, 2
Jensen, A., 233
Johnson, D., 145, 152*n*.
Johnson, R. W., 4, 20*n*.
Johnson, W., 144, 152*n*.
Jones, J., 247
Jones, R. L., 12, 18*n*., 240
Journal of Afro-American Issues, 231
Journal of School Psychology, 233
Journal of Special Education, 229–232, 238, 240, 247, 251, 252

Kagin, E., **5**, 18*n*., 61, 82*n*., 157, 182*n*., 238
Kaiser, H. A., 51, 57*n*.
Kamin, L. J., 12, 18*n*., 218, 224*n*.
Kaminsky, B. P., **150, 151**
Kapplan School Supply Corporation, **149**
Kendrick, S. A., 232
King, D. L., 72, 82*n*.
Kohn, M., 236
Koppitz, E. M., 199, 212*n*.
Kozloff, M., 219, 224*n*.
Kuder-Richardson correlation, 130
Kuhlmann Tests of Mental Development, 27

Labeling the mentally retarded
(Mercer), 243
Lacey, H., 50, 57*n*.
Lambert, N. M., 8, 11, 15, 16, 18*n*., 47–50, 57*n*., 61, 82*n*., 86, **88**, 92*n*., 95, 107*n*., 113, 115, 125*n*., 145, **146, 147,** 152*n*., 157ff., 159,

161–63, 170, 182*n*., 183*n*., 221, 224*n*., 237, 238
Language Development, in behavior scale, 24, **46**, 48, 53, **53**, 164, 166, 168, 170, 178–180, 249
Loasa, L. M., 16, 19*n*., 93, 107*n*.
Larry P. v. *Riles,* 16, 158
Lauro, C., 144, 152*n*.
Learning
and adaptive behavior, 40
and disabled, 216–217
Learning Accomplishment Profile, **149**
Leland, H. W., 1–3, **5,** 7, 11–14, 18*n*., 19*n*., 21ff., 22, 25, 28, 30, 33, 36, 40, 42*n*., 45, 57*n*., 61, 67, 82*n*., 86, **88,** 90, 92*n*., 106, 107*n*., 116, 125*n*., **147,** 159, 167, 183*n*., 218, 224*n*., 238, 239, 249
Leland, M., 12, 13, 16, 17, 18*n*.
Lemert, E. M., 75, 82*n*.
Levine, M., 228
Levine, S., 61, 81*n*., **88,** 92*n*., **148**
Lewis, J. F., 2, 85, 86, **88,** 92*n*., 94, 107*n*., 113, 116, 145, 146, 152*n*., 185ff., 198, 202, 209, 212*n*.
Link, R., **150**
"Lions in search of more Christians"
(MacMillian & Jones), 240
Littell, W., 240
Livingston, S. A., 145, 152*n*.
Loeffler, F., 228
Long, N. J., 105, 107*n*.
Loubser, J. J., 61, 81*n*.

Mainstreaming, 187
MacMillian, D. L., 12, 18*n*., 240
Mannheim, K., 1, 2*n*., 215, 224*n*.
"Manual on Terminology and Classification in Mental Retardation, A," 86, 177
Marr, J., 144, 152*n*.
Mastenbrook, J., 106, 107*n*., 217, 220, 224*n*.
Matuszek, P., 10, 19*n*., 143, 152*n*.
McCarthy, J., 240
McClelland, D. C., 240, 241
McIntosh, E., 241
McKenna, B., 11, 18*n*.

McLean, J., 12, 17n.
Measles, red, 201
Measured Intelligence (MI), 51. *See
    also* Intelligence; IQ
"Measurement of adaptive behavior"
    (Nihira et al.), 250
"Measurement of change in adaptive
    behavior, The" (Foster & Fos-
    ter), 234
Measures of vision, Hearing, and
    Weight/Height, in SOMPA, 185,
    199–200
Medical model, 61ff., 185, 188–191,
    197–202, 211, 242, 243, 251
Medication use, in behavior scale, 47,
    47
Meier, J. M., 218, 219, 224n.
Meningitis, 201
Menstruation, in behavior scale, **52**
Mental age, 60
"Mental deficiency" (Penrose), 251
Mental deficiency, definitions of, 59ff.
Mentally retarded and society, The
    (Begab & Richardson, eds.), 244
Mental retardation (MR). *See also*
    Educable mentally retarded;
    Trainable mentally retarded
and adaptive behavior, 65
assessment of, 10, 94, 247
classification of, 12, 16, 25–26, 35,
    40–41, 244
in classroom, 181
community-based card, 31, 251
definition, 12, 60, 96–97, **97,** 157, 186,
    216, 217n., 217, 219, 228–232
diagnosis of, 8n., 93, 159, 169, 252
educables, 15
and ethnicity, 14, 205, 242–245
goals of, 239
identification of, 12, 15, 186
and institutionalization, 8, 13, 16, 26,
    27, 48, 51, 227, 241–242, 249
and intelligence, 22, 26, 61, 70, 229
and labels, 178
and learning, 116, 142
and litigation, 158
models on, 242
and norms, 36

organic defect in, 243
and potential, 25
and productivity, 49
and responsibility, personal, 56
reversibility in, 28, 37
and rights, individual, 24–25
and school, 85
and self-esteem, 229
and social expectations, 47
survey on, 88
treatment, evaluated, 247
Mental Retardation, journal, 227, 228,
    238, 251
Mental Retardation (Baroff), 228
Mental Retardation Abstracts, 239
"Mental retardation and adaptive be-
    havior" (Leland), 238
Mercer, J. R., 1, 2, 2n., 4, **5,** 7, 8, 8n.,
    10, 11, 13–17, 18n., 19n., 59ff.,
    61, 70, 82n., 85, 86, **88,** 91, 92n.,
    93, 94, 105, 106, 107n., 113, 116,
    142, 145, **146,** 152n., 185ff., 195,
    196, 198, 202, 205, 209, 212n.,
    217–219, 217n., 221, 223, 224n.,
    230, 235, 241–246, 251
Meyers, C. E., 16, 18n., 61, 82n., 238,
    248
Mirro, M., 144, 152n.
Mix, B. J., **150**
Moen, M., 227
Money, handling, in behavior scale, **53**
Morrow, H. W., 3ff, 17n., 85ff., 93ff.,
    115ff., 141ff., 215ff., 227ff.
Morse, W. C., 105, 107n.
Motor skills, **52, 150, 151**
"Multi-dimensional model . . ."
    (Buck), 231
Multiple-regression analysis, 163–166,
    194, 196, 209, 246
Muma, J., 83, 83n., 215, 216, 222,
    224n., 229
Murphy, M. C., **150**

Nagler, B., 12, 19n., 247
National Association of State Consul-
    tants in School Psychology
    (NASCSP), 85, 116
National Health Surveys, 201

Need assessment, on adaptive behavior survey form, 96ff., **109–112**

Neer, W., 247

Nesbit, M. J., 93, 105, 107n.

Neuromotor Development, in behavior scale, 51, 52, **52**

Newman, R. G., 105, 107n.

Nicoll, R. C., 8, 18n., 47–50, 57n., 115, 125n., 170, 182n., 237

Nihira, K., 2, **5, 6,** 7–9, 12, 13, 15, 18, 19n., 29, 32, 42n., 43n., 45ff., 47, 49, 57n., 61, 67, 82n., 86, **88,** 90, 92n., 115, 125n., 126n., **147,** 158, 159, 167, 168, 183n., 219, 225n., 239, 247–251

Nihira, L., 251

Nirje, B., 3, 19n.

Nomenclature, 1

"Non-biased assessment of minority group children" (Garza), 234

Nonconforming behavior, in behavior scale, 168

Normalization, theory of, 3. See also Norms

"Normalized behavior in community placement" (Nihira & Nihira), 251

Norm-reference measures, 10, 33, 34, 145, 153, 154, **155.** See also Norms

Norms
and ABS, 119, 129, **133, 134**
and age, 220
and assessment, 142–143
and behavior, 69–70
concept of, 62
and EFG, **175,** 176
and ethnicity, 130
as expectations, 191–192
pluralistic, 186
in rating forms, 126–127
and reference groups, 165

Number and Time Concepts, in behavior scale, 24, **46,** 50, **53,** 54, 164, 166, 168, 170, 179, 180, 249

Oakland, T., 10, 12, 16, 19n., 115, 126n., 143, 152n., 251, 252

Oakwood Resident Movement Scale & Curriculum, **150, 155**

O'Brien, J. J., **148**

Odd Mannerisms, in behavior scale, 250

Office of Civil Rights, 4, **6,** 19n.

"On defining mental retardation" (Baumeister & Muma), 229

"Operationalizing a nonbiased appraisal process" (Tucker), 252

Opton, E., 16, 18n.

Orleans, P., 242

Pacific State Hospital Project, 13–14, 16, 17

Page, E. R., 24, 43n.

Parent Interview Manual (Mercer & Lewis), 185, 185n., 202, 207

Parsons State Hospital Project, 12–14, 16, 17, 106

Parton, D., 50, 57n.

Pathological model. See Medical model

Patients, physicians, and illness (Jaco, ed.), 243

Peer groups, roles in, 77–78, **146,** 193, 206. See also Roles

Pellagra, 62

Penrose, L., 251

Personal hygiene, in behavior scale, **52, 53, 150**

Personal Independence. See Independence, in behavior scale

Personal Maladaptation, in behavior scale, **47,** 48, 248

Personal Self-sufficiency, in behavior scale, 49–52, **52**

Personal-Social Responsibility. See Responsibility, in behavior scale

Philips, I., 12, 19n.

Phillips, L., 105, 107n.

Phylogenetic/ontogenetic evolution, 64

Physical Development, in behavior scale, 24, **46,** 48, **150,** 164, 166, 172, **172,** 173, 179, 249

Physical Dexterity Tasks, in SOMPA, 185, 190, 197–200, 202, 209

Piaget, J., 21, 43n.

Pluralistic model, and SOMPA, 185,
    193–195, 208–210, 246
Pneumonia, 201
"Policy statement, A . . ." (Mercer),
    244
Polio, 201
Popham, W. J., 130, 133n.
"Position paper on the measurement of
    adaptive behavior" (Harbin &
    Haigh), 235
Predictive validity, 130, **134,** 229–230.
    See also Validity
Prenatal/Postnatal Inventory, 201
Preschool Attainment Record, **150**
Preschools, 73
President's Committee on Mental Re-
    tardation, 3, **7,** 19n., 216, 222,
    225n.
Primary deviance, 75
*Proceedings of the First Congress of
    the IASSMD* (Richards, ed.),
    239
*Proceedings of the National Associa-
    tion of Superintendents,* 234
*Proceedings of the 79th Annual Con-
    vention of the American Psy-
    chological Association,* 248
Productivity, in behavior scale, 49
Profile Summary Sheet, 181
Project News, 234, 247
Prosocial Behavior, in behavior scale,
    50
Prugh, D. G., 105, 107n.
"Psychoeducational assessment in the
    seventies . . .", symposium,
    237
Psychological assessment, and adap-
    tive behavior, 3ff.
    approaches, 16–17
    definitions, adaptive behavior, 4,
        5–7, 7–9, 153
    definitions, psychological assess-
        ment, 9–11
    functions of, 10
    historical perspective, 11–12
    nonbiased, 4, 11, 15–17
    products of, 1, **155**
    projects on, 12–16

social context of, 7
texts on, 4
Psychological Bulletin, 240
Psychological Corporation, **146**
Psychological Disturbances, in be-
    havior scale, 47, **48,** 165, 171,
    177, 250
Psychometrics
    function of, 211
    prerequisites of, 143
    technology of, 153
Public Law 93-380, 9, 85
Public Law 94-142, 3–4, 9, 217, 218n.,
    220
Public transportation, use of, in be-
    havior scale, 52, **53**
Punishment
    and delay, 36
    and motivation, 36
Pupil Appraisal Committee, 137

Questionnaire, on adaptive behavior,
    87ff, **87**
    on ABS—PS, 101–104, **101–104**
    on adaptive behavior tests, 98–101,
        98–101
    on alterations, 100, **100**
    concept/definition, 96–98, **97**
    need assessment, 96ff.
    procedure, 95, **96**
    results, 95–96
    on roles, 205–207
    and standardization, 205ff.
    survey form, **109–112**
    on tests, 98ff.
"Quo vadis, AAMD" (Clausen), 232

Race, change, and urban society (Or-
    leans & Sage, eds.), 242
Raffeld, P., **150**
Ramirez, M., 73, 82n.
Raisin in the Sun (Hansberry), 113
Rebellious Behavior, in behavior scale,
    47, 48, 164, 165, 171, 249
Record Form, 185n.
"Region IV Education Service Center
    Conference . . ." (McCarthy),
    240
Reliability, 117, **120,** 221

of ABS, 33–34
of ABS-PS, 167–169
defined, 130
types of, **134**
Reporting Service for Children, **151**
"Response to educational uses of tests,
    A . . ." (Bernal), 229
Responsibility, in behavior scale, 25,
    31, 34, 35, 40, **46**, 48–50, 55, **55,**
    56, 166–168, 171, 178, 179, 249
Reward, and delay, 36
Reynolds, D., 247
Rhesus monkeys, surrogate-reared, 72
Rheumatic fever, 201
Richards, B. W., 239
Richardson, S. A., 244
Rimland, B., 219, 225*n.*
Riverside Project, 60–61, 67, 186, 187,
    205, 243
Robb, G. P., 4, 20*n.*
Robbins, R. C., 61, 82*n.*
Robinson, H. B., **6**, 7, 20*n.*
Robinson, N. M., **6**, 7, 20*n.*
Rogers, D., 15, 17*n.*, 233
Roles
    and ABIC, 205–207
    and adaptive behavior, **5**, 8
    of children, 76
    nonacademic, in schools, 204, 206
    in peer groups, 77–78, **146**, 193, 206
    in social systems, 60, 65–66, 69, 90
Roller, J. D., **150**
Rosman, B., 236
Ross, A. O., 50, 57*n.*, 218, 219, 225*n.*

Sailor, W., **150**
Sander, L. W., 71, 82*n.*
Santa Cruz Co., 88, 92*n.*
Santa Cruz County Office of Educa-
    tion, **147**
Sattler, J., 4, 20*n.*, 218, 225*n.*
Scarlet fever, 201
Scheff, T. J., 191, 212*n.*
School
    adjustment to, 236
    diagnosis in, 86
    rules in, 78–79

School Functioning Level (SFL), 185,
    202, 208
School Psychology Digest, 246
Schwartz, B., 251
Secondary deviance, 75
Secure base
    described, 203
    in social entry, 72
Self-abusive Behavior, in behavior
    scale, **47**, 48, 161
Self-concepts, **148**
Self-destructive Behavior, in behavior
    scale, 250
Self-direction, in behavior scale, 25, **46,**
    48, 55, 164, 166, 168, 171, 179,
    249
Self-help Skills, in behavior scale, 51,
    52, **52**
Self-maintenance roles, 79, 206–207
Self-reliance, measurement, 159
Sensory deficiency, 32
Sensory Development, in behavior
    scale, 51, **52**
Sensory-motor development, 28
Sequin, E., 11, 157
Sex differences, in ABS—PS, 166, 168,
    171
Sexually Aberrant Behavior, **47**, 161,
    250
Shellhaas, M., **5**, 12, 13, 18*n.*, 19*n.*, 29,
    43*n.*, 45, 57*n.*, 61, 67, 82*n.*, 86,
    88, 90, 92*n.*, **147**, 158, 159, 167,
    168, 183*n.*, 239, 249, 250
Shoaee, M., 22, 25, 36, 42*n.*
Simon, T., 60, 81*n.*
Situated functioning, 70
Situationally retarded, 70
Smith, D. E., 28, 42*n.*
Snellen Test, 200
"Social adaptation assessment . . ."
    (Allen et al.), 228
Social adjustment, 66
Social & Prevocational Information
    Battery, **150, 155**
Social Competence Scale, 236
"Social competence scale and symp-
    tom checklist, A . . ." (Kohn
    & Rosman), 236

Social competency, 11, 64, 236
Social-cultural Aspects of Mental Retardation (Mercer, ed.), 242
Social-deviance view, in sociology, 191
Socialization
    anticipatory, 203
    in behavior scale, 25, **46,** 48, 55, **56,** 164, 166, 171, 169, 180, 249
Social maladaptation, in behavior scale, 32, 48, 248
Social Participation, in behavior scale, 50
Social quotient, problem with, 9
Social responsibility
    in behavior scale, 48–50, 171
    categories of, 36–38
Social roles. *See* Roles
Social skills, in behavior scale, **150, 151**
Social statuses, 69
Social-system model, 230
    adaptive fitting, 70–71
    adaptive trajectories, 74–75
    adaptive typography, 75–76
    components of, 68–70
    developmental sequencing, 76–80
    entry in, 72–74
    medical model, 65ff.
    on retarded, 242, 243
    and SOMPA, 185, 191–193, 202ff.
    system components, 68–70
Social value, efficiency of, 11
Sociobehavioral studies in mental retardation (Meyers et al., eds.), 238, 248
"Sociocultural factors in educational labeling" (Mercer), 244
Sociocultural Scales, 195–197
"Socioeconomic bias . . ." (Neer et al.), 247
"Sociological perspectives on mild mental retardation" (Mercer), 242
SOMPA Profile Folder, 185
SOMPA Technical Manual (Mercer), 185, 196, 198, 202, 209
South Dakota Code, on mental deficiency, 59
Spanish version, of ABIC, 205

Spearman, C., 61, 64, 82n.
Spearman-Brown correlation, 130
Special education, 10, 15, 142–43, 171ff., **172.** *See also* Mental retardation
Specific item content, 117
Speech Development, in behavior scale, **54**
Spencer, L., 250
Spencer-Booth, Y., 72, 82n.
"Standardization of a public school version of the AAMD ABS)" (Lambert et al.), 238
Standardized tests, 10
Statistical model, 243
Stereotyped Behavior, in behavior scale, **47,** 48, 165, 168, 171, 250
Sternfield, A. E., **150, 151**
Stillman, R., 88, 92n., **148**
Strauss, J., 232
"Struggle for children's rights, The" (Mercer), 246
Student Assessment Manual (Mercer & Lewis), 185, 209
Student Assessment Manual and Record Form, 185n., 199
Student Assessment Model (Mercer & Lewis), 198, 200
Student Record Form, 209
"Study of adaptive behavior" (Nihira & Shellhaas), 250
"Study of environmental demands, A" (Nihira), 247
Symptoms Checklist, 236
System of Multicultural Pluralistic Assessment (Mercer), 246
System of Multicultural Pluralistic Assessment (SOMPA), 2, 14, 68, 85, **88,** 91, **99,** 113, 116, **146, 155,** 185ff., 230, 245, 246, 251
    assessment models of, 188ff.
    development of, 186–188
    measuring instruments, 195ff.
    norms for, 145
    Profile Folder, 185n.

Table manners, 23, **52**
TARC Assessment System, 129, **150**

Tarjan, G., 238, 248
"Testing for competence rather than for intelligence" (McClelland), 240
"Test 'validity,' 'bias,' and 'fairness' " (Mercer), 245
Texas Education Agency, **7,** 20*n.,* 93, 94, 107*n.,* 217, 225*n.*
Texas Regional Resource Center, 86, 94, 116–117
Texas State Board of Education, 93
Texas State Learning Resource Center, 180, 183*n.*
Texas workshops, 93, 117
Thomas, D., 47, 48, 57*n.*
Time, in behavior scale, **53,** 54
T.M.R. Performance Profile for the Severely and Moderately Retarded, **150**
Today's Educational Consultant, 240
Toilet training, 49, 52, **52**
Tomiyasu, Y., 47, 57*n.*
Trainable mentally retarded (TMR), 48, **103,** 161–167, 169, 171, 237. *See also* Mental retardation
Training School Bulletin, The, 241, 251
Transition agent, in social system, 72–73, 203
Trauma Inventory, 201
Tuberculosis, diagnosis of, 62
Tucker, J. A., 4, 11, 17, 20*n.,* 93, 105, 106, 108*n.,* 115, 126*n.,* 142, 144, 152*n.,* 154, 156*n.,* 217, 218, 225*n.,* 252

Unacceptable Behavior, in behavior scale, **47,** 48
Unacceptable or Eccentric Habits, in behavior scale, 250
Unacceptable Vocal Habits, in behavior scale, 165, 171, 250
University of California, Berkeley, 159
University of California, Riverside Project, 14, 16
University of Texas, Dallas, **148**
Untrustworthy Behavior, in behavior scale, 47, **48,** 164, 165, 171, 249
U.S. Public Health Service, 201, 210*n.*

Validity, 117, **138,** 245
of ABS, 33–34, 220–222
of ABS—PS, 161–167, 169
of social system measure, 193
of SOMPA, 190
types of, 130, **134**
"Validity of the AAMD ABS . . ." (Lambert), 237
Variance, 247
Vayda, S., 22, 25, 36, 42*n.*
Vineland Social Maturity Scale (VSMS), 27, 35, 48, **88,** 91, 98, **99,** 132, **151,** 228, 241, 251
Vineland Training School, 60
Violent and Destructive Behavior, 249
Visual acuity, 190, 200
Visual Acuity Inventory, 201
Vocabulary Activity, 25
Vocal Habits, in behavior scale, **47**
Vocational Activity, in behavior scale, **46,** 48, **149,** 163–166, 168, 179
Vocational Rehabilitation agency, 70
Voisin, F., 11, 157, 215
Vort Corporation, **148**

Waldrop, M., 50, 57*n.*
Walker, J., 144, 152*n.*
Walls, R. T., 141, 143, 152*n.,* 252
Warren, S., 241
Wayne State University, 68*n.*
Wechsler, D., 185, 212*n.*
"Wechsler Intelligence Scale for Children" (Littell), 240
Wechsler Intelligence Scale for Children—Revised (WISC—R), 51, 185, 194, 195, 202, 207–209, 211, 231, 240, 244, 246. *See also* Intelligence; IQ
Wechsler Preschool and Primary Scale of Intelligence (WPPSI), 185, 208. *See also* Intelligence; IQ
Welch, R. J., **148**
Werner, T. J., 141, 143, 152*n.,* 252
Wesman, A., 232
"When you're up to your waist in alligators . . ." (Mercer), 246
"Who is normal?" (Mercer), 243
Whooping cough, 201

Wilcox, M. R., 15, 18*n.*, 115, 125*n.*,
    159, 182*n.*
Williams, R. L., 10, 20*n.*, 145, 152*n.*,
    218, 225*n.*
Wilson, J. B., 12, 20*n.*, 252
Windmiller, M., 15, 11, 18*n.*, 48, 86, **88,**
    92*n.*, 95, 107*n.*, 145, **146, 147,**
    152*n.*, 161, 171, 183*n.*, 221,
    224*n.*, 238
With bias toward none (Oakland ed.),
    252
Withdrawal
    in behavior scale, **47,** 165, 168, 249

    in family, 241
    social, 36
Wolman, B. B., 4, 20*n.*
Work habits/performance, in behavior
    scale, **55**
Writing/reading, in behavior scale, **53,**
    54

Y.E.M.R. Performance Profile for the
    Young and Mildly Retarded, **151**
Young, E., 144, 152*n.*
Ysseldyke, J., 10, 11, 19*n.*, 93, 107*n.*,
    223, 224*n.*